THE END OF UTOPIA

THE
END
OF
UTOPIA

*Politics and Culture in
an Age of Apathy*

RUSSELL JACOBY

BASIC
BOOKS

A Member of the Perseus Books Group

Copyright © 1999 by Russell Jacoby.

Published by Basic Books,
A Member of the Perseus Books Group

All rights reserved. Printed in the United States of America.

No part of this book may be used in any manner whatsoever without written permission except in the case of brief quotations embodied in critical articles and reviews. For information, address Basic Books, 10 East 53rd St., New York, NY 10022-5299.

A CIP catalog record for this book is available from the Library of Congress.
ISBN 0-465-02000-3

10   9   8   7   6   5   4   3   2   1

For Sarah and Sam, again

CONTENTS

ACKNOWLEDGMENTS

As usual by both necessity and choice I keep my acknowledgments brief. For my most diligent and devoted readers, Naomi Glauberman and Brian Morton, my deepest thanks. I am grateful to Paul Breines, Robert Brenner, and Robert Hill for commenting upon various chapters; and I am deeply indebted to Steve Fraser for taking on this book and to Jo Ann Miller of Basic Books for saving it.

PREFACE

During the years I worked on this book the major American political events consisted of charges of rape in the army, adultery in the air force and improper sexual activity in the White House. These accusations followed a spellbinding trial in which a sports celebrity was charged with murdering his wife. Of course, these happenings did not exhaust the news of the day. Yet other events, such as changes in welfare regulations or the settlement of cases against tobacco companies, were not especially compelling. The world situation—to audaciously generalize—has been equally uninteresting or depressing; it has been characterized by progress toward a European Union, on the one hand, and sectarian bloodletting and disintegrating states, on the other.

To be sure, anyone can draw up a list stressing the positive—a peace agreement in Northern Ireland—or the negative—the spread of AIDS in Africa. Yet politics has become dull, which does not mean benign. At worst, it is defined by economic collapse, despotism and fratricidal violence. At best, liberal regimes resist challenges by regressive religious and nationalist movements. We are increasingly asked to choose between the status quo or something worse. Other alternatives do not seem to exist. We have entered the era of acquiescence, in which we build our lives, families and careers with little expectation the future will diverge from the present.

To put this another way: A utopian spirit—a sense that the future could transcend the present—has vanished. This last statement risks immediate misunderstanding, since *utopia* today connotes irrelevancies or bloodletting. Someone who believes in utopias is widely considered out to lunch or out to kill. I am using *utopian* in its widest, and least threatening, meaning: a belief that the future could fundamentally surpass the present. I am referring to the notion that the future texture of life, work and even love might little resemble that now familiar to us. I am alluding to the idea that history contains possibilities of freedom and pleasure hardly tapped.

This belief is stone dead. Few envision the future as anything but a replica of today—sometimes better, but usually worse. Scholarly conclusions about the fall of Soviet communism ratify gut feelings about the failures of radicalism. A new consensus has emerged: There are no alternatives. This is the wisdom of our times, an age of political exhaustion and retreat.

These attitudes infiltrate all of life and take a toll. For the young, the world appears less enchanting. Amid European and American affluence, prospects look poor. Recent reports of sharp declines in birth rates in wealthy European nations identify a new cynicism or pessimism. Young adults fear that dark clouds are gathering. "I believe we are seeing a fundamental shift in human behavior," states one Swedish expert, explaining falling Swedish birth rates. The belief that the future will be better than the present is gone. "Young people now seem to have a sense that living for today is about the best they can do." To have children appears too risky and expensive. "There is a perception—shared even in vastly different countries like Sweden and Italy," summarizes this report, "that what was possible for previous generations is not possible for this one."[1]

Falling birth rates are not my concern, but collapsing intellectual visions and ambitions are. In this book I chart a cultural retreat; radicals have lost their bite and liberals their backbone. In the face of superior force or the experience of history, retreat is not dishonorable. Defeat "registers the constellation of forces, not the quality of insight, theory and even practices," I once wrote in a book on defeated traditions.[2] To return to the drawing boards, to reconsider the past: These are estimable choices. The problem is not the defeat, but the intellectual weariness and dissembling, the pretense that every step backward or sideways marks ten steps forward. The hype about multiculturalism is a prime example. A return to a familiar idea of pluralism is presented as a conceptual and political break-through.

At the dawn of another new century, Samuel Coleridge wrote to his friend William Wordsworth. Two hundred years ago, in 1799, he suggested that Wordsworth contest the widespread malaise and resignation. "I wish you would write a poem, in blank verse, addressed to those, who, in consequence of the complete failure of the French Revolution, have thrown up all hopes of the amelioration of mankind, and are sinking into an almost epicurean selfishness, disguising the same under the soft titles of domestic attachment and contempt for visionary *philosophes*."[3] I have not written a poem, but I would like to think that in its defense of visionary impulse this book partially fulfills Coleridge's bidding.

Los Angeles
January 1999

THE END OF UTOPIA

— 1 —

THE END OF
THE END OF
THE END OF IDEOLOGY

In September 1955, several hundred writers and scholars from Raymond Aron to Arthur Schlesinger, Jr., assembled in Milan's National Museum of Science and Technology to discuss "the future of freedom." Their outlook was roughly liberal and anticommunist, their mood, upbeat. Stalin had died; the new First Secretary of the Soviet Communist Party, Nikita Khrushchev, spoke of detente and peace. Western Europe and the United States were prospering. Perhaps Marxism had a future in the underdeveloped nations, but elsewhere its day seemed past. One participant observed that an "atmosphere of a post-victory ball" prevailed. "There was," noted Edward Shils, "a sometimes rampant, sometimes quiet conviction that Communism had lost the battle of ideas with the West."[1]

"In most Western societies, the ideological controversy is dying down," stated Aron in an opening address. History has "refuted the exaggerated hopes placed in Revolution." Aron admitted that tensions still "arise" over equality, employment, wages and inflation, "but the reasonable anxieties they evoke do not give rise to any fundamental conflict."[2] Serious people now agree on the basic framework of the welfare state.

Several months later, Khrushchev startled the delegates to the Party Congress with a secret speech denouncing Stalin as a murderer, liar and maniac. Of 139 members of a previous Central Committee, 70 percent had been "arrested and shot," Khrushchev announced. "Or let us take the matter of the Stalin Prizes," he continued. "Not even the tsars created prizes which they named after themselves."[3] After decades in which Stalin had been deified, the hold-no-punches indictment stunned the delegates. The transcript of the speech underlined the response: "Animation in the hall," "Tumult in the hall."

Not only in the hall. News of the "secret" speech caused dismay among loyal Communists around the globe. For many critics, including those who had gathered in Milan, the Khrushchev speech only confirmed the ideological dissolution. Moreover, communism suffered other blows in the mid-1950s: widespread protests in East Berlin, riots in Poland and a Soviet invasion of Hungary to put down a revolt. The Berlin strikes on June 17, 1953, inspired Bertolt Brecht's mordant poem "The Solution":

> After the uprising of the 17th June
> The Secretary of the Writers Union
> Had leaflets distributed in the Stalinallee
> Stating that the people
> Had forfeited the confidence of the government
> And could win it back only
> By redoubled efforts. Would it not be easier
> In that case for the government
> To dissolve the people
> And elect another?[4]

Raymond Aron's *The Opium of the Intellectuals*, his criticism of Marxism, appeared just before the Party Congress. Aron, who had been a principal organizer of the Milan conference, evoked what he called "the end of the age of ideology," or "the end of the ideological age."[5] Ideology meant revolution and utopianism: These were finished. No one could pretend that an alternative to advanced capitalism existed.

"Imperfect and unjust as Western society is in many respects, it has progressed sufficiently . . . so that reforms appear more promising than violence and unpredictable disorder." Nor could we return to a pure laissez-faire economy; undiluted capitalism was also obsolete. Liberalism and socialism were no longer pure doctrines or pure opposites. "Western 'capitalist' society today comprises a multitude of socialist institutions." The old ideologies were over. In a foreword to an American edition, published after Khrushchev's speech, Aron wondered, "Is there still a need to denounce the opium of the intellectuals?" He asked, "Didn't Stalin carry off with him in death not only Stalinism, but also the age of ideology?"[6]

Aron joined a chorus of voices in Europe and the United States that intensified during the 1950s. The authors proclaimed, celebrated and sometimes lamented the end of ideology and utopia. They did not simply glorify unvarnished capitalism; rather, they argued that the new economic and political realities had advanced beyond both Adam Smith and Karl Marx. The welfare state encompassed politics; modifying, not transforming, liberal capitalism defined the future. Nevertheless, their emphasis lay on the demise of the radical vision.

The term *end of ideology* may have first appeared in the writings of Albert Camus, the French essayist and novelist. In a 1946 piece for *Combat*, the Resistance newspaper paper he edited, Camus criticized the recent efforts of French socialists to reconcile Marxism and ethics. For Camus this could not be done; the Marxist belief that ends justify the means legitimates murder. The socialists had to choose to either accept or reject Marxism as an "absolute philosophy." In doing the latter socialists would "show that our time marks the end of ideologies, that is, absolute utopias which in reality destroy themselves."[7]

Several years later a junior Harvard professor, H. Stuart Hughes, used the term *end of ideology* in a report on the mood of European intellectuals. Hughes observed that the "leftist European intellectual" now realized "with considerable sense of shock" that he preferred capitalism to communism. "The end of the *mystique* of the

Left is the clearest sign of what has happened" since the war. The left lacks conviction and ideas, he stated in his 1951 essay "The End of Political Ideology."[8]

Many scholars and commentators in the 1950s presented kindred arguments. Judith N. Shklar titled the last chapter of her *After Utopia: The Decline of Political Faith* "The End of Radicalism." Radicalism, she wrote, "has gone totally out of fashion." It requires a "minimum of utopian faith" that people can transform their social environment, but today this spirit is lacking. Socialism "has not been able to recover the lost spirit of utopian idealism and is neither radical nor hopeful today." She concluded, "All that need really be stated is that socialism no longer has anything to say."[9]

Seymour Martin Lipset agreed. "'Politics is now boring,'" he stated in his 1960 *Political Man*, quoting a Swedish journalist. "'The only issues are whether the metal workers should get a nickel more an hour, the price of milk should be raised, or old-age pensions extended.'" For Lipset, as for Aron, "the fundamental political problems of the industrial revolution" no longer give rise to ideological disputes. He put it emphatically: "This very triumph of the democratic social revolution in the West ends domestic politics for those intellectuals who must have ideologies or utopias to motivate them to political action."[10]

Daniel Bell's *The End of Ideology* offered the sharpest formulation. The old nineteenth-century ideologies were "exhausted," undermined by the horrors of Soviet communism and the success of liberal capitalism. "Such calamities as the Moscow Trials, the Nazi-Soviet pact, the concentration camps, the suppression of the Hungarian workers, formed one chain [of events]; such social changes as the modification of capitalism, the rise of the Welfare State, another." At the end of the 1950s, Bell stated, "the old passions are spent" and "the old politico-economic radicalism . . . has lost its meaning." The situation seemed clear: "The ideological age has ended." As Bell put it, ". . . In the Western world, therefore, there is a rough consensus among intellectuals on political issues: the acceptance of a Welfare State; the desirability of decentralized power; a system of mixed economy and of political pluralism."[11]

The End of Ideology, published in 1960, closed with reflections on the fate of younger intellectuals in a world that had put radicalism and utopianism to rest. The new generation, with "no meaningful memory" of old debates, finds itself in a society that has rejected "apocalyptic and chialistic visions." "There is a restless search for a new intellectual radicalism," but nothing is found. Ideology is "intellectually devitalized"; politics offers "little excitement." Social reforms do not provide a "unifying appeal." "Whether the intellectuals in the West can find passions outside of politics is moot."[12]

Two years later Bell brought out a slightly revised edition of *The End of Ideology* registering a small shift in political realities. Between 1960 and 1962 something had appeared on the scene: a new left. "To close the book" on ideology, Bell now added, "is not to turn one's back upon it. This is all the more important now when a 'new Left,' with few memories of the past, is emerging." Bell wondered where it was going and what its politics entailed.[13]

For good reason. In the early 1960s history was speeding up and radicalism found a new life; ideological conflict was intensifying, not weakening. Fidel Castro swept into Havana in 1959, and two years later the United States broke off relations with Cuba. Castro and his comrade-in-arms "Che" Guevara appeared to many as romantic heroes, inspiring revolution throughout the Americas. Students protesting segregation in the southern states galvanized support from youth in the North. A new politics was spreading across the land.

"Walking through Harvard Square" in 1960, recalls Todd Gitlin in his history of the 1960s, "I saw a poster tacked on a telephone pole." It announced a rally against nuclear weapons with a speech by Erich Fromm and music by Pete Seeger and Joan Baez. "The previous year, I might have passed such a notice with barely a glance, but this one was irresistible." Something had changed, and not simply for Gitlin. That night the arena was jammed with six thousand people.[14]

The new left and the 1960s resist a brief summary; it remains disputed when the "1960s" began, what they accomplished or when they ended. For some conservatives, the 1960s are only too alive, the origin of America's malaise, drug problem and underclass. A fairer account might credit the 1960s with ending the war in Vietnam and creating a new awareness of racial and social inequalities. Few doubt that the 1960s marked a period of relentless disputation. Not only a political revolution, but a revolution in life, morals and sexuality was discussed, and sometimes pursued. The 1960s slogan "The personal is political" meant that private life, once considered outside of politics, was now the subject of manifestos and criticism. The 1960s buried talk of "the end of ideology."

At least this is what many believed. Already in 1960, C. Wright Mills, the radical sociologist, denounced the "end-of-ideology" proponents as smug conservatives, tired liberals and disappointed radicals. "Ultimately, the end-of-ideology is based upon a disillusionment with any real commitment to socialism." Its partisans believe "that in the West there are no more real issues. . . . The mixed economy plus the welfare state plus prosperity—that is the formula. U.S. capitalism will continue to be workable." For Mills this was bunk; the end of ideology was "on the way out." A new left was emerging that was not afraid to be utopian. "Is not our utopianism a major source of our strength? . . . Our theoretical work is indeed utopian—in my own case, at least, deliberately so. What needs to be . . . changed, is not merely first this then that detail . . . [but] the *structure* of institutions, the *foundation* of policies."[15]

For the next several decades the end-of-ideology thesis took a beating. The civil rights movement, black power, antiwar protests, national liberation struggles, feminism—the world seemed drenched in revolution and ideology. "What is the evidence for the increasingly fashionable thesis of the gradual extinction of ideology in the West?" asked an observer in 1967. He found little, and argued in an essay titled "The End of the 'The End of Ideology'" that ideology was "waxing stronger than ever."[16] Bell's argument, stated another commentator, smacked of the past. "The sixties have now passed their half-way mark and it seems that perhaps Bell's death sentence was a bit premature."[17] "One would have thought, a few years ago," stated another analyst, "that the age of ideology was at an end." The emerging student movement, however, refuted the idea.[18]

In 1968, using Bell's phrase as an epigraph, Christopher Lasch blasted the notion of the end of ideology. "All of Western society faces insurrectionary threats from within," stated Lasch. "Vietnam has exploded the cold-war consensus. . . . Riots threaten to become a permanent feature of urban life." Militant blacks attack America and support Third World revolutions. Students are rebelling in Paris, Berlin, Rome and Madrid. For Lasch, postindustrial society generated new conflicts. We are witnessing "a revival of ideology."[19]

"Not so very long ago," summarized a reviewer in 1972, "Raymond Aron, Daniel Bell and Seymour Martin Lipset, among others, were confidently predicting the decline of ideological fervor in the Western industrialized countries. . . . This was wrong. . . . The past two decades have been characterized by a growth and proliferation of total ideologies."[20] Little seemed more bankrupt than the notion of a widespread agreement in the welfare state and pluralism. Nothing seemed more ridiculous than the pronouncement of the demise of fundamental political fissures, the end of ideology.

Until today. In 1989 communism collapsed in Eastern Europe; the disintegration of the Soviet Union soon followed. History does not repeat itself, but sometimes it comes close. When Erich Honecker, the East German leader, learned of the mass demonstrations in Leipzig in October 1989, he asked, referring to the strikes of 1953, "Is it another 17th of June?"[21] It was, and worse, since this time the people dissolved the state and indicted Honecker for crimes against its citizens.

The events of 1989 mark a decisive shift in the Zeitgeist: History has zigged or zagged. No simple lesson follows, but it is clear that radicalism and the utopian spirit that sustains it have ceased to be major political or even intellectual forces. Nor is this pertinent simply to adherents of the left. The vitality of liberalism rests on its left flank, which operates as its goad and critic. As the left surrenders a vision, liberalism loses its bearings; it turns flaccid and uncertain.

Bell had it right, only he did not draw out all the consequences—and he jumped the gun. To use Bell's words from 1960, responsible political thinkers believe in "the acceptance of a Welfare State; the desirability of decentralized power; a system of mixed economy and of political pluralism." Who objects to these now? However, Bell missed a fundamental irony—the defeat of radicalism bleeds liberalism of its vitality.

To be sure, reading the Zeitgeist leaves room for argument. Many pretend that nothing has changed. With bravado or blindness they repeat familiar adages. In 1995 Paul Lauter, a leftist English professor, denounced "the end of ideology" as the rant of quacks: "The academy has always had its share of charlatans, lowlifes, and scurvy reprobates: they produced an Aryanized version of the classics, faked twin-studies, . . . history without black writers, and my favorite bit of academic nonsense, the 'end of ideology.'"[22]

Lauter is hardly alone. Nevertheless, the evidence is everywhere that the wisdom of "lowlifes" speaks to the present better than the dicta of well-heeled English professors. A seismic shift in political and cultural realities has taken place. To put it bluntly, the demise of communism eviscerates radicalism and enfeebles liberalism.

Francis Fukuyama's much discussed *The End of History and the Last Man* partly addressed this issue. His argument reformulated with a philosophical flourish the more prosaic "end-of-ideology" proposition.[23] Fukuyama added Hegel and Alexandre Kojève, a Russian-French Hegelian, to Daniel Bell.[24] In an article that preceded the book, Fukuyama stated that "the triumph of the West, of the Western *idea*, is evident first of all in the total exhaustion of viable systematic alternatives to Western liberalism."[25] Even the language evokes *The End of Ideology*, whose subtitle referred to the "exhaustion" of political ideas.

Fukuyama sensed an affinity between his and Bell's positions and tried to distance himself from Bell. The "ultimate triumph of Western liberal democracy," he wrote, does not lead "to an 'end of ideology' or a convergence between capitalism and socialism . . . but to an unabashed victory of economic and political liberalism."[26] Yet this was exactly Bell's argument, not a "convergence," but the victory of welfare or liberal capitalism. Fukuyama defends the same proposition.

He admits isolated Marxists may exist "in places like Managua, Pyongyang or Cambridge," but radicalism now lacks historical force or future. Misgivings cloud Fukuyama's good cheer. With the demise of a radical opposition, passion and idealism also depart; only commercial regulations and tariffs remain contentious. Alluding to the fact that the brilliant Kojève ended his days organizing a trade group, the European Common Market, Fukuyama regretted that a "Growing 'Common Marketization'" defines the future. In the original article Fukuyama ended on a bittersweet note that recalls Bell's doubts. Fukuyama expressed "nostalgia" for the history of big ideas and robust ideologies:

> The end of history will be a very sad event. The struggle for recognition, the willingness to risk one's life for a purely abstract goal, the worldwide ideological struggle that called forth daring, courage, imagination, and idealism will be replaced by economic calculation, the endless solving of technical problems, environmental concerns and the satisfaction of sophisticated consumer demands. In the post-historical period there will be neither art nor philosophy, just the perpetual caretaking of the museum of human history.[27]

Fukuyama's argument has provoked extensive and damaging criticism, but at least half still stands.[28] In the book version Fukuyama perceived a "worldwide liberal revolution" or a "Universal History of mankind in the direction of liberal democracy"; he announced not simply the end of ideology, but the end of history. However, history did not end; and liberal democracy will not triumph everywhere. Authoritarianism and despotism have a glorious future. On these issues Fukuyama overplayed his hand. Moreover, he paid no mind to a paradoxical result of defeated leftism, the loss of liberal resolve and clarity.

Yet his statement that the hour of radicalism is past rings true. Apart from a few diehards in stray capitals and campuses, intellectuals have become willy-nilly liberals.

> In our grandparents' time, many reasonable people could foresee a radiant socialist future in which private property and capitalism had been abolished. . . . Today, by contrast, we have trouble imagining a world that is radically better than our own, or a future that is not essentially democratic and capitalist. Within that framework, of course, many things could be improved . . . homeless . . . minorities . . . jobs. . . . We can also imagine future worlds that are significantly worse that what we know now. . . . But we cannot picture to ourselves a world that is *essentially* different from the present one, and at the same time better.[29]

Fukuyama stated a verity that many refuse to acknowledge. Today socialists and leftists do not dream of a future qualitatively different from the present. To put it differently, radicalism no longer believes in itself. Once upon a time leftists acted as if they could fundamentally reorganize society. Intellectually, the belief fed off a utopian vision of a different society; psychologically, it rested on self-confidence about one's place in history; politically, it depended on the real prospects.

Today the vision has faltered, the self-confidence drained away, the possibilities dimmed. Almost everywhere the left contracts, not simply politically but, perhaps more decisively, intellectually. To avoid contemplating the defeat and its implications, the left now largely speaks the language of liberalism—the idiom of pluralism and rights. At the same time, liberals, divested of a left wing, suffer from waning determination and imagination.

At best radicals and leftists envision a modified society with bigger pieces of pie for more customers. They turn utilitarian, liberal and celebratory. The left once dismissed the market as exploitative; it now honors the market as rational and humane. The left once disdained mass culture as exploitative; now it celebrates it as rebellious. The left once honored independent intellectuals as courageous; now it sneers at them as elitist. The left once rejected pluralism as superficial; now it worships it as profound. We are witnessing not simply the defeat of the left, but its conversion and perhaps inversion.

Of course, this interpretation of the recent past can be challenged. Why charge radicals with the grievous misdeeds of Stalinism? Why accuse the wider left of the crimes of Soviet Marxism? For the last forty years, certainly in the United States, the left harbored little sympathy for Stalinism or Stalinist regimes in Eastern Europe. Sift through stacks of leftist tracts, newspapers and leaflets of the 1960s and 1970s and you will be hard-pressed to find a single word praising East Germany or Poland.

The new left broke with the old left on this very issue—Stalinism. The new left wanted nothing to do with authoritarian leaders, bureaucratic functionaries and barracks communism. For this reason, the new left scandalized not simply conservatives, but stolid Communists, who considered it too anarchistic. Communist parties almost everywhere reacted with horror to the new left. *Anti-Communist Myths in Left Disguise*, a typical book by a Communist apparatchik from the 1970s, attacked new leftists as anarchists and libertines.[30]

It is possible to go further: The new left helped break up Stalinism. "Here and there," writes the critic Paul Berman in his *Tale of Two Utopias*, "the leaders of the revolutions of '89—a Václav Havel in Czechoslovakia, an Adam Michnik in Poland—turned out to be the same heroic persons, now adult liberals, who as young radicals had helped lead the movements of '68, just to show the relation of one uprising to the next."[31]

Michnik at least half agrees. "For my generation," he has written, "the road to freedom began in 1968." He admits that "at first glance," rebelling students in Berkeley and Paris, on one side, and those in Warsaw and Prague, on the other, shared little. The former rejected democratic liberties and championed the Communist project; the latter championed democratic liberties and rejected communism. "Nevertheless, I think there were also some common threads:

the anti-authoritarian spirit, a sense of emancipation, and the conviction that 'to be a realist means to demand the impossible.'"[32]

Havel also found sustenance in 1960s culture, partly derived from a 1968 visit to New York. The Czech dissident movement, writes Berman, was an "odd" confirmation of "some of the wilder youth-culture theories that became popular circa 1969 in the American New Left." When Czech authorities banned a rock group, the Plastic People, Havel and others rallied to their defense in a committee that eventually became Charter 77, which spearheaded the opposition for the next ten years. Almost confirming the argument, after less than a month in office, the new Czech president Havel invited Frank Zappa to Prague; he was met by ecstatic fans, "hippies from 1968, preserved in amber" (in Berman's words).[33] "The Czechs were delighted to point out," Timothy Garton Ash observed, "that '89 is '68 turned upside down."[34]

Yet to credit the new left for undermining Stalinism is a stretch. Perhaps it played a small role in Czechoslovakia and Poland; nothing more. Nor is there a need to be simplistic about the new left; what "the" new left did over twenty-odd years cannot be neatly categorized. Some individuals despised the old left; some came out of the old left and never abandoned Stalinism; other individuals and splinter groups reembraced it.

For instance, in 1972, a mainstream American publisher, Doubleday, brought out a collection of Stalin's writings edited by H. Bruce Franklin, a new-leftist English professor. His introduction began this way: "I used to think of Joseph Stalin as a tyrant and butcher who jailed and killed millions, betrayed the Russian revolution, sold out liberation struggles." Franklin continued, "But to about a billion people today"—a billion and one including Franklin—"Stalin is the opposite of what we in the capitalist world" believe. According to Franklin, who is now a chaired professor at Rutgers University, Stalin was an authentic liberator, a true leader who is revered by working people throughout the world.[35] This stuff was hard to take in 1972—indeed, it would have been hard to take in 1932—but it was not representative of the new left.

No matter. Setting forth the history of the new left is important, but most people ignore it. Anarchists, Trotskyists and new-leftists might despise Stalinism, but they partake in the wider left and share its fate. This is indisputable. The demise of the Soviet Union and its Communist allies eviscerates the idea of socialism. Intellectually cogent protests in the name of an unsullied socialism or "classical" Marxism are both necessary and useless.[36] "With the final collapse of the Soviet system," writes the French leftist André Gorz, "it is not just a variety of socialism that has collapsed. . . . What has also collapsed is the conception of 'authentic' socialism (or communism)."[37]

Numerous critics and observers have seen the handwriting on the wall, although their interpretations differ. Eric Hobsbawm, a veteran Marxist historian, admits: "Those of us who believed that the October Revolution was the gate to the future of world history have been shown to be wrong." He concedes that today "there is no part of the world that credibly represents an alternative system to capitalism," which "has once again proved that it remains the most dynamic force in world development."[38] Robin Blackburn, editor of *New Left Review*, concurs: "The ruin of 'Marxist-Leninist' Communism has been sufficiently comprehensive to eliminate it as an alternative to capitalism and to compromise the very idea of socialism. The debacle of Stalinism has embraced reform Communism, and has brought no benefit to Trotskyism, or social democracy, or any socialist current."[39]

For the left in South America, writes Jorge E. Castañeda, "the fall of socialism in the Soviet Union and Eastern Europe represents the end of a stirring, effective, nearly century-old utopia. Indeed, the very notion of an overall alternative to the status quo has been severely questioned. . . . The idea of revolution itself, central to Latin American radical thought for decades, has lost its meaning."[40]

Exactly. Socialism may not be dead, but confidence in a new and different society is. Instead of championing a radical idea of a new society, the left ineluctably retreats to smaller ideas, seeking to expand the options within the existing society. Immediately after noting the link between "'89" and "'68," Ash observes the difference, the absence of a new socialism or utopia. The Eastern European left does not reach for a new society beyond capitalism; rather, it supports parliamentary democracy, rule of law and a market economy—the familiar institutions of Western Europe and North America.[41]

Michnik concurs. He notes the "common threads" linking '68 and '89, but emphasizes the contrast. "At that time," he writes of the 1960s, "we defined ourselves as socialists and people of the left," but now "this formula" gives rise to "an internal protest." After living in a Communist "utopia" for forty years, he can no longer "subscribe" to its ideology.[42] Michnik is not alone. As the English-Czech scholar Ernest Gellner stated shortly before his death, "No one, virtually *no one* has a good word to say for Marxism itself. . . . Never was a sinking ship abandoned with such alacrity and unanimity, never was an experiment condemned so conclusively."[43]

Even Misha Glenny, who tries in his informed study of the East European revolutions to salvage socialism, comes up short. His very title, *The Rebirth of History*, implies that Francis Fukuyama's idea of the "end of history" (and socialism) is misleading. To a degree he is surely right. When he witnessed Alexander Dubček, who had been deposed by the Soviets twenty years earlier, addressing a half million cheering Czechs in 1989, Glenny along with the throngs melted into tears. "It was the only way to comprehend what I was witnessing— the rebirth of a history that the forces of reaction thought they had killed off forever."[44]

Other observers agree that the events of 1989 could be read not as the end of history, but its beginning. The long night of repressive communism had lifted. In 1989 several hundred thousand Hungarians gathered for a massive state funeral, the reburial of their president, Imre Nagy, executed following the Soviet invasion of 1956; this was an act of liberation and sadness. "The somber and sometimes even tearful mood of the huge crowd," writes a historian, "testified to the depth of the emotional burden of powerlessness and humiliation that Hungarians had felt since 1956."[45] Now they were taking charge of their fate.

Nevertheless, as David Marquand observes, "The crowds that thronged the squares of eastern Europe" were "acting in the spirit" of the French or American, not the Bolshevik Revolution. "They were protesting *against* the October Revolution" and against Marxism.[46] Even Glenny admits that for Eastern Europeans "the vocabulary associated with socialism is identified with economic failure and political repression." The "socialism" that survives in Eastern Europe consists of little more than a skepticism about the market and a desire to preserve a social-security network.[47]

In other words, this "socialism" does not differ from a Western end-of-ideology liberalism bound to the welfare state and planning small improvements to it. The point is, everywhere the left becomes practical, pragmatic and liberal. "We perhaps need to rethink and reconstruct the concept of socialism," writes Douglas Kellner, a leftist professor, in an essay titled "The Obsolescence of Marxism?" "Perhaps socialism should be seen more as a normative ideal than as a historical force."[48]

Socialist thought, writes Norman Birnbaum in an overview of the plight of socialism, is "defensive," with no grand, new projects or hopes. European socialists are "chastened . . . content with very small stakes, afraid to ask more of themselves and their electorates."[49] "The brute fact," summarizes Stanley Aronowitz, is that "there is little to distinguish the U.S. left from yesterday's everyday social welfare liberalism. . . . Most appalling, we live in a time when the left has run out of ideas."[50] One of the left's savviest thinkers concedes that the outlook is grim. "None of the political currents that set out to challenge capitalism in this century has morale or compass today," concludes Perry Anderson in a lengthy encounter with Fukuyama. The "socialist vision" has "fallen into radical doubt."[51]

What is true of the socialists need hardly be proved for those closer to the center: liberals. The differences between these political categories have never been clear, but it can be safely assumed that if leftists have abandoned a belief in a different future, liberals commit themselves more than ever to the welfare state. As the philosopher

Richard Rorty puts it, "We liberals have no plausible large-scale sce-
nario" for the future; we have no ideas analogous to those of "our
grandfathers . . . for changing the world."[52] We must junk the big
proposals and ideas that misled us in the past. "I hope that we can
banalize the entire vocabulary of leftist political deliberation." We
must drop the term *capitalism* and "conclude that bourgeois democratic welfare states are the best we can hope for."[53]

In an era without a left, political philosophers like Michael J.
Sandel use a new or refurbished vocabulary to revive liberalism. He
tells us in his well-received book *Democracy's Discontent*, that we
need a new "political agenda informed by the civic strand of freedom." What does that mean? The answer must be, not much or not
clear. Goodwill and earnestness mark Sandel's book, but its language turns soapy with incessant calls for civic virtue and republican
freedoms. "A political agenda informed by civic concerns would in-
vite disagreement about the meaning of virtue and the forms of self-
government," he writes with mounting excitement. If this says little,
Sandel clarifies that the agenda faces two specific challenges: "One
is to devise political institutions capable of governing the global
economy. The other is to cultivate the civic identities necessary to
sustain those institutions, to supply them with moral authority they
require." Or, he writes that "to revitalize the civic strand of freedom" Americans "must find a way to ask what economic arrangements are hospitable to self-government, and how the public life of a
pluralist society might cultivate in citizens the expansive self-under-
standing that civic engagement requires."

This is liberalism that has lost its moorings. Sandel runs on about
moral authority and civil allegiances. The terms sound edifying and
almost religious, but their meaning is obscure. The nouns pile up in
neat mounds across the page: civic virtue, civic identity, moral authority, common identity. To be sure, Sandel on occasion specifies
activities that exemplify new citizenship. The practices seem worthy,
but not particularly fresh or original; nor do they require a new
rhetoric. He points to "sprawlbusters," people who oppose national

chain stores in their communities, or to new urbanists seeking to "build communities more hospitable to a vibrant civic life."[54]

These are not stray examples of an earnest and woozy liberalism. The chatter on civic virtues and republican purpose fills endless essays and talks. In well-appointed lecture halls poker-faced professors gather to reflect on the crises of America before adjourning for the banquet dinner. What they offer is not wrong, but uplifting and vague. "A more communitarian version of liberalism," writes Thomas A. Spragens, Jr., a Duke University professor, "would permit liberalism to recapture some of the normative complexity and moral weight that characterized its inception." Like Sandel, Spragens finds practical implications in this rhetoric. Liberals "seek to design social institutions and policies in ways that promote civic friendship and a sense of common purpose. . . . They will seek to promote institutions, such as the public schools, that bring people from different backgrounds together. . . . And they will champion a public rhetoric of common identity and inclusiveness."[55]

Political theorists crank this stuff out by the truckload; perhaps someone is buying. It is hard to protest the sentiment and ethos, but it is also hard to know what it means aside from a general support for the liberal state and democratic politics. The problem is, this liberalism has turned vapid because a left that kept it honest has disappeared or turned liberal or both. A left constituted the liberal backbone; as the left vaporized, the backbone went soft. The decline or fate of liberalism without a left might be glimpsed in the distance traveled since John Stuart Mill, whose name is often invoked by today's liberals.

To put it crudely, page for page, sentence for sentence, Mill's writings delivered a kick that contemporary liberals never match. The new liberals have adopted an idiom that is uplifting without being transcendental, profound without being deep. The emergence of a watery liberalism derives not simply from a lack of talent or genius. Rather, Mill partook of a socialist world; he was drawn to utopian socialism and wrote sympathetically about socialism.[56]

His grip of economic realities may be one reason his prose and ideas retained an earthy radicalism his successors relinquish. One example: Mill defended private property, but he challenged as unacceptable "landed property," that is, private ownership of tracts of land:

> When the "sacredness of property" is talked of, it should always be remembered, that any such sacredness does not belong in the same degree to landed property. No man made the land. It is the original inheritance of the whole species. Its appropriation is wholly a question of general expediency. When private property in land is not expedient, it is unjust. . . . It is some hardship to be born into the world and to find all nature's gifts previously engrossed. . . . To reconcile people to this . . . it will always be necessary to convince them that the exclusive appropriation is good for mankind on the whole, themselves included. But this is what no sane being could be persuaded of.[57]

*   *   *

Everywhere a return to market or civic thought can be charted. In an era of ideological decomposition, leftists advance only the most modest goals and ideas. "Many politically engaged intellectuals," writes sociologist Jeffrey Alexander, have adopted ideas about the market as rational or liberating. "We are witnessing the death of a major alternative not only in social thought but in society itself."[58]

Some left-leaning observers argue that the old political categories have lost their meaning. "Time has chopped away" at the differences between liberal and leftist, writes Michael Tomasky in his book, *Left for Dead*, which tries to resuscitate a left. "No one today can talk seriously about dismantling capitalism, for example, which was the main project of the left in America. . . . Similarly, no one can talk seriously about the possibility of world socialism."[59]

For Tomasky, minor reforms of the market constitute the outermost boundaries of political aspiration. "The first principle of a new left program is to . . . produce a strategy to protect working families in the age of globalization." The problem is less the commendable goals, however, than the limited means. Inasmuch as global capitalism is irreversible, Tomasky argues that a left should not resist international trade agreements, but "push for inclusion" of an "equalization tax" so that goods made cheaply in the Third World cannot undersell American goods.

It hardly need be underlined that the notion of protective tariffs is not radical; and in fact a hint of a fundamental transformation does not tinge his pages. Tomasky attacks corporations and over-compensated executives, but believes that in an era of sound bites, "only when a presidential candidate or a party leader or some other major figure" repeatedly attacks the ills "will these conditions begin to change." As is so often the case, the language of the practical reformer becomes spongy and vague. In addition to exemplary speeches, he calls for a "rhetoric . . . aimed at galvanizing working people around a positive idea—the potential they have as political partners to make corporations and politicians respond to them."[60]

Robert Kuttner's *Everything for Sale*, closer to the liberal middle, exudes an even more cramped spirit; all he wishes to do is modify the market. He sees himself as a critic of the pure laissez-faire economy and an exponent of the "mixed economy," a creation as American as Alexander Hamilton or Lyndon B. Johnson. He believes that the capitalist system is a "superior form of economic organization" that sometimes needs to be supplemented, corrected and modified, for instance, in the field of health care. He offers a cogent criticism of the proposal, and often reality, that the profit-making corporations minister to the health needs of a population.

Again, Kuttner has many reasonable things to say, but no one will pretend he is offering a strikingly different vision for America; his prose and pose bear the stamp of Washington think tanks. He seconds a proposal to create a new category of a "responsible corporation" that would receive tax breaks in exchange for decent environmental and employee provisions. Among other conditions, to qualify a corporation would "have to contribute at least 3 percent of payroll to a portable, multi-employer pension plan, along the lines of plans offered by the TIAA/CREF teacher's pension fund."

This proposal also calls for a "Tobin-style tax on short-term trading of securities."

The idea, presented in the language of Washington bureaucrats, is less than riveting and is hardly comprehensible to the uninitiated. Some of his other proposals score low on the plausibility scale. To counter profound American political apathy, Kuttner suggests a "policy jury," something like a mock jury in which "ordinary citizens" are charged with resolving difficult public-policy issues. After specialists make presentations, the juries come to a verdict. Why bored Americans, who barely vote or read newspapers, might take a week off to listen to experts drone about national health plans or reforming the tax code is not immediately obvious. However, Kuttner knows about the process firsthand:

> I participated in one of these affairs, whose subject was the budget deficit. I was the expert witness, opposed by Republican Representative Vin Weber. . . . Each of us was backed up by a team of specialists. . . . Twelve ordinary people, compensated with a trip to Washington and a modest honorarium, spent the better part of a week boning up on fiscal issues. At the end of the week they voted to cut defense spending."[61]

Kuttner grandly notes that a foundation and a university footed the bill for this experiment in civic virtue. One need not be a right-wing crank to wonder if the monies could have been better spent than wining and dining several teams of specialists and twelve outsiders for "the better part of week"; nor does one have to be a cynic to wonder about the "ordinary citizens" dragged into this affair. In any event, the proposal hardly comes to terms with political apathy.

Paul Starr, who co-edits a political magazine with Kuttner, puts it forthrightly. Once socialism inspired liberalism with ambitious ideas of transformation, but no more; it is time to call it quits. The socialist project "has been thoroughly discredited." Liberalism has no need of socialism. "Socialism is simply not our appointed historical destiny." For Starr, the old dream must be surrendered; the point is to modify, not transform. "Reform capitalism, yes; replace it, no."

He calls for the end to an old love affair. "When socialism was young and full of fervor, some liberals were understandably infatuated. . . . But the romance should be over once and for all."[62]

Even a robust effort to invigorate radicalism like Ralph Miliband's *Socialism for a Skeptical Age* presents itself mildly and soberly: "A socialist government would give a very high priority to the achievement of full employment and would seek to turn the right to work into a reality." He continues that "a fundamental aspect of policy would be the provision of ample facilities for retraining and the renewal of skills."[63] Once upon a time leftists and radicals talked of liberation or the abolition of work. Now the talk is about full employment and retraining the workforce.

Ira Katznelson, a leftist political scientist, explains why he believes that socialism "must undergo an astringent tapering" and become "self-limiting." In genteel prose he writes that socialism must "give up the impossible dream of a future entirely without exploitation" and embrace "meliorative" goals, "while recalling to liberalism the inherently social qualities of its own cherished norm of human autonomy."[64] Pass the sherry. Katznelson is to socialism as Sandel is to liberalism.

Other socialists hold up, once again, familiar Scandinavian models. "It is a useful thing to try to make the question of what could be a viable socialism in an advanced industrial society more specific," writes the socialist Bogdan Denitch in *After the Flood*. For instance? "Something like a more advanced Sweden."[65] Charles Derber in *What's Left?* offers as a model Basque cooperative factories in Mondragon, Spain. "Mondragon is not a household name, but it should be and may soon become so," he writes optimistically. In Mondragon, he finds worker-owned and -managed enterprises that could be emulated.[66]

Even hard-boiled socialists confirm the widespread drift into policy proposals. Socialists now present themselves as practical businessmen. They have dispensed with radical sentiments and foggy utopias. John E. Roemer, a well-regarded leftist thinker, opens his *A Future for Socialism* by noting the collapse of Soviet communism, but he argues that an "alternative socialism" or "market socialism" is still possible and desirable. He wants a socialism that would aim for both "efficiency *and* equality." He sketches out a realistic model, which turns on what one of his champions calls "a relatively simple device": the distribution of coupons.[67]

The simple scheme is relatively complex, requiring the establishment of nonconvertible "coupons" giving ownership in corporations and companies. These are delivered to citizens in an egalitarian manner—and are given up at death—bestowing on all equal ownership in society's wealth. They cannot be sold or surrendered, which prevents new inequalities from arising. The benefits are numerous: "One should expect, then, that the poor will be the controlling group in most firms, as they own the majority of coupons. . . . Thus, the firms will choose their levels of investments in the interest of the poor."[68]

Is this plan practical or possible? It presupposes a completely egalitarian redistribution of assets. All citizens receive the same amount of coupons and ownership in society's resources. Donald Trump and the hotel maid will get equal shares in what was once his hotel. What are the prospects for this? Nil. To put it another way, these are practical reforms that require a revolution.

The scheme presents itself as a limited proposal that has been methodically thought out, an example of a new nonutopian and tough-minded socialism. Indeed, Roemer includes an appendix in which he calculates to the tenth of a cent the profit dividend each adult in the United States would have received if the "coupon economy" had been in operation during the postwar decades. For instance, he estimates that in 1989 each adult would have received $310.414—much worse than in 1988, when everyone would have pocketed $820.794.[69]

Socialism here has contracted to the idea of equality defined by coupons, incentives and competition. Fight for socialism and win $310.41. Roemer admits that socialists should consider themselves "victorious" if they "can design systems that bring about the degree of income equality and level of public services that exist in the Nordic social democracies."[70]

This is not a stray example. Much contemporary socialist thought seeks to be practical in market terms. Another leftist emphasizes that "pragmatic market socialism" has little to do with past social-ism. James A. Yunker, a professor of economics, advocates a social-ism devoted to equality in which corporate power will be concentrated in what he calls a Bureau of Public Ownership. He re-grets that in the past socialists damned capitalism too broadly. Al-though their intention was to galvanize support for socialism, "these ill-considered charges against capitalism may have seriously weak-ened the socialist cause by suggesting that its adherents were mostly harebrained enthusiasts driven by utopian fantasies."

His "pragmatic market socialism," on the other hand, is a "very precise and conservative formulation of socialism." Yunker demon-strates how conservative it is. His market socialism will "some-what" increase the equality of income distribution with "the emphasis on the adverb 'somewhat.'" That is all. "Neither will it necessarily have any significant beneficial effect on recognized social problems . . . such as alienation, crime, drug abuse, racism, sexism, environmental degradation, militarism and imperialism."[71] This is a socialism suitable for capitalism.

Donald Weiss, a leftist professor, argues in *The Specter of Capital-ism and the Promise of a Classless Society* that recent events have re-futed much but not all of Marxism. The idea of a classless society "not only is desirable but is becoming increasingly feasible." How is it possible to achieve a classless society, when everything seems to militate against it? Easier than even Roemer suspected—dismantle public education.

For this Marxist, public education perpetuates class differences. "A competitive market in education would bring us nearer to the goal of the classless society than our public system can get us." So-cialism, or what remains of the socialist idea, namely a classless soci-ety, can be introduced by a "voucher system . . . an economically essential moment of the overthrow of classes."[72] At the *fin de siècle*, Marxism seeks an afterlife as a more perfect capitalism.

Another venture to fan the flames that will warm no one belongs to Michael Albert, a long-term socialist writer and publisher. His *Thinking Forward* combines agitprop and academic chit-chat with a dreary vision of the future. Albert is so pleased with his idea of "participatory economics" that he has given it an acronym, PARECON; and with a keen sense of its import he titles his last chapters, "Reactions to PARECON" and "What's Next for PARECON?" He wants to distinguish "PARECON" from market socialism.

Some sense of the beast comes across in his description of its aim: "To reduce to a minimum (if possible to zero) the possibility of socially counterproductive self-advancement; to prevent some people from 'living better' than others unless they had undergone greater personal sacrifice." If this sounds a bit grim, he assures us that in PARECON "esteem and social recognition for outstanding abilities that create great social benefits for others will be very high." Lest this leave the masses unmoved, Albert's elegant prose might provoke them: "The difference in a participatory economy from all those that have gone before is not that nobody will ever have to perform a task they dislike, but that any task in anyone's job complex that is not gratifying is there because it would be unfair if it were absent."[73]

Those who never fell in love have less to fear. Perhaps for this reason, some of the sharpest criticism of the market comes not from socialists or liberals, but from conservatives free of guilt and apology. The terms here may not precise. What is conservativism today? In any event, two writers associated with *Business Week* have written a more spirited attack on market capitalism than anyone on the contemporary left. William Wolman and Anne Colamosca, in *The Judas Economy: The Triumph of Capital and the Betrayal of Work,* do not simply defend wage workers, but question the success of unfettered capitalism. The unraveling of the Soviet empire signified a Western victory in the cold war; it also "damaged the case for milder forms of state intervention, ranging from democratic socialism to such gentle free market reforms as America's New Deal." Not only heirs of Marx, but those of Franklin D. Roosevelt and Lyndon B. Johnson lost out.

Today even the left-wing parties extol the private sector, doubting the government's ability to serve the public. Yet Wolman and Colamosca recall a truth the left tries to soft-pedal:

The economic pathology of communist and socialist states does not by itself prove the case against government. The state has done enough good and the unfettered free market enough harm in the industrial countries of the West during the twentieth century to raise serious concerns about the ultimate impact of the right-wing drift of economic policy throughout the industrial world.

To be sure, these authors harbor no far-reaching vision of the future. They anticipate crises and limited employment, but call for only limited reforms, "grounded in the possible," a better balance between labor and capital. In short, they believe "capitalism must be saved from itself."[74]

* * *

The issue is the decline of a utopian vision that once imbued leftists and liberals. The point is hardly that improved air, enhanced welfare or a broader democracy is bad. The question, rather, is the extent a commitment to reasonable measures supplants a commitment to unreasonable ones—those more subversive and visionary. Can liberalism with a backbone exist if its left turns mushy? Does radicalism persist if reduced to means and methods? Does a left survive if it abandons a utopian hope or plan? "The idea of utopia," commented T. W. Adorno some years ago, has "disappeared completely from the conception of socialism. Thereby the apparatus, the how, the means of socialist society have taken over any possible content."[75]

To be sure, even those with little familiarity with Marxism know its founders denounced "utopian" socialism and prized "scientific" and practical approaches. This is only half right. Marxism and utopianism did not exist as simple opposites.[76] Yet it is true that the utopian spirit remained alive mainly among the dissenting leftists from Paul Lafargue and William Morris to Walter Benjamin and Ernst Bloch. These thinkers protested an idea of the future as an improved model of the present, where labor was not abolished or minimized, but simply better compensated. On this very issue, Lafargue,

Marx's son-in-law, penned in 1883 a caustic pamphlet attacking the fetish of work, *The Right to Be Lazy.*

Lafargue argued that not only economists and moralists, but socialists and laborers, believe that more work is the cure for social and personal ills. His pamphlet opened with a parody of the opening of *The Communist Manifesto:* "A strange delusion possesses the working classes. . . . This delusion is the love of work, the furious passion for work." The religion of work has spread throughout society, maiming and crippling individuals, although Lafargue notes that the rich preach work, but choose leisure.

Though the ancient world understood that work was a curse, modern industrial society spreads its gospel. The working class, Lafargue hopelessly hoped, must reject the work fetish. It must demand "the Rights of Laziness," restricting labor to three hours and "reserving the rest of the day and night for leisure and feasting."

> If, uprooting from its heart the vice which dominates it and degrades its nature, the working class were . . . not to demand the Rights of Man . . . not to demand the Right to Work which is but the right to misery, but to forge a brazen law forbidding any man to work more than three hours a day, the earth, the old earth, trembling with joy would feel a new universe leaping within her.[77]

On this topic Walter Benjamin as well excoriated the conventional socialists, who "resurrected" the "old Protestant ethic of work" and believed that factory labor constituted "technological progress." Against these cramped ideas, Benjamin returned to utopians like Charles Fourier, "whose fantasies, which have so often been ridiculed, prove to be surprisingly sound."[78]

For a practical world Fourier's writings are anathema; he dreamed of androgenous planets, a libertine sexual order and a paradise of food. Even the poorest would eat five times a day with a choice of twelve types of soup, twelve types of bread and wine and twelve dressings for meat and vegetables. Unlike Kuttner, who proposes policy juries, Fourier commended tasting juries; he anticipated, as his biographer puts it, "a day when the wars of civilization would be replaced by what amounted to international cooking contests."[79] No one has attacked more extravagantly the religion of commerce. "Wisdom, virtue, morality, all these have fallen out of fashion: everybody worships at the shrine of commerce. A nation's true greatness, what the economists regard as its true glory, is to sell more pairs of trousers to the neighbouring empire than its buys from them."[80]

Over the years and against conventional wisdom, utopians sustained a vision of life beyond the market. Amid the revolutionary surges following World War I, the Hungarian Georg Lukács set forth a theory of the "old and new culture" in which he argued that the socialist economy was not the goal; it was simply a precondition for humanity to advance to a new and humane culture. Most radicals do not understand that political power and economic reorganization is not the end-all, stated Lukács. The goal is not a new economic order, but freedom from an obsession with economics.

> We can clarify this with a very simple example: someone is racking his brain over a complex scientific problem but during his work he contracts an unrelenting toothache. Clearly, in most cases he would be unable to remain in the stream of his thought and work until the immediate pain is relieved. The annihilation of capitalism, the new socialist reconstruction of the economy, means the healing of all toothaches for the whole of humanity.[81]

"The healing of all toothaches for the whole of humanity": That this statement can no longer be thought, much less restated, bespeaks the end of utopia.

— 2 —

THE MYTH OF
MULTICULTURALISM

W hy . . . put recipes for cheese balls on revolutionary flags?"
asked O. B. Hardison, Jr., the classicist, in his book on American
cultural identity. He was referring to the national motto, *E Pluribus
Unum* ("One out of Many" or "Out of Many, One"), which appears on coins and official symbols of the United States. According
to Hardison, the motto derives from a poem of Virgil that gave a
recipe for a cheese ball, a favorite of Roman farmers. "You put all
the ingredients of the cheese ball into a bowl, says Virgil, mix them
together, and—presto!—from many you get one."[1]

Oddly little consensus exists as to where the American motto
came from or what it means.[2] If Virgil was the ultimate source, the
exact phrase does not appear in the Roman poet; in fact, the motto
shows up in the works of no Latin writer. The originators of the
great seal of the United States, who sanctioned the saying, included
Jefferson, Adams and Franklin. They commissioned a Swiss-French
artist to design the seal, and either he or Franklin borrowed the
words from a well-known English journal, *The Gentleman's Magazine*, where *E Pluribus Unum* regularly ran on the title page.

The Gentleman's Magazine, in turn, had picked it up from an
earlier periodical published in London by a French Huguenot,
Pierre Antoine Montteux, who seemed to have invented the motto.
In affixing *E Pluribus Unum* to his journal, Montteux meant al-

most the opposite of what the motto is often said to signify. "That which is prefixed to this *Miscellany*," Montteux wrote in 1692, referring to *E Pluribus Unum,* "implies that tho' only one of the many Pieces in it were acceptable, it might gratify every reader."[3] For Montteux, many do not make one; rather, he believed his magazine succeeded if only one contribution out of the many pleased the reader.

In adopting the epigram for *The Gentleman's Magazine*, its editor, Edward Cave, seemed to have something else in mind. Cave's magazine often consisted of material abridged from other sources. *E Pluribus Unum,* implied the editor, made one issue out of many separate pieces, a common practice of the day. Early English magazines often sported mottoes that alluded to their diversity. Cave also copied the motto, "More in Quantity and Greater Variety than any Book of the Kind and Price."[4] His use of *E Pluribus Unum* may have had less to do with cheese balls than advertising.

Cave, who also had the habit of pinching, altering and fabricating material for his magazine, earned a reputation as a literary buccaneer.[5] Moreover, Montteux, who invented the slogan, led a less than sterling life and died, strangled, in a brothel.[6] In short, *E Pluribus Unum,* the elevating motto of American cultural pluralism, not only lacks a clear classical legacy, it is shot through with ambiguity and scandal. One nineteenth-century historian who reflected on this tangled history found the story shameful:

> We have been singularly unfortunate in our choice of a motto, and it would be difficult to find one more infelicitous or more inappropriate for a great nation than "E pluribus unum." Surely nothing could be more unbecoming or more insignificant ... a motto of modern, plebeian, and non-classic origin, with no literary or historic associations ... a motto utterly void of all religious or moral tone ... a motto that may mean either union or disunion, according to one's sympathies, and which, unhappily, meant the latter in the mind of its originator. .... Every citizen who has the best interests of his country at his heart must regret that our present motto was so unfortunately chosen and is so utterly unfit for a great republic.[7]

However, this unedifying motto and the pluralism it implies or belies have bewitched the American republic from its beginning—and never more than in recent years, when an interest has become an obsession.[8] Few causes have won such widespread enthusiasm as pluralism and its incarnations as multiculturalism, cultural diversity and cultural pluralism. The phrases kick off a thousand speeches and articles; they appear in hundreds of essays and books. Government officials, college administrators, corporate executives, museum curators and high-school principals—to name just a few—declare their commitment to multiculturalism. One sign of the times: The American Council on Education published a guide to programs and publications on cultural diversity that runs four hundred pages.[9]

Even conservatives, who might be expected to swim against the current, often jump in, confining their objections to fringe deformations, not the thing itself. Publicly at least, they hesitate to forcefully protest a larger multiculturalism. To establish its credentials, a conservative foundation put out a magazine called *Diversity* edited by an African American with the name David S. Bernstein.[10]

Liberals and leftists run the show. They define themselves by their enthusiasm for multiculturalism—the more you support it the more virtuous you are. Lawrence Levine's *The Opening of the American Mind*, the liberal rejoinder to Bloom's *The Closing of the American Mind*, brims with enthusiasm for multiculturalism. "We have rediscovered that sense of excitement, that sense of as yet unrealized possibilities. . . . Scholars have finally set about exploring and amending and expanding the notions of pluralism."[11] For liberals or leftists to challenge multiculturalism is like questioning recycling.

Multiculturalism was not always so popular. Horace M. Kallen, who virtually copyrighted the term *cultural pluralism,* stated in 1924 that the idea was "popular nowhere in the United States." He knew why. Vast immigration and World War I aggravated the public's fears of foreigners; Americanization and assimilation, not pluralism and diversity, became the watchwords. For Kallen, the revived Ku Klux Klan exemplified a repressive American conformity. "The alternative before Americans is Kultur Klux Klan or Cultural Pluralism."[12]

Seventy years later everyone—except for a few conservative dissenters—has joined Kallen in celebrating "cultural pluralism." "We are all multiculturalists now," concludes Nathan Glazer. We can "still argue about the details," but multiculturalism is here to stay; its victory is "complete."[13] Once "cultural pluralism had been a minor movement in the history of the American academic and literary intelligentsia," writes the historian David A. Hollinger. By the 1990s, however "a sea change had taken place." Since the earlier discussion, "the most striking difference" is "the sheer triumph . . . of the doctrine that the United States ought to sustain rather than diminish a great variety of distinctive cultures." Now "opponents of this idea" are "very much on the defensive in national politics, the mass media, public education and academia."[14]

Even backers of a radical multiculturalism, who revile a liberal variant, proclaim they ride the crest of history. Christopher Newfield and Avery F. Gordon, two University of California professors, rebuke Rush Limbaugh, the conservative commentator, for his attacks on multiculturalism, observing he "rightly feels marginal to a diversity that is becoming an accomplished fact in the realm of culture."[15] The language is revealing. Diversity commands the mainstream; the conservative nay-sayer is on the margins.

How come? Has a program supported by Kallen and a few other dissenting intellectuals simply won everyone over? Has a new and varied immigration forced recognition of cultural diversity? Have cultural groups become more assertive and Americans more tolerant, liberal and cosmopolitan? Is the applause for multiculturalism a straightfoward success story, one of increasing enthusiasm for an increasingly diverse America? Or is it the result, as Nathan Glazer believes, of "the failure to bring a larger share of blacks into the common society?"[16] Each of these explanations expresses a partial truth, but a vital part of the story has been omitted.

Multiculturalism also plugs a gaping intellectual hole. Stripped of a radical idiom, robbed of a utopian hope, liberals and leftists retreat in the name of progress to celebrate diversity. With few ideas on how a future should be shaped, they embrace all ideas. Pluralism becomes the catch-all, the alpha and omega of political thinking. Dressed up as multiculturalism, it has become the opium of disillusioned intellectuals, the ideology of an era without an ideology.

The issue is not cultural pluralism itself. Ideas of diversity (and its kin: pluralism, variety, cultural pluralism and multiculturalism) are neither false nor objectionable; on the contrary, they are true and attractive. Diversity characterizes the natural, physical and cultural worlds—and we generally take delight in differences, not uniformity. Most people, and probably most philosophers, prefer pluralism and diversity to totality and the absolute. William James, for instance, complained of the "glut of oneness" with its dogmatic rigidity, which is threatened by "the slightest suspicion of pluralism, the minutest wiggle of independence."[17]

The problem is not a preference for pluralism, but its cult. The fetish sabotages a sober inspection of reality by catering to the American love of quantity. The lingo of pluralism underwrites the basic hype that more is better—more things, items, cars and cultures. Multiculturalism is obviously better than monoculturalism; a world of differences trumps a world of uniformity. But what exactly is multiculturalism?

The ideas of multiculturalism, cultural pluralism and diversity turn sacrosanct. They become blank checks payable to anyone in any amount, lacking meaning or content. They not only suggest a politics, but often replace politics. However, even with adjectives like *radical* or *transformative* attached, what politics do they designate? Apart from the wish to include more voices in the curriculum or different faces at the office, no vision drives multiculturalism. A term bandied about in discussions of multiculturalism, *inclusiveness* suggests conformity. The document drawn up by activists for a New York state education reform was titled *A Curriculum of Inclusion*. The goal of including more people in the established society may be laudable, but hardly seems radical. The rise of multiculturalism correlates with the decline of utopia, an index of the exhaustion of political thinking.

Several questions are rarely asked, much less answered, in the discussions of multiculturalism. How pluralistic is cultural pluralism? What are the real differences between cultures? What do the words *culture* and *pluralism* signify? Why did they become the preferred terms? How and why have cultural analyses replaced economic and sociological approaches? What is the relationship of politics to cultural pluralism?

To get at the terms *culture* and *pluralism* would require volumes, especially the word *culture*. Here only a few strands of this story and a few of its consequences can be discussed.

*   *   *

"When I hear the word culture, I reach for my gun." This famous line comes from a 1933 German play, *Schlageter*, by Hanns Johst. A more accurate rendering of the German runs, "When I hear the word culture . . . I release the safety on my Browning!" The name Browning—in Europe more than the United States—became identified with automatic and semiautomatic guns designed by the American John M. Browning. Gavrilo Princip, who commenced World War I by assassinating Archduke Franz Ferdinand, used a Browning .32-caliber semiautomatic pistol.[18]

Johst, a playwright and poet, shifted from the expressionism of World War I to the Nazism of World War II. "With loving dedication and unswerving loyalty," Johst inscribed *Schlageter* to Adolf Hitler. The work expressed typical nationalist and anti-intellectual contempt for liberalism, encapsulated in the idea of "culture." In the play a World War I veteran chides his pal for lapsing into liberalism.

> And the last thing I'll stand for is ideas to get the better of me! I know that rubbish from '18, . . . fraternity, equality, . . . freedom, . . . beauty and dignity! . . . No, let 'em keep their good distance with their whole ideological kettle of fish *[Weltanschauungssalat]*.. . . I shoot with live ammunition! When I hear the word culture . . . I release the safety on my Browning![19]

"Culture" here implies liberalism and the Enlightenment, everything the Nazis despised. Yet it was not only the far right that loathed culture, but the far left as well. With an unsettling kinship to Johst's formulation, the Martinique psychiatrist Frantz Fanon wrote in *The Wretched of the Earth*, "When the native hears a speech about Western culture, he pulls out his knife—or at least makes sure it is within reach."[20] This view of culture roughly parallels that of Johst; talk of fraternity, equality, beauty and dignity drives the native to violence.

The disdain for culture expressed by Johst and Fanon is not identical, however. Both despise the deceit of culture, but for opposite reasons. For Johst, culture is in itself a fraud, the cheap talk of weaklings; for Fanon, culture deceives by reneging on its promises. Johst and the Nazis hated culture itself; Fanon hated its hypocrisy, a very different notion.

Liberals also denounced culture. John Bright, a nineteenth-century orator and liberal member of Parliament, complained that when people "talk about what they call *culture* . . . they mean a smattering of two dead languages of Greek and Latin." Frederic Harrison, a follower of Comte and positivism, concurred. "Perhaps the silliest cant of the day is the cant about culture. Culture . . . applied to politics . . . means simply a turn for small fault-finding, love of selfish ease, and indecision in action."[21]

All quarters targeted what might be called a classical notion of culture that emerged with the Enlightenment. Ideas about education, cultivation and progress drenched "culture," which implied a notion of progress. "The words *enlightenment, culture,* and *education [Bildung]*," wrote Moses Mendelssohn in 1784, "are newcomers to our language. . . . Linguistic usage, which seems to want to create a distinction between these synonymous words, still has not had the time to establish their boundaries."[22] "All cultural progress," wrote Kant fifteen years later, "represents the education of man. . . . The most important object of culture . . . is man . . . endowed with reason." Kant called this process the gift of "becoming civilized through culture."[23] To Fichte culture was the "exercise of all powers towards the end of full freedom."[24]

This concept of culture, attacked from the right and left, limped into the twentieth century, but did not survive. For conservatives it was too liberal, for leftists too elitist. Liberal anthropology struck the decisive blows. In 1952 two anthropologists, A. L. Kroeber and Clyde Kluckhohn, published a historical survey charting the fluctuating fate of the term *culture*. "The most generic sense of the word 'culture'—in Latin and in all the languages which have borrowed from the Latin root—retains the primary notion of cultivation or becoming cultured. . . . A second concept to emerge was that of German *Kultur*, roughly the distinctive 'higher' values or enlightenment of a society."[25]

According to Kroeber and Kluckhohn, the older and restricted meaning of culture had slowly ceded to a more expansive and scientific definition. They dated the more scientific version from E. B. Taylor's nineteenth-century *Primitive Culture*, which offered a dispassionate definition of culture as a "complex whole which includes knowledge, belief, art, law, morals, customs and any other capabilities and habits acquired by man as a member of society." Older usages assuming a hierarchical order still lingered, however. Even "intellectual and semi-intellectual circles" reverted to obsolete definitions. Kroeber and Kluckhohn wanted to hasten the victory of an objective and plastic notion of culture—that was the point of their book. "There would be no need for this monograph," they said, if people generally used the scientific term.[26]

The key work undermining the classical definition may have been Ruth Benedict's 1934 *Patterns of Culture*, a twentieth-century anthropological best-seller.[27] Benedict surveyed three peoples—the American Indians of the southwest Pueblos, those of the Northwest Coast and the Dobu of Melanesia—arguing not only against biological determinism, but for the relativity of cultures. "Social thinking at the present time," she concluded, "has no more important task before it than that of taking adequate account of cultural relativity."[28]

Twenty-five years later Margaret Mead noted that when Benedict began *Patterns of Culture*, her definition of "culture" belonged only to the "vocabulary of a small and technical group of professional anthropologists." Now it had become common usage.[29] Since these remarks, the anthropological concept of culture has completely swallowed the older notion. Culture has severed links to cultivation and reason and become any ensemble of activities. As one historian has put it, today's multiculturalists are "the intellectual descendants of Benedict."[30]

The newer definition did not win without protest. From Matthew Arnold in *Culture and Anarchy* to T. S. Eliot in *Notes Towards the Definition of Culture,* some scholars and critics sought to preserve "culture" as the realm of education, art and improvement. For instance, in the 1920s the classicist Werner Jaeger wrote that the new terminology led to a "leveling" in which antiquity became simply one "culture" out of many. The "anthropological concept" has made culture "a mere descriptive category which can be applied to any nation, even to the 'culture of the primitive.'"[31]

This countermovement, largely by conservatives, was futile; liberals, leftists, sociologists, psychologists and anthropologists—among others—rejected as reactionary any hierarchical view of culture or any distinction between an elite "culture" and common "civilization." Neither Marxists nor psychoanalysts saw any justification in separating "culture" from "civilization." "I scorn to distinguish between culture and civilization," wrote Freud.[32]

The gain was obvious. In the name of liberalism and science, anthropologists effectively dispatched as prejudiced the narrow idea of culture, which often was implicitly or explicitly racist. Earlier definitions, tied to ideas about education and cultivation, necessarily included judgments; some societies or groups might be less cultivated or practiced in the arts of freedom. The new concept implied no evaluation; cultures could not be ranked or rated. They were all equal. Culture became a fact of human life. For many anthropologists, the new concept of culture delivered a death blow to pseudo-scientific racism.

From the beginning of his career almost to his death in 1942, Franz Boas, the main figure in American anthropology, forcefully argued that human differences were cultural, not biological. In 1906 W. E. B. Du Bois invited Boas to address a black audience at Atlanta University, where the anthropologist championed the abilities of the American Negro. "To those who stoutly maintain a material inferiority of the Negro race and who would damper your ardor by their claims, you may confidently reply . . . that the past history of your race does not sustain their statement, but rather gives you encouragement." No scientific evidence supports the idea of Negro inferiority.[33] Boas's influence "in matters of race can hardly be exaggerated," writes the historian Carl N. Degler. "He accomplished his mission largely through his ceaseless, almost relentless articulation of the concept of culture."[34]

The anthropological notion of culture exuded a liberal and egalitarian ethos; this is its appeal and its truth. Yet *culture* also lost any specificity, becoming everything and anything. When *culture* is defined as an "ensemble of tools, codes, rituals, behaviors," not simply every people, but every group and subgroup has a "culture." The shift toward symbolic perspective by anthropologists further flattened and extended the turf; no longer is culture restricted to the "ensemble" of activities of a people, but *any* activity of *any* group might form a culture or subculture. Everything is culture. An essay by the anthropologist Clifford Geertz analyzes "common sense" as a "cultural system."[35] Kroeber and Kluckhohn had admitted that anything might constitute a "culture." What determines a particular culture is simply "convenience" and the "level of abstraction."[36]

The conceptual loss seems small. What is the danger if every group can be viewed as a "culture"? If every activity can be viewed culturally? A short step, however, leads from considering common sense a cultural system to treating the "culture" of drug addicts, soccer moms or fans of *Star Trek*. Of course, everyone has his or her own list, but the upshot is that each configuration forms a culture. Yet this can be questioned; different traits might not constitute a distinct culture.

The elastic notion of culture served well to undermine prejudice and ethnocentrism. Any damage was not obvious and, initially, was unimportant. Yet social usefulness does not equal truth. A conceptual bill went unpaid, and over the years costs have mounted. A return to a hierarchical notion of culture is not desirable, but an advance to some precision may be. Without considering what separates one culture from another, talk of multiculturalism succumbs to myths and illusions. If we cannot establish what defines a unique culture, how can we understand the relationship between two or more cultures or multiculturalism? To put this sharply, multiculturalism relies on an intellectual rout, the refusal or inability to address what makes up a culture.

In the conceptual defeat, culture is subjectivized. Culture becomes whatever any group or researcher wants it to mean. No one challenges that a collection of people constitutes a separate culture. At the same time the jargon of cultural diversity obscures social and economic realities, which turn either irrelevant or uninteresting. Multiculturalists see only culture and hardly attend to economic imperatives. Yet how can culture subsist apart from work and the production of wealth? And if it cannot, how can culture be apprehended without considering its entanglement in economic realities?

If the economic skeleton of culture were put on the table, patter about diversity might cease; it would be clear that the diverse cultures rest on the same infrastructures. What does it mean if two different cultures partake of identical economic activities? What does it imply if the same jobs, housing, schools, modes of relaxing and loving inform "two" cultures? To put this differently: What does cultural pluralism signify in the absence of economic pluralism?

Perhaps the question seems meaningless. Yet the apparent lack of meaning signals the intellectual retreat. The economic structure of society—call it advanced industrial society or capitalism or the market economy—stands as the invariant; few can imagine a different economic project. The silent agreement says much about multiculturalism. No divergent political or economic vision animates cultural diversity. From the most militant Afrocentrists to the most ardent feminists, all quarters subscribe to very similar beliefs about work, equality and success. The secret of cultural diversity is its political and economic uniformity. The future looks like the present with more options. Multiculturalism spells the demise of utopia.

No one contests the importance of jobs and wages in everyday life, but even the remaining Marxists lose interest. For decades critics have deplored the narrow materialism of Marxism; much of this criticism has been to the point. The critics succeeded beyond their wildest dreams, however. Economic Marxism became cultural Marxism. The valid criticism of a reductionist Marxism passed into a complete surrendering of its materialist core. Today Marxism trades in spirits, texts, images and echoes and flourishes only in departments of literature and English. Derrida's book on Marx, aptly titled *Specters of Marx*, deals with ghosts and reflections. Nineteenth-century Marxism was materialistic and determinist; late-twentieth-century Marxism is idealist and incoherent.[37]

Outside of Marxism, the same tendencies prevail. Culture is sexy, economics pedestrian. Strife about wages and work seems boring. Conflicts involving gays, lesbians or women, notes Stanley Aronowitz, provoke attention and discussion. "In contrast, a national 1993 Mineworkers' strike competes with the obituary columns for space on the back pages of the daily press."[38] David Bromwich has wondered whether intellectuals today would oppose an economic slavery if it lacked any racial or cultural dimension.[39] The question is hardly moot as economic inequalities augment and harden.

To the degree that culture subsumes everything, politics loses meaning. Of course, adherents of cultural pluralism often write of its politics. They reiterate endlessly the proposition that all of society and its constructs are political: texts, contexts, readings, authors, books, curriculums. Yet when everything is political, nothing is—or nothing is more political than anything else. "Recoding" a text is as politically charged as refashioning state power. Evidently multiculturalism is political, but how exactly? In the main, as advanced by radicals and academics, politics becomes simply a series of slogans about marginalization, power, discourse and representation. These terms address real problems, but they fail to specify any particular politics. Marginal groups want power or representation, but how or why does this reflect cultural differences or an alternative vision?

*   *   *

In the long run intellectual history cannot be divorced from political and social history. The onset of Nazism in the 1930s and the cold war in the 1950s affected the fate of the idea of pluralism; these events brought a notion of pluralism to the surface as an antipode to a new term, perhaps a new reality: totalitarianism.

The word *totalitarianism,* referring to Italian fascism, first appeared in the 1920s. After 1933, some critics extended it to Nazism. With its program of *"Gleichschaltung"* (total coordination of society) and the "total state," Nazism could properly be dubbed totalitarian. Yet the label really entered popular and scholarly discourse once Soviet communism fell under its rubric. Initially the Soviet Union and Nazi Germany seemed fundamentally different, and few sought to include them under one conceptual framework. Indeed, for much of the 1930s the two countries were sworn enemies.

Of course, this changed dramatically in August 1939 with the signing of the nonaggression pact between Germany and the Soviet Union. After this date, many liberal thinkers looked at Nazism and Soviet communism as related systems, adopting the term *totalitarianism* as the preferred label for both.[40] At a scholarly symposium held in Philadelphia soon after the pact, a speaker noted that the basic encyclopedia in the social sciences jumped from "torts" to "totemism" with no reference to totalitarianism.[41] Abbott Gleason, a professor of Russian history, writes that within a few months the word entered common discourse. "In the years 1940 and 1941 . . . the terms *totalitarian* and *totalitarianism* became . . . coin of the realm" in newspapers and periodicals. [42]

Around this time observers rediscovered pluralism and diversity as the essence of liberalism, which they contrasted to both monolithic

Nazi and Communist regimes. At the 1939 symposium a speaker listed "anti-pluralism" as a principle of the totalitarian and the "monistic" states. "Pluralism, a doctrine defended by liberalism, negates the very character of the totalitarian state."[43] Over the next several decades this perspective on totalitarianism with its ode to Western pluralism enjoyed great success. Its impact was probably aided by the fact that its leading exponents were refugees from European Nazism and communism, scholars of considerable intellect and prestige such as Hannah Arendt, Karl Popper, F. A. Hayek, Jacob Talmon, and Isaiah Berlin.[44]

For several reasons most writings on totalitarianism targeted Marxism and communism, not Nazism. Marxism possessed an intellectual credibility and heft, absent in Nazism, a mishmash of nationalist and anti-Semitic notions. For scholars analyzing the sources of totalitarianism, Marxism offered something to bite into. The intellectual substance of Nazism was nil. Moreover, communism preceded and outlasted Nazism; after 1945 and the onset of the cold war, totalitarianism signified the Soviet Union. Nazism had disappeared. "The term *totalitarian*," writes the historian Andrzej Walicki, "came to be applied to every country in which a party calling itself communist remained in power."[45] For Western liberals the main threat to freedom came from Marxism and communism.

The 1952 study of totalitarianism by the Polish-Israeli historian Jacob Talmon, who identified himself as someone who "has lived through the traumatic experiences of Nazism and Communism," says virtually nothing about the former.[46] "From the vantage point of the mid-twentieth century," Talmon wrote in the first paragraph of *The Origins of Totalitarian Democracy*, "the history of the last hundred and fifty years looks like a systematic preparation for the headlong collision between empirical and liberal democracy on the one hand, and totalitarian democracy on the other."[47]

Totalitarian democracy meant communism, not Nazism. This reading of history surprised even some of Talmon's students and followers; Nazism and genocide disappeared. Yehoshua Arieli, chairman of the Talmon Memorial Foundation, cited these same opening sentences and commented, "The phenomenon of the Holocaust as key to the understanding of the modern human condition is in a curious way overlooked." It does not fit into "the interpretative account" that Talmon gives of the "last one hundred and fifty years."[48]

Writings on totalitarianism posited a rough equivalence of Nazism and communism; they were both total systems straitjacketing life and thought. However, insofar as Marxism, not fascism, was the object of study, a shift in emphasis, and perhaps logic, took place. Pluralism was celebrated against the left; and the denunciation of the total system imperceptibly became the denunciation of utopia, as if they were obviously linked. Are they? In fact, totalitarianism and utopianism are not necessarily related; at least without distending the concept of utopianism into obscurity, it would be difficult to find a utopianism within Nazism. Yet the liberal consensus successfully established a rough equivalence of utopianism and totalitarianism, setting both against liberal pluralism. Damning totalitarianism meant damning utopianism.

These ideas found their most popular exposition in a best-seller published at the end of World War II, *The Road to Serfdom*, by F. A. Hayek, an Austrian economist and philosopher who had settled in England. For Hayek, communism and fascism were "merely variants of the same totalitarianism," which he argued in a chapter titled "The Great Utopia." Yet his real concern was the increasing socialist sentiment of his new home and the dangers of a welfare state. He called his book a "warning to the socialist intelligentsia." "Democratic socialism" relied on general and utopian ideas, he believed, that brought an end to individual liberty.[49]

Karl Popper's writings also did much to spread the belief that utopianism equaled totalitarianism and both undermined pluralism. As with Talmon and Hayek, the argument unfolded mainly against the left. His 1945 *The Open Society and Its Enemies* opened with Plato and lavished chapters on Hegel and Marx, but in two volumes hardly mentioned Nazism. It closed with a ringing defense of "our Western civilization" as "essentially pluralistic."[50]

In addition to Hannah Arendt, whose *Origins of Totalitarianism* attacked the Soviet and Nazi systems for relying on "total" ideologies,[51] Isaiah Berlin must be credited for establishing pluralism as a liberal creed. He decried the total and ideological approach, "the single all-embracing, all-clarifying, all-satisfying plan"; he feared the totally planned society that might eventually cast aside "the infinite variety of persons."[52]

Few ideas in political thought have enjoyed as much success as Berlin's propositions about "two concepts of liberty"; they have elicited a shelfload of commentary. Berlin proposed that historically two varieties of freedom existed, negative and positive. The former constitutes the domain of noninterference, where the individual is free from external control; the latter relies on an image of freedom and inexorably leads in the direction of control, regulating how people will live. Since not all individuals will support the same plan or vision, "positive" freedom requires coercion; for Berlin "positive" freedom constituted "the heart of many of the nationalist, communist, authoritarian and totalitarian creeds of our day." He concluded "Two Concepts of Liberty" by praising pluralism and denouncing total plans.[53]

Berlin, Popper, Arendt and the others carried the day. In the 1940s and 1950s the prevailing wisdom held that diversity and pluralism were the defining features of American society in particular and the wider tradition of Anglo-American liberalism in general. Totalitarian societies, on the hand, resting on "ideology" and "utopia," were inherently dictatorial. "Pluralism is a characteristic feature of democracy," which is opposed to the "uniform and monolithic . . . and 'totalitarian'" societies, stated one summary of the scholarly consensus.[54] As World War II receded into the past, analyses of totalitarianism increasingly concentrated on Marxism and the Soviet Union. The cold war infused the idea of pluralism.

Berlin is again illustrative. Though his critique of totalitarianism remained abstract, his concrete examples frequently came from Marxism; indeed, his entire argument about "positive" liberty necessitating total control hardly makes sense for Nazi, racist or nationalist ideologies. These doctrines did not presuppose a "positive" liberty they sought to enforce; they assumed no idea of liberty. Berlin's work addresses communism and Marxism, not Nazism and fascism; it was tilted against the left, not the right. In other words, Berlin's ideas partook of the cold war.

He was "rather proud," according to one account, to be a "Cold-War Liberal."[55] His credentials could hardly be contested. During the war in Vietnam, Berlin did not want to criticize the Americans. "It is frightful that Vietnamese villages should be bombed and the innocent continuously killed," he wrote. "But it seems to me even more dreadful to abandon people. . . . How is one to guarantee that . . . a precipitate and total American withdrawal would not cause other South-east Asian governments to be intimidated into knuckling under to régimes which many of their citizens would surely hate?"[56]

The cold war shaped and colored American pluralism. In the typical interpretation, against totalitarianism a series of contending and diverse groups constituted the genius of American society—its remarkable pluralism. This often repeated proposition explains why 1960s critics and scholars turned against pluralism with a vengeance. Pluralism became identified with the establishment. With the onset of the civil rights movement and the Vietnam war, younger critics objected to a picture of a benign America defending the world from totalitarianism.

What was so pluralistic about segregation? Or bombing Hanoi without voting a declaration of war? The notion of pluralism and its opposite, totalitarianism, seemed less a theory than a conformist defense of American society—exactly when racial and antiwar protests challenged American righteousness. "It is obvious that in using the totalitarian model," wrote Alfred G. Meyer, a Soviet specialist, "American scholars were also celebrating Americanism and at the same time succumbing to cold-war hysteria."[57]

In a history of the word *totalitarianism,* Abbott Gleason provides a generational account of disenchantment with the ideology of pluralism. "My initial rejection of these views [of totalitarianism and

pluralism] . . . began in college," he writes, "took on a more coherent form in the civil rights movement, [and] continued in opposition
to the Vietnam war." Protesting students came to believe that major
financial and political powers in the West—capitalism itself—evis-
cerated pluralism. "Many younger scholars found the Manichaean
division into good and evil, white hats and black hats, democrats
and totalitarians implausible and, after a while, insufferable. . . . The
term *free world*, so often used as an antonym to *totalitarian*, seemed
increasingly hollow."[58]

Critiques of pluralism formed the backbone of many leftist political
writings from the 1960s. A collection of "dissenting" pieces on power
and community targeted the "myth" that American society is "pluralistic." "The main substantive theme that unites all these essays is our
rejection of that myth; our conviction that the concept of democratic
pluralism has been ideological and obscurantist, in that our political
order is neither genuinely pluralistic nor always democratic."[59]

Henry S. Kariel's 1961 book *The Decline of American Pluralism*
argued that the state and corporations undercut pluralism.[60] Michael
Rogin, a Berkeley political scientist, opened his 1967 study of Mc-
Carthyism with an attack on the idea of pluralism; he noted that
American intellectuals gravitated toward pluralism under the impact
of the 1950s conformity and anticommunism.[61] The idea of "pluralism" meant political retreat. The historian John Higham in a comprehensive survey noted that "those radicals who pay heed to the
theory of pluralism denounce it."[62] These references can be easily
multiplied. For several decades the idea of pluralism exuded political
conformity and cold-war anticommunism. A new generation of
scholars and critics coming of age in the 1960s denounced it.

No longer. The interpretation of totalitarianism that damned
utopianism alongside Nazism and communism proved dominant;
the battle cry of pluralism easily overran all stations. No prisoners
were taken, but no soldiers were found. Critics of pluralism spawned by the 1960s vanished almost without a trace. Why? No single
reason explains the renewed popularity of pluralism. The rapid
demise of socialism knocked the intellectual breath out of leftists;

lacking confidence or belief in a complete social restructuring, they retreated to partial beliefs in partial cultures—pluralism. Liberals needed little encouragement; they were always attracted to pluralistic ideas, and freed from sharp criticism from a left, they redoubled their commitment.

Pluralism, the ideology of the market and the individual, becomes the bedrock principle for liberals and leftists. Pluralism returns as radicalism ebbs. Nor is this wholly objectionable. Not every age spawns bold ideas about society. In its various forms, perhaps pluralism is the best our era has to offer. Yet the retreat is presented as an astounding advance. A familiar if not banal idea, pluralism, is dubbed cutting edge. Painted with "culture" or christened multiculturalism, it becomes a mythology of our time.

*   *   *

The literature on multiculturalism includes much that is reasonable and necessary. It is surely fair that various histories, long slighted, should get a hearing in curriculums; it is desirable that people of all kinds populate the stories children read and the books they study. We want students to know that there were black scientists, Jewish gangsters and women artists. We want curriculums to reflect the complexity of history and society.

These projects remain urgent and legitimate. Yet they constitute only a fraction of a multicultural argument that goes far beyond revising curriculums to address vast tracts of life and letters. Outside of the curriculum debates (and sometimes within them), multiculturalism easily loses its bearings. Driven by abstract "culture" and a formalist "pluralism," multiculturalism gives rise to programs and notions that lag far behind social and economic developments. Hundreds of essays on "cultural identity" fling out references to Derrida and Foucault with little purchase on their topic. Endless discussions of multiculturalism proceed from the unsubstantiated assumption that numerous distinct "cultures" constitute American society.

Only a few historians or observers even consider the possibility that the opposite may be true: that the world and the United States are relentlessly becoming more culturally uniform, not diverse. Serious reflections about cultural pluralism must at least consider the relentless forces of cultural homogenization and ask the questions, "How can pluralism exist within uniformity?" "What is the possibility of multiple cultures within a single consumer society?" To ask is partially to answer, for it is possible that cultural diversity and social homogeneity are connected inversely. The call for cultural identity may arise as a response to its demise.

No group is able, and few are willing, to stand up to the potent homogenizing forces of advanced industrial society. All Americans, from African Americans to Greek Americans, buy the same goods, look at the same movies and television, pursue the same activities and have—more or less—the same desires for success. From the angle of marketing, these groups may show up as distinct consumers of music or sports, but this hardly constitutes fundamental identities. All differences between groups have not disappeared; this is obvious. Yet they may progressively decline. Exactly for this reason, they assume increasing importance for individuals. It is the rootless, not the rooted, who fetishize their roots.

The revival of ethnic identity amid its real decline may be news to the dogmatic exponents of multiculturalism, but not to historians of immigration and assimilation. One highly regarded historian of immigration, Marcus Lee Hansen, formulated a generational "law" that speaks to this very issue. He called the law "the principle of third-generation interest," which can be summed up in the maxim, "What the son wishes to forget the grandson wishes to remember."

According to Hansen, first-generation immigrants, burdened with "material cares," paid little heed to the old-world culture from which they came. Their sons and daughters, taunted by native-born Americans, wanted to escape from the foreign language, religion and family customs; and they adopted a "policy of forgetting." "Nothing was more Yankee than a Yankeeized person of foreign descent." It is the next generation, the third, that remembers with pride its roots and common heritage.[63] In current terms, it is the third generation that fuels cultural identity and revival, the enthusiasm for multiculturalism.

Since its formulation in 1937, Hansen's "law" has provoked much attention and criticism.[64] In many ways his argument is too simple. Yet it captures a feature of immigration that remains pertinent: the renaissance of cultural identity in the context of its real decline. The sons and daughters who want to remember and honor their past are third-generation Americans; they are American born and educated; they no longer "feel any inferiority."

Their confidence, perhaps comfort, in their American identity allows them to cultivate their past. They carry with pride their national or ethnic identity, but what does it mean? They are also assimilated and lack the language, customs and practices of their grandparents. Polish Americans do not speak Polish. African Americans know little of Africa. This is a truth that current multiculturalists do not know or want to know. To put it sharply: Multiculturalism is not the opposite of assimilation, but its product.

Many multiculturalists decorate their pronouncements with rote dismissals of the "melting pot" and assimilation, but a closer look and a more precise use of terms render their arguments questionable. Nathan Glazer and Daniel Moynihan's 1963 *Beyond the Melting Pot* stated flatly, "The point about the melting pot . . . is that it did not happen."[65] This is easy to quote, but with a more careful examination of the terms and meaning, it is more plausible to argue the reverse: The point about the melting pot is that it did happen—and is happening.

In fact Glazer and Moynihan are clear; they do not mean "distinctive language, customs and culture" persist or proliferate in American society; these are "lost" by the third generation. They refer to the reality that New York blacks, Jews and Italians retain identities as interest and pressure groups, concentrating in certain occupations and geographic areas. By surveying neighborhood associations and political positions on welfare or schooling, Glazer and Moynihan argue that ethnic identity subsists. Yet they deny that the groups have any particular cultural component; nor do they broach the idea that the ethnic blocs offer any fundamentally different political vision. On the contrary, New York ethnic groups participate in mainstream political life like mayoral elections.

The other classic study from the early 1960s, Milton M. Gordon's *Assimilation in American Life*, using a much wider canvas than New York City, came to a roughly similar conclusion. Ethnic identity remains surprisingly "hardy," yet Gordon also means sociologically, not culturally. Apart from "minor modifications in cuisine, recreational patterns, place names, speech, residential architecture, sources of artistic inspiration, and perhaps a few other areas," he states, "over the generations . . . the triumph of acculturation in America" has been "overwhelming." Where it has been blocked is sociologically. For Gordon this means that each ethnic, religious and national group has its "own network of cliques, clubs, organizations, and institutions."[66]

Gordon calls this "structural pluralism," in contrast to "cultural pluralism," which hardly exists. The term *structural* may mislead, implying a density to pluralism that Gordon does not mean. He found that groups separate along the lines of friendship patterns and associations, but not culturally. "Structural" separation does not depend on cultural separation. Black people hang out with black people and worship in black churches; Jews hang out with Jews and worship in synagogues. This does not mean these groups represent different cultures. Or as Gordon states, it is possible for separate groups "to continue their existence even while the cultural differences between them become progressively reduced and even in greater part eliminated."[67]

In 1981 another sociologist, Stephen Steinberg, published a tough-minded book, *The Ethnic Myth*, that appraised the talk of an ethnic upsurge and cultural identity. "The thesis advanced here," he stated,

> is that the ethnic revival was a "dying gasp" on the part of ethnic groups descended from the great waves of immigration of the nineteenth and early twentieth centuries. That is to say, the revival did not signify a genuine revitalization of ethnicity, but rather was sympto-

matic of the atrophy of ethnic cultures and the decline of ethnic communities. Placed in historical perspective, the revival appears to have been doomed from the outset, inasmuch as it could not possibly reverse trends that have been in the making for several generations.

For Steinberg as for other sober commentators, cultural and ethnic groups cannot sustain themselves against the homogenizing force of American society. "Increasingly, cultural values and life-styles are shaped by influences alien to the ethnic milieu—the mass media and popular culture, on the one hand, and educational institutions committed to universal values, on the other." What remains is weak and symbolic ethnicity.[68] In a new preface to *The Ethnic Myth,* Steinberg laments the "book's utter failure" to dispel "myths and misconceptions" about race and ethnicity. "To oppose these ideological currents is like swimming upstream—one starts out with a burst of energy, makes some headway, but eventually succumbs to the unrelenting downstream force."[69]

Another sociologist, Richard D. Alba, has also documented the ineluctable forces of assimilation. Using indexes of languages spoken, residential neighborhoods and intermarriages, he argues that "the social bases for ethnic distinctiveness are eroding among Americans of European ancestry. . . . As older, currently more ethnic generations are replaced by their children and grandchildren, who are less ethnic on average, the groups as a whole become less ethnic."[70] None of this is easy to refute.

Other investigators dismiss the widespread alarm that new immigration threatens the status of English. "Recent immigrants are in fact learning English," writes the social scientist Geoffrey Nunberg, "at a faster rate than any earlier generations of immigrants did— and by all the evidence, with at least as much enthusiasm. Whatever 'multiculturalism' may mean to its proponents, it most assuredly does not involve a rejection of English as the national lingua franca." For instance, new figures show that for recent Hispanic arrivals "becoming American entails not just mastering English, but also rejecting the language and culture of one's parents."[71]

These simple and perhaps unpalatable truths go virtually without comment in the babble about multiculturalism. The United States is not becoming more, but less, multilingual. It is a relentlessly monolingual society—much more than other societies. Kallen's favorite example of a harmonious and diverse society was Switzerland, where bi- and tri-lingualism are common. In the United States, on the other hand, fewer and fewer students study and acquire proficiency in foreign languages.

In his damning study of the American curriculum, *Tourists in Our Own Land*, Clifford Adelman, of the U.S. Department of Education, documents the precipitous decline in the serious study of languages. One might imagine that enthusiastic multiculturalists might be alarmed. After all, language and culture sustain each other. Yet they rarely mention it. "In all the contemporary discussions of 'multiculturalism' and 'cultural diversity,'" Adelman complains, "we hear little, if anything, about native language and language maintenance, let alone do we see native speakers of English reaching out to immerse themselves in another culture through second language acquisition." Without studying another language, he states, people "will never be more than tourists."[72] In different terms, without acquiring another language, which few Americans do, learning about Africa through Kwanzaa is like learning about Germany through Oktoberfest.

The inescapable forces of Americanization do not ensure that all groups participate in society with the same success. Those excluded because of racial or ethnic injustice, however, do not necessarily constitute a distinct culture. Suffering does not engender a culture. With the best of intentions, in 1959 the anthropologist Oscar Lewis introduced the term *the culture of poverty* to fathom the endemic impoverishment of Mexican families. Lewis himself was a lifelong socialist—with a fear of anti-Semitism that led him to change his name from Lefkowitz. He had first subtitled *Five Families* "The Anthropology of Poverty," but the subtitle of the published book ran "Mexican Case Studies in the Culture of Poverty." The book and phrase "culture of poverty" proved popular; however, critics roundly denounced Lewis for implying that unique cultural traits, and not economic conditions, led to poverty.[73]

Nevertheless, "the-culture-of" approach enjoys unparalleled success; few attend to the economic content of the "culture." Nor, as the anthropologist Charles A. Valentine trenchantly argued years ago, is much attention given to the relationship of the culture or the subculture to the larger society. "Clarification of these matters is very much overdue, if only because it has become so intellectually stylish to discover 'cultures' everywhere in national and international life." By logic or observation something sets a "subgroup" apart from a larger society or culture. What exactly? Without considering the wider frame, what appears distinct is mythologized, as if each group lived in a separate universe.[74]

For those who care to look, the evidence is everywhere that distinct cultures are not so distinct. In his provocative book on poor black children in Philadelphia, *On the Edge*, Carl H. Nightingale found that these kids increasingly have succumbed to consumer society, which preys on their vulnerability. Precisely because they are excluded and humiliated, they become fanatical devotees of name brands, gold chains and pricey cars—insignias of American success.

"As soon as they are able, the kids begin to demand the basic building blocks of the b-boy outfit. Already at five and six, many kids in the neighborhood," Nightingale reports, "can recite the whole canon of adult luxury—from Gucci, Evan Piccone, and Pierre Cardin, to Mercedes and BMW. . . . From the age of ten, kids become thoroughly engrossed in Nike's and Reebok's cult of the sneaker." Then comes the fascination with rappers and drug dealers. The "ubiquitous rap tapes" show "a preoccupation with consumption and acquisition that never characterized the old soul and R&B hits." The lure of the local drug dealers arises from their "glorification of blackness . . . with virtuoso performances of conspicuous consumption." Nightingale concludes that "the cult of consumption has permeated the emotional and cultural life of poor urban African-American kids" with devastating consequences.[75]

No group wants to hear that it lacks culture, but that is not the issue; rather, the question is how different the various cultures are from each other and from the dominant American culture. For instance, scholars from Melville Herskovits to Sterling Stuckey have documented the persistence of African tales, songs and language in the American black experience.[76] This is a valid and valuable endeavor, but it does not mean that today African Americans constitute a distinct culture—any more than do Italian Americans, Japanese Americans or Jewish Americans.

Little suggests that any group except the most marginal and inflexible can maintain, or even wants to maintain, a distinct culture within American society. Such groups do exist, but typically play little role in multiculturalism, because they want to be left out rather than let in. For instance, the Amish rarely figure in discussions of multiculturalism—not simply because they are a small group, but because they are too far outside the mainstream. Their absence, however, highlights the unspoken conformity of multiculturalism, in which the multiple cultures want, more or less, the same things. Unlike other American "cultures," the Amish reject the use of electricity, automobiles and most modern consumer goods; their clothing, mainly sewn by themselves, has changed little over a century. They are almost preindustrial and communitarian.

Many outsiders may find this interesting or endearing, but nothing more. As one scholar of the Amish has commented, tourists are "enchanted" by the Amish, and academics tout their mental health and ecological soundness. "Despite these accolades" few outsiders cast aside "technological convenience" to "submit themselves to the collective order of Amish life."[77] As Randy Testa, who lived with the Amish, has written, "Being Amish is not a 'life-style'":

> I would not want to become Amish. Nor could I. One could convert to Catholicism and still be a used-car dealer, an investment banker, or the owner of a beauty salon. These occupations do not exist within Amish society. . . . Being Amish is a faith and a completely encompassing way

of life. For better or worse, conversion to the Amish faith would mean leaving the worldly world behind.[78]

The simple truths of Americanization would not surprise the originators of the idea of cultural diversity. "Cultural pluralism," as Kallen formulated it eighty years ago, may have been a brave effort to preserve cultural identity in the face of a repressive Americanization. It was this and something more—or less; it was also a half step in ineluctable cultural accommodation.

Kallen, born in Silesia, was brought to the United States by his father, an orthodox rabbi. As the oldest and, until the eighth child, the only son, Kallen was expected to follow his father into the orthodox rabbinate. Yet the father's implacable religious world repelled the son, who considered him "strict" and "authoritarian." "I didn't like him," admitted Kallen, who regularly fled from home as a boy. Only when his father was dying did they reconcile, at which time Kallen penned a grudging appreciation. "He was the last of the old school of Jews, who made absolutely no concession to their environment."[79]

Kallen wanted Judaism to make concessions to the environment and move toward the mainstream, becoming "secular, humanist, scientific, conditioned on the industrial economy, without having ceased to be livingly Jewish." Kallen and the others who joined him in the program of "cultural pluralism," like the African American Alain Locke, may have been more successful than they wished. Today the terms *cultural pluralism, multiculturalism* and *cultural diversity* do not designate different lives, but different lifestyles in American society. The "diverse" cultures all dream of, plan for and sometimes enjoy the same American success. Only the ideologues of multiculturalism have not heard the news.

*   *   *

The dearth of economic and sociological analyses, the inflation of cultural approaches, the assumption that cultures fundamentally diverge, the failure or inability to consider the forces of assimilation and homogenization and the lack of any political vision or alternative all characterize current discussions of multiculturalism. The politics that emerges either ratifies familiar (and estimable) sentiments about respecting all groups or pretends to a subversiveness that has no foundation.

A recent collection exemplifies the anemic concepts and timid politics of liberal multiculturalism. The authors of *Multiculturalism* assume that cultures fundamentally conflict and ponder how liberalism can reconcile antagonistic demands. The volume pivots about "The Politics of Recognition," an essay by an esteemed liberal philosopher, Charles Taylor. For Taylor, "recognition" is not simply a courtesy we owe one another, but a "vital human need" based on the fact that life is "dialogical"; we define ourselves through contact with others. Unfortunately "with the modern age" the "need for recognition" often goes unmet. "Misrecognition" implies more than disrespect. "It can inflict a grievous wound, saddling its victims with a crippling self-hatred."

It gets worse. Classic liberalism handed out recognition evenly or at least tried, sometimes successfully, to ignore differences of class or gender or race. Unfortunately, the principle of equality clashes with a new idea or need, what Taylor calls the "politics of difference" grounded in the "age of authenticity," which he dates from Rousseau and Herder. According to Taylor, authenticity is the notion that "there is a certain way of being human that is *my* way. I am called upon to live my life in this way. . . . Being true to myself means being true to my own originality." Taylor seeks to reconcile the "equal recognition" that basic liberalism bestows and a special recognition required by "authenticity" that underlies multiculturalism.

Taylor happily gnaws on this nut: How can the egalitarianism of classic liberalism be reconciled with a multiculturalism demanding special recognition for specific cultures? Yet to get at the fruit, he glosses over serious issues. For starters, what is authenticity and how is it achieved? For Taylor "authenticity" sustains the differences that constitute multiculturalism, but he mythologizes the concept, a favorite of continental existentialists like Martin Heidegger. The level-headed Canadian philosopher teams up with murky Heideggerians.

As T. W. Adorno argued in his polemic against the Heideggerians, *The Jargon of Authenticity*, "authenticity" itself is a suspect concept; it claims a profundity it has not earned. The term evokes inwardness and rootedness, assuming a mythic, formal and empty cast. Someone is or is not "authentic," based on what? Objectivity is jettisoned, wrote Adorno, while "subjectivity becomes the judge of authenticity." The notion of authenticity ends in tautologies; the self constitutes the self. "Man is he, who he is," stated Heidegger, the prime exponent of the cult of authenticity.[80]

Although Taylor's formulations lack the mock profundity of the Heideggerians, they partake of the same logic and jargon. Authenticity "accords moral importance to a kind of contact with myself, with my own inner nature. . . . It greatly increases the importance of this self-contact by introducing the principle of originality: each of our voices has something unique to say." Authenticity mythologizes the self; at worst it follows orders. Even Taylor's phrases betray the deceit. "I am called upon to live my life in this way." Who is calling? Authenticity claims a radical individualism while dragging out the genealogical tables to expel the unauthentic. It reeks of mysticism and the police.

Moreover, Taylor glides from the mythology of authentic individuals to that of authentic cultures, an even more dubious idea. Presumably certain authentic cultures need special recognition. What cultures and what sort of recognition? Apart from regular references to Quebec, a fog descends. Like many commentators, Taylor simply posits that "all societies are becoming increasingly multicultural," as if this were self-evident; and he assumes that the majority culture threatens minority cultures without bothering to tell us what minority cultures he's referring to or what is distinct about them.

It even might be questioned whether Quebec represents a distinct culture. The French language dominates in Quebec, but does a language make a culture? Not really, in the opinion of many historians. Language is "merely one, and not necessarily the primary way of distinguishing between cultural communities," states Eric Hobsbawm. "The political claims to independence in Poland or Belgium were not language-based. . . . Nor was the Irish movement in Britain."[81] Language quarrels do not necessarily indicate two cultures clashing. If Quebec becomes an independent nation, would an observer conclude that Montreal and Toronto represent different cultures?

In any event, Taylor fails to get very far. The notion that life is "dialogical" and requires mutual recognition cannot be contested, but also hardly needs affirmation. The belief that "withholding of recognition can be a form of oppression" sounds like psychobabble, the philosophical version of the self-esteem chatter applied to cultures as a whole. What mangles people are bad or no jobs, decaying communities, tattered human relations and defective education rather than "misrecognition," whatever that might mean.

Reality gives Taylor and his philosophical colleagues the creeps, however. Taylor derives the "homogenizing" trends in society from a "conception" of equal rights, not a social reality. His commentators pick up the baton, operating with notions of "culture" that are threatened or threatening, but they skimp on details. Michael Walzer tells us that the dominant culture endangers minority cultures. "Some nationalities or social unions or cultural communities are more at risk than others," and, if this is too vague, he audaciously explains: "The public culture of American life is more supportive, say, of this way of life than of that." The "say" here is priceless, the philosopher's announcement of a bold foray while shuffling the old lecture notes.

Taylor and his colleagues address real conflicts. Yet the jargon of recognition, authenticity and cultural self-esteem muddies the waters. They hardly ponder what constitutes a culture and what is multiculturalism within a single society. In fact, they slip from multiculturalism to cultural differences, "ways of life" and even "ways of viewing the world," as if these were all the same. This allows several contributors to write of women as a "disadvantaged" culture suffering from failed recognition. What culture do women constitute? Does it vary from society to society? The conceptual slackness of these judicious thinkers enables the arguments to unfold; it is much easier to write of cultural differences in advanced industrial society, which obviously exist, than different cultures, which may not.

For instance, it is possible to point to Christmas, Chanukah and Kwanzaa as illustrating cultural differences; it is less possible to discuss them as representing different cultures within American society. A sober view of these holidays, in fact, might conclude that they register not differences, but similarities. In the Anglo-American world Christmas always entailed popular celebrations, but not till the nineteenth century did it mean shopping and exchanging gifts. Santa Claus himself emerges out of a "motley compound" of images to become a gift giver. "Toy and confectionary shopkeepers," writes the historian Leigh Eric Schmidt, "with their prime interest in children as a market, led the way in using Santa Claus."[82]

Partly because it falls in December, Chanukah, a minor holiday, has become a major holiday for Jews and has taken on one of the trappings of Christmas, the giving of gifts, which it did not originally include.[83] A black activist professor invented Kwanzaa, situated between Christmas and New Year's Day, to give African Americans an alternative to Christmas; it was intended to remain noncommercial, for example, through the exchange of homemade gifts, but has increasingly surrendered to market forces.[84]

These realities do not intrude upon the philosophical quest for authenticity and recognition. Taylor wrestles with the conundrum, concluding, "There must be something midway between the inauthentic and homogenizing demand for recognition of equal worth, on the one hand, and the self-immurement within ethnocentric standards, on the other." There must be, but Taylor only suggests caution. "The presumption [of equal worth] required of us is not peremptory and inauthentic judgments ... but a willingness to be open to comparative cultural study of the kind that must displace our horizons in the resulting fusions."[85]

The timid conclusions, chalky language and toothless concepts are hardly rare among political philosophers; in fact, they thrive on this stuff. They cannot get enough of it. Taylor's distinguished commentators fall over themselves in their enthusiasm for his essay. "Extraordinarily rich" and "remarkable," rejoices Susan Wolf, a Johns Hopkins University philosophy professor. They have never read anything quite as stimulating. The collection suggests a liberalism that has lost its bone and muscle.

Nevertheless, Taylor and the liberal philosophers are clear and honest thinkers next to those further to the left. In the multicultural sea, leftists sail ahead by huffing and puffing about power, difference and marginalization; they fill endless essays and books with talk of radical and transformative multiculturalism. What is subversive is never quite specified. The relentless repetition of terms like *counterhegemonic, disruption* and *contestation* suggests a nagging doubt; the terms must be included in every sentence lest the edifice collapse. Homi K. Bhabha, a University of Chicago professor, is a master practitioner:

> Cultural difference must not be understood as the free play of polarities and pluralities. . . . The jarring of meanings and values generated in the process of cultural interpretation is an effect of the perplexity of living in the liminal spaces of national society. . . . Cultural difference, as a form of intervention, participates in a logic of supplementary subversion similar to the strategies of minority discourse. The question of cultural difference faces us with a disposition of knowledges or a distribution of practices that exist beside each other, *abseits* designating a form of social contradiction or antagonism that has to be negotiated rather than sublated. The difference between disjunctive sites and representations of social life have to be articulated without surmounting the incommensurable meanings and judgements that are produced within the process of transcultural negotiation.[86]

The radical program on multiculturalism might be characterized as jargon attached to an air compressor. A recent collection, *Mapping Multiculturalism*, exemplifies the genre. Its editors want to establish that real multiculturalism surpasses liberal assimilation or pluralism;

true multiculturalism is more robust and threatening. They offer a three-point guide to pick the real McCoy from "the crowd of pretenders." First, real multiculturalism has been "more hospitable" to "a whole range of perspectives" on "gender, sexuality, new panethnicities, and new 'nations' like Queer Nation" than has ordinary pluralism. Second, real multiculturalism "has strongly endorsed racially based group identities and *antiessentialism* at the same time." Finally, a "transformative multiculturalism" seeks "political parity." "A real multiculturalism requires political as well as cultural inclusion, requires the sharing of power among relevant groups."[87]

This stuff would take pages to unravel. At its best, it represents familiar liberalism parading as something more. If multiculturalism is defined as being "open" to "new perspectives," then few could oppose it. At its worst, it represents the conservative nightmare come true—mindless relativism. Multiculturalism means embracing whatever comes tearing down the turnpike of history; every truck is dubbed a culture and some even get tagged "nations," as in "Queer Nation." The question is how gender or "panethnicity" constitutes a new culture, much less a nation. About this the authors say nothing. Critical thought requires conceptual care and precision; nowadays this has been exchanged for cheerleading and academic bombast.

The statement that multiculturalism endorses with equal enthusiasm racial and nonracial groups (in the parlance, antiessentialism) relies on an old sleight of hand. If you cannot figure it out, say both. The demand for political power and parity is the nub of the matter, however. On the basis of equality it is possible to demand more women in the military, more African Americans in government or more Latino policemen, but what does this have to do with multiculturalism?

The multicultural dynamic is assumed, but rarely explained; individuals apparently pop up as carriers of divergent cultures. Presumably the black policeman, like the black law professor, represents a different culture than the nonblack colleague. The multiculturalists pretend to liquidate false generalizations while trading in them.

Even a term like "Eurocentrism" is objectionable, as if a homogenous European culture existed—as if Adolf Hitler and Anne Frank represent the same Europe.[88] Nor is it accurate historically. "Far from being Eurocentric," writes the classicist Karl Galinsky, the Greco-Roman world "encompassed all of the Mediterranean, including North Africa and Egypt, much of the Near East, and at times, sizable portions of the Middle East extending as far as Afghanistan and the Indus Valley."[89]

None of this matters. The main goal is power or empowerment or jobs or resources. The call for power sounds radical and serious, especially coupled to multiculturalism. In fact, power devoid of a vision or program means little; it is a demand that certain people get more authority and clout. Again, increased representation of women or African Americans in various fields can be defended straightforwardly in the name of equality. As desirable as this goal may be, it suggests little of multiculturalism and nothing of subversion. Do black mayors represent a different culture? Or female Supreme Court judges? And should they? After the rhetoric is stripped away, the call for power and its decayed psychological form, empowerment, suggests a converging politics, monoculturalism. Everyone wants a bigger piece of the same action.

Of course, the partisans put up a firestorm of revolutionary rhetoric. Aside from the reasonable proposals to redraw curriculums and textbooks, the demands have precious little to do with multiculturalism. For instance, two professors want a multiculturalism that goes beyond a benign study of various groups or "simplistic . . . exposure to different cultures." Rather, Ted Gordon and Wahneema Lubiano argue that multiculturalism requires a "reconsideration and restructuring of the ways in which knowledge is organized . . . and used to support inequitable power differentials." This means that "those of us interested in a transformative multiculturalism must insist that it cannot be held to exist within dominance."

The uncertain English reflects the uncertain politics. What could it mean that multiculturalism cannot "exist within dominance"? Is this a call for revolution? Subversion? Not exactly. "It is important that minority people be part of *all* levels of the University chain of command, that they be an empowered presence at the levels of policy-making." A "transformative multiculturalism" must address the university "relations to staff workers and their racial, gender, and class makeup."[90]

These positions, which are very common, betray an unlimited ability to mythologize. To participate in policymaking constitutes revolutionary multiculturalism. To challenge the "organization of knowledge" may be desirable, but what does that mean and what does cultural pluralism have to do with it? Like other exponents of radical multiculturalism, Gordon and Lubiano refer vaguely to minority and non-Western knowledge as if they inherently subverted domination and hierarchy. How? Does Chinese culture undermine hierarchy? Does Hinduism?

To improve relations with staff workers and increase minority possibilities may also be highly desirable, but what have they to do with multiculturalism? Do various staff workers represent different cultures? With Lubiano and other enthusiasts, multiculturalism becomes a shorthand for anything desirable. "Radical multiculturalism," she writes, "can include attempting to influence decisions such as whether to focus on high-tech military research, Department of Defense contracts, or fuel air explosives instead of contributing to research based on meeting housing needs."[91]

Once past the jabber about hegemony, difference and domination, this politics is defined by appointments and jobs, the not-so-revolutionary demand to be part of the university bureaucracy or the corporate world. In cruder terms, radical multiculturalists want more of their own people in the organization. This is fully understandable, but it is not radical, and it is barely political. It suggests patronage, not revolution.

The discussions of "marginalization" often evidence rank bad faith. One could say the Amish or Hasidic Jews are marginalized; yet they themselves do not proclaim their marginality, either because they do not see it or because it does not trouble them—they have no interest in joining the mainstream. On the other hand, the radical multiculturalists, postcolonialists and other cutting-edge theorists gush about marginality with the implicit, and sometimes explicit, goal of joining the mainstream. They specialize in marginalization to up their market value. Again, this is understandable; the poor and excluded want to be wealthy and included, but why is this multicultural or subversive?

For instance, an exponent of Native American studies denounces the educational imperialism of Eurocentric education. Native traditions "challenge, at root," the "dominant-subordinate construction" and the "social hegemony" of Euro-American superiority. Up to now Eurocentrism "marginalizes Ethnic Studies or American Indian Studies or Gender Studies," states M. Annette Jaimes Guerrero, a California professor. What must be done? Head for the hills? Blow up the mainstream institutions? Not exactly. "American Indian Studies will need to be able to stand on its own as a fully accredited discipline with departmental status and even with a broader institutional standing."[92]

This is typically argued without losing a beat. Ethnic studies is marginalized; it threatens the core of Western domination. Conclusion? We want the Western overlords to give us more support and money. Once upon a time revolutionaries tried, or pretended to try, to make a revolution; they harbored a vision of a different world or society. Now dubbed radical multiculturalists, they apply for bigger offices.

Another effort to carve out a radical, even socialist, multiculturalism has been made by Nancy Fraser, a well-regarded political theorist. For all its vigor, it also surrenders to jargon and platitudes. Part of its failing may be due to historical innocence. Fraser states grandly that "the interimbrication of culture and political economy is a leitmotiv of all my work." Whatever "interimbrication" might mean, Fraser seems unaware that many earlier political thinkers such as Emile Durkheim and Max Weber wrestled with the relation of culture and political economy. Her own intellectual world rarely reaches back beyond 1980.

Fraser is not happy with those, like Taylor, who see multiculturalism based on failed "recognition." This implies that more esteem or appreciation would settle grievances. She wants to supplement the exclusively "cultural" outlook with one targeting "socioeconomic injustice." People suffer from joblessness, pollution and ill health, which cultural recognition will not heal. Fraser separates the two dimensions, cultural and economic injustice. The first calls for "some sort of cultural or symbolic change" or what she calls "recognition," which is Taylor's concern. The latter calls for "political-economic restructuring of some sort" or "redistribution," which Fraser wants.

As a good political scientist, she realizes the real world does not fit her categories; most collectivities are "bivalent," suffering from both cultural and economic injustice. For instance, African Americans are not simply the object of cultural insults, but economic injustice. The difference between liberalism and radicalism (or in her lingo, affirmative and transformative remedies) pivots on the cures to this "bivalent" suffering. Mainstream multiculturalism supports affirmative remedies, which may undo disrespect, but leave intact fundamental structures. Transformative remedies, inspired by deconstruction, change the underlying foundation.

How is this accomplished? She explains, "By destabilizing existing group identities and differentiations, these [transformative] remedies would not only raise the self-esteem of members of currently disrespected groups; they would change *everyone's* sense of self." Fraser trumps liberal psychobabble about self-esteem by promising to change everyone's self—and "destabilize" groups to boot. She understands the vagueness of her program and helpfully provides one example: homosexuality and homophobia. Liberal remedies seek to "revalue gay and lesbian identity." Her approach promises much more. Transformative remedies, "associated with queer politics," seek to "deconstruct the homo-hetero dichotomy . . . so as to destabilize all fixed sexual identities." They aim to "sustain a sexual field of multiple, debinarized, fluid, ever-shifting differences." So ends her clarifying example.

Should children be raised in a family lacking stable sexual identities? Of course, such a pedestrian concern never darkens this advanced theorizing. Fraser simply supposes that radicalism demands more destabilizing, fluid and multiple differences. Why? Are these always desirable and liberating? Though it is hardly a counterargument, most people probably think they already suffer from too much instability. Why should the radical project seek to render everything fluid and multiple?

None of this is explained because it is inexplicable. Despite its theoretical pretense, radical thought dishes out the adolescent cliché that what is fixed is bad and what moves is good. Fraser regularly repeats that radicals destabilize gender and race. Her feminism replaces "gender dichotomies" by "networks of multiple intersecting differences that are demassified and shifting." What "multiple intersecting differences" are and why they are desirable is not evident. Her real inspiration comes from the market and consumerism, where quantity, change and hype constitute the game.

Fraser still occasionally uses the term *socialism,* and even once the term *utopia,* but her idiom sinks them. To make her program sound political, she throws in hackneyed slogans to awaken leftists who slumbered through the demonstration of "interimbrication." Academic blather and political clap-trap fit seamlessly together.

> Transformative redistribution to redress racial injustice in the economy consists of some form of antiracist democratic socialism or antiracist social democracy. And transformative recognition to redress racial injustice in the culture consists of antiracist deconstruction aimed at dismantling Eurocentrism by destabilizing racial dichotomies.[93]

Bereft of ideas, leftists and liberals enthusiastically celebrate cultural pluralism to fill the void. They string together buzzwords like *cultural identity, authenticity, counterhegemonic, representation, transformative* and *destabilizing,* which elicit nods from the camp followers; and they add a couple of stale political slogans as proof of their political righteousness. This vast literature is animated by a meager vision. The demise of utopia makes way for the party of multiculturalists.

— 3 —

MASS CULTURE AND ANARCHY

Can it be denied that to live in a society of equals tends in general to make a man's spirits expand, and his faculties work easily and actively? . . . Can it be denied, that to be heavily overshadowed, to be profoundly insignificant, has, on the whole a depressing and benumbing effect?. . . " This is Matthew Arnold, the nineteenth-century poet and critic, in "Democracy," an essay he published in tandem with one titled "Equality."[1] With spirit and force these pieces reaffirmed Arnold's egalitarian and democratic convictions.

To those familiar with recent "culture wars," the references might be surprising. The Arnold that filters through these polemics appears as an uncompromising defender of high culture against popular culture; he is the quintessential antidemocratic elitist. For conservatives he is a hero, a stalwart defender of cultivation and learning. Many works, from William J. Bennett's *To Reclaim a Legacy* and Dinesh D'Souza's *Illiberal Education* to Roger Kimball's *Tenured Radicals,* honor Arnold as upholding traditional standards, a nineteenth-century rock against the mass culture and relativism of the late twentieth century.

"Instead of aspiring to gain a thoughtful acquaintance with (as the Victorian poet and critic Matthew Arnold famously put it) 'the best that has been thought and said,'" runs a typical passage, "these new forces in the academy deliberately blur the distinction between high culture and popular culture."[2] The Arnold who defended "the best that has been thought and said" and defined culture as a passion for "sweetness and light"—for many conservatives this *is* Arnold.

Conversely, for leftists and some liberals he is a repellent elitist and reactionary. They view Arnold's central text, *Culture and Anarchy*, as nothing more than a thinly veiled defense of the old establishment against the new democratic society. "Matthew Arnold," writes his most recent biographer, "seems to have become a sort of easy shorthand . . . for a notion of cold cultural arrogance, an elitist disdain for mass culture."[3]

Although both right and left misread Arnold—if they read him—the issue is less Arnold than the understanding of mass culture. Over the decades the lure and dazzle of mass culture has exponentially intensified; its audience extends in every direction. The position staked out by some conservatives, which has little changed over time, speaks for itself; they sanction fortifying the dikes. The position staked out by liberals and leftists, which has changed, raises questions. Once upon a time they believed in a new and better culture for people. No longer. In the name of democracy they anoint the daily fare of entertainment and movies; their confidence in a transformed future has evaporated.

Arnold serves as a symbol in the culture wars, but he deserves better; he offered an approach to mass culture that should be resuscitated. Along with John Stuart Mill and Alexis de Tocqueville, Arnold endorsed democracy and equality. At the same time the great nineteenth-century liberal thinkers did not fetishize these categories; they remained alert to outcomes and contexts, assailing "leveling," the "tyranny of the majority" or "uniformity." They understood that supporting equality and democracy did not entail approving all its configurations. On the contrary, they often protested what in today's idiom might be called mass culture. They were democrats and egalitarians willing to criticize everyday culture and opinions no matter how entrenched or popular.

In the current climate, their willingness shows up as unacceptable elitism. Contemporary political thinkers lack the boldness of the nineteenth-century liberals. That people are equal and should be treated equally is one matter; that their thoughts and activities are equal is another. The second does not follow from the first or, at least, it does not directly follow; it must first pass through history and society. This means that the principle of human equality and its concrete expression in society are not the same. By virtue of inferior education or destructive conditions, equal people develop unequally. This is not an insult, but an observation—and indeed, an observation on which pivots a criticism of society. Mill and Arnold perfectly understood this, as did twentieth-century critics like Dwight Macdonald. Today this wisdom seems lost.

Scholars and critics have surrendered to an inexorable logic of equality. "Since all people are equal, then everything they do must be equal" goes the reasoning. Loyal to this logic, they reject criticism of mass culture as elitist because it supposes that some things are superior to others. They view the criticism of culture advanced by Arnold or Macdonald as demeaning. In place of the old elitism new critics embrace mass culture as complex terrains of subversion and contestation.

These approaches open doors to studying topics from jazz to comic books that earlier scholars ignored. This is all for the good. Yet in casting aside as elitist truth, individuality and perfection—notions that animated Arnold and Mill—today's critics also close the door to a different future; they ratify the status quo in the name of democracy. Despite their claims of subversion, they subvert the effort to go beyond the existing society; they block the utopian impulse that pervaded the critique of mass culture.

The Renaissance scholar John C. Olin detected a utopian note in Arnold's call to turn "a stream of fresh and free thought upon our stock notions and habits" and in his hope that "culture," as the development of perfection, would be "the great help out of our present difficulties." Arnold sought, wrote Olin, "an intellectual and moral enlightenment. . . . It is a democratic social ideal."[4] The nineteenth-century critic denounced the culture of his day in the name of something better, a more thoughtful and graceful culture. Today most observers and scholars reject this as naive and elitist. In confounding criticism and elitism, they back themselves into a world without exit.

*   *   *

Almost thirty years ago the German poet and essayist Hans Magnus Enzensberger complained of what he called the "cultural archaism" of the left. He charged that the new left analyzed the media through a single concept, manipulation, that saw the masses as dupes. For Enzensberger not only was the manipulation thesis unsatisfactory, it meant that young political activists spurned contact with television, preferring preindustrial modes. Ironically the left, which presented itself as the future, looked backward. Young leftists disdained the mass media.

Of course, this was the not the whole story. Some activists, notably Abbie Hoffman and Jerry Rubin in the United States, utilized the mass media, mainly television. "It wasn't through traditional political organizing—reading books, and getting leaflets and hearing arguments," stated Rubin about the cascading campus riots in the late 1960s. "It was through being turned on by something they saw on television." Though this may be partly a self-delusion, Rubin's enthusiasm for television represented a minority opinion.[5]

Enzensberger's observation captured the widespread sentiment. Few cared to understand what the media did or how it operated; the new left generally viewed the media as the enemy's fiefdom. In Berkeley, Enzensberger noted, students assailed computers as a symbol of oppression.

During the May events in Paris [1968] the reversion to archaic forms of production was particularly characteristic. Instead of carrying out agitation among workers with a modern offset [press], the students printed their posters on the hand presses of the École des Beaux Arts.

The political slogans were hand-painted. . . . It was not the radio head-quarters that were seized by the rebels, but the Odéon Theatre.[6]

Today the situation has completely changed. Few subscribe to notions of manipulation and fewer scorn the mass media. A "cultural archaism" that abhorred the mass media developed into a leftist "cultural studies" that more or less adores it. Of course, a straight line does not lead from the 1960s hostility to the media to its embrace thirty years later. Nor is a capacious cultural studies the single outcome of the 1960s.

Yet a fundamental shift in intellectual sensibilities has taken place, and the distance traveled is most visible in cultural studies, which is left-wing in its origin and orientation. *Cultural studies* defies a brief description; very broadly it denotes an academic field spanning several specialties that has moved away from studying past works of high culture to analyzing contemporary popular culture from pornography to sports. A democratic and populist impulse permeates the field.

Even the most cursory look at its new anthologies finds lengthy and appreciative articles on rock videos, menswear, TV talk shows and soap operas. A recent collection includes studies by "second-generation" professors "who no longer feel obliged to make the case that [television] serials are an appropriate object of scholarly inquiry." Articles like "The Role of Soap Opera in the Development of Feminist Television Scholarship" suggest a new world of academic studies.[7] To earlier sensibilities the notion of "feminist television scholarship" is itself jarring, much less the role of soap operas within that scholarship.

The transition does not simply signify a regression. As Enzensberger argued, the thesis that evil managers tricked passive masses suffered from grave weaknesses. Earlier critics often subscribed to this supposition. "Ours is the first age in which many thousands of the best-trained individual minds have made it a full-time business," wrote Marshall McLuhan in his 1951 study of advertising, "to get inside the collective public mind . . . in order to manipulate, exploit, [and] control."[8]

Few today would second this statement from *The Mechanical Bride*. Even McLuhan rapidly backed off. He reflected a few years later that he had attempted "a defense of book-culture against the new media. . . . My strategy was wrong, because my obsession with literary values blinded me to much that was actually happening."[9] Or, as he stated more emphatically later, he decided to give up the moralizing of *The Mechanical Bride* for "no-point-of-view."[10] Although McLuhan hardly caused the shift, he led the way. Within a few years he glided from critic to booster of the mass media.

Several reasons might be offered to explain the wider transformation among critics and scholars. The war in Vietnam convinced skeptics that politics gets played out in the mass media; from the war footage on television to the Pentagon Papers in newspapers, activists and radicals concluded that the mass media could shape public opinion. At the same time, the generation that drew this lesson grew up with the mass media and came to prize it.

In his book on intellectuals and popular culture, *No Respect*, Andrew Ross outlines what he calls the transition from "the last generation of American intellectuals to swear unswerving allegiance to the printed word and the dictates of European taste" to his own generation, immersed in American popular culture. Unlike the last generation, the new does not reject out of hand "commercialization" or "the creativity of consumption."[11] Coming of age with television formed the basis for an appreciation; it did not shock, as it did the previous generation, but seduced and charmed. "Television culture," writes James B. Twitchell in his *Carnival Culture*, "is my culture. . . . I've watched it all my life. I was weaned on that Zenith [of his parents]. . . . At some mysterious point in the 1950s, television ceased to be just an odd-looking gizmo . . . and entered the bloodstream. It became us. It is who we are."[12]

"I've watched several hours of television every day for most of my life," writes David Marc in his book on television and literacy, "and that adds up to tens of thousands of life-time hours in front of the set." This experience, shared by many of his generation, prompted a very different approach than that of earlier critics. Television unsettled the older critics, according to Marc. "All feared the threat of a total corporate takeover of culture. All dreaded the consequences of the outmoding of their craft. 'Us' was *Kultur* . . . 'them' was television."[13]

"Us" were elitists and often European refugees, which made their criticism of mass culture questionable. Elites have always made Americans uneasy. Sociologists like Herbert Gans and Edward Shils added their expertise to this suspicion: The critics of the mass media were not only elitists, they were elitists losing their status in the fluid American society. The critics belonged to a prebourgeois order of courts and patrons threatened by American democracy. To salvage their status, they fetishized elitist creativity and scorned the larger audience.

The critics faced a "drastic downward social mobility" and consequently "produced an ideology of *ressentiment* expressed . . . in the formulation of the mass culture critique." For Gans, this was strictly un-American. "Most of the critics," he observed, have been "Europeans or Americans who were descendents from the European elite or who modeled themselves on it."[14] Real Americans love mass culture.

In an often cited attack, Shils stated that the criticism of mass culture derived from "disappointed political prejudices" and "resentment" against American society. "Whereas in Europe an educated person of the higher classes could . . . avoid awareness of the life of the majority of the population, this is impossible in the United States. What is a vague disdain in Europe must become an elaborate loathing in America."[15] Or as another commentator put it, the United States does not provide a "sheltered niche for [the European] intellectuals or accord them the deference and caste-privileges which they regard as their due."[16] For American scholars, and in particular those raised after World War II, the criticism of mass culture evoked snobbishness and privilege.

One historian believes that "the harried, often intemperate, attacks" by older intellectuals on mass culture should be seen as "acts of exclusion and self-definition." They demonstrated authority by denouncing mass culture. "To be a serious intellectual in America required that one be opposed to the insidious, levelling forces of mass culture; showing too much respect for mass culture," writes George Cotkin, "could even bring forth doubts about one's own intellectual credentials." This "anxiety" blinded observers to "richness of mass and popular culture."[17] Cotkin's generation, free of anxiety, embraces mass culture.

The oeuvre and reception of Dwight Macdonald reflects the shifting perspective on mass culture.[18] By virtue of his essays and journalism, Macdonald, who died in 1982, belongs in the ranks of leading twentieth-century American intellectuals. His 1963 article in the *New Yorker* on the "invisible poor," which drew attention to Michael Harrington's neglected *The Other America*, is usually credited with reigniting the American debate on poverty.[19] Several of Macdonald's essays remain the most uncompromising assaults on mass culture—and in the course of various revisions, he hardened, not softened, his position, for instance, retitling his "Theory of Popular Culture" first a "Theory of Mass Culture" and then "Masscult and Midcult" to indicate his disenchantment. "It is sometimes called 'Popular Culture,'" he explained, admitting he had used the phrase himself, "but I think 'Mass Culture' a more accurate term, since its distinctive mark is that it is solely and directly an article of mass consumption, like chewing gum."[20]

Macdonald, a maverick leftist, reviled mass culture as base and exploitative. Nor did he curb his criticism because it might sully his democratic credentials. "Whenever a Lord of Masscult is reproached for the low quality of his products, he automatically reposts, 'But that's what the public wants, what can I do?'" For Macdonald, however, the rejoinder does not wash: It does not consider that the "wants" of the public do not arise spontaneously, but are conditioned and manufactured. In his earlier and more Marxist terminology, he stated:

> Mass culture is imposed from above. It is fabricated by technicians hired by businessmen; its audiences are passive consumers, their participation limited to the choice between buying and not buying. The

Lords of *kitsch*, in short, exploit the cultural needs of the masses in order to make a profit and/or to maintain their class rule.[21]

Macdonald was well aware of the charges of elitism. "For some
reason, objections to the giving-to-the-public-what-it-wants line are
often attacked as undemocratic and snobbish. Yet it is precisely because I do believe in the potentialities of ordinary people that I criticize Masscult." He could not understand how leftists could defend
mass culture—or the masses. "To Marx's 'fetishism of commodities'
I would counterpoise our modern fetishism—that of the masses."[22]
In 1959 he gave a talk on mass culture to a student group that was
soon to play a role in the new left. Their response surprised him.

> What I was not prepared for was the reaction to my attacks on our
> mass culture. These were resented in the name of democracy. Holly-
> wood to me was an instance of exploitation rather than satisfying of
> popular tastes. But to some of those who took to the floor after my
> talk, Hollywood was a genuine expression of the masses. They seemed
> to think it snobbish of me to criticize our movies and television.[23]

This response by these early new leftists anticipated the future. Although several sympathetic biographies of Macdonald have appeared, for contemporary cultural-studies scholars Macdonald is, at
best, irrelevant and, at worst, unacceptable. In *Left Intellectuals and
Popular Culture* a young historian, Paul R. Gorman, sets forth the
new conventional wisdom. Macdonald today, we are told, "is most
often invoked as an example of 'what went wrong' with mass culture criticism." Contemporary critics and writers "now generally
agree that the analyses put forth by Macdonald and his fellow critics
were misguided." Newer and more sophisticated work "denies that
people are directly manipulated." The successors to Macdonald
operate with "a more flexible conception of 'culture,'" and they disdain judging with "fixed values." Gorman welcomes this new phase,
calling it "the decline of criticism."[24]

A move toward celebration can probably be charted in the aban-
donment of the term "mass culture" as derogatory and elitist. "The

phrase 'mass culture,'" writes historian Patrick Brantlinger, "originated in discussion of mass movements and the effects of propaganda campaigns, film, and radio shortly before the outbreak of
World War II." From the outset, he notes, it "has carried negative
connotations."[25] The term "mass culture" seems to have been
spawned by notions of "mass society," which in turn derived from
the "masses," which were generally viewed as a danger; the term
was "interchangeable with *hoi polloi*, rabble, canaille, the great un-
washed."[26]

For observers from the nineteenth century to the present, the
"masses," as well as mass society, mass psychology and mass culture, threatened civilization. The masses were sometimes crowds,
mobs and rabble. Freud's 1922 booklet, *Group Psychology and the
Analysis of the Ego*, which considers one threat to civilization,
might be more accurately translated as *Mass Psychology and the
Analysis of the Ego (Massenpsychologie und Ich-Analyse)*.[27] Even
Matthew Arnold used the term gingerly, as too derogatory. Referring to the spurious culture delivered to the English population, he
stated "Plenty of people will try to give the masses, as they call
them, . . . "[28]

Previous generations of leftists rarely bothered to criticize mass
culture because they thought its flaws were self-evident; moreover,
many were convinced that the prevailing culture would vanish with
the bourgeoisie itself. Popular and mass culture was bourgeois culture. In the future society all would enjoy the elite culture. One veteran of the Communist movement recalled the teachings he heard as
a youth: "The saxophone is not a real instrument . . . jazz and certainly popular music were all capitalist expressions. In my adolescent mind there was a day when the Revolution would come, and
there would be no popular music. . . . Everybody would listen to
Beethoven."[29]

Others believed that the working class incarnated not only a superior economic and social system, but a superior culture.[30] In its crud-
est form the adherents of the Soviet "proletarian culture" movement
supposed that workers must "immediately create" their own "so-

cialist forms of thought, feeling and daily life."[31] Devotees of "socialist realism" called for a break with bourgeois decadence and pessimism; new revolutionary art would be "optimistic," "joyous" and "heroic."[32] Even those distant from the Soviet approach believed that the culture of the working class was different from and superior to the culture of the middle class; it anticipated a more humane future.

Today few still believe this—certainly not exponents of cultural studies. Herein lies a revealing irony: Contemporary cultural studies, with its sympathetic interpretations of mass culture, largely derives from a British socialism that sought to keep mass culture at bay. The British radicals wanted to salvage a distinct class-based culture. They subscribed to the idea of a working-class culture, which they saw endangered by mass culture. "The threat to . . . traditional working-class life," writes one account, was "crucial for the early development of cultural studies."[33]

Richard Hoggart's *The Uses of Literacy*, usually dubbed a founding work in cultural studies, celebrated working-class culture and railed at mass culture for submerging it. To current leftists, the socialist Hoggart probably sounds like a conservative:

> Most mass-entertainments are in the end what D. H. Lawrence described as "anti-life." They are full of corrupt brightness, of improper appeals and moral evasions. . . . They tend towards a view of the world in which progress is conceived as a seeking of material possessions, equality as moral leveling and freedom as the ground for endless irresponsible pleasure. . . . They tend towards uniformity. . . . Working people . . . are . . . being presented continually with encouragements towards an unconscious uniformity. This has not yet been found hollow by most people because it is expressed most commonly as an invitation to share in a kind of palliness, even though in a huge and centralised palliness.[34]

Hoggart became the first director of the Birmingham Centre for Contemporary Cultural Studies, a key institution in the promotion of cultural studies. Other main contributors to cultural studies such as E. P. Thompson and Raymond Williams also devoted themselves to documenting and defending working-class culture. Thompson's classic *The Making of the English Working Class* can be viewed as a long argument for the centrality of working-class culture. "The making of the working class," he stated, "is a fact of political and cultural, as much as of economic history."[35]

Williams devoted much of his life to resisting mass culture. "I thought the Labour government had a choice," Williams reminisced about the post–World War II period: "Either for reconstruction of the cultural field in capitalist terms, or for funding institutions of popular education and popular culture that could have withstood . . . the bourgeois press. . . . I still believe that the failure to fund the working-class movement culturally" led to its demise in the 1950s.[36]

Williams also spent fifteen years as a teacher in adult education, mainly under the auspices of the Workers' Educational Association. As one account put it, "Williams wanted very much to work in adult education because of class loyalty and identification."[37] Nor was he an exception. Hoggart and Thompson also dedicated themselves to adult education. They committed themselves to teaching (and listening to) an adult population largely composed of working individuals who could not afford the time and money for a regular university education; these educators hoped to salvage a working-class culture. As Williams stated, "It was distinctly as a vocation rather than a profession that people went into adult education—Edward Thompson, Hoggart, myself."[38]

The British adult education group, itself the successor to a working-class education movement, gave rise to cultural studies. Tom Steele, who has written a history of its origins, observes that cultural studies "began as a political project of popular education amongst adults." However, he continues, few traces of these allegiances surface in contemporary cultural studies. Students now think that it "sprang fully-armed from the side of a university department of English." Practitioners of cultural studies do not know, forget or cast aside the original cause and motivation.[39]

In a lecture near the end of his life Williams tried to set the record right: "We are beginning, I am afraid, to see encylopaedia articles dating the birth of Cultural Studies from this or that book of the late fifties. Don't believe a word of it. That shift of perspective . . . began in Adult Education; it didn't happen anywhere else."[40]

Today to speak of adult education or salvaging working-class culture as political projects sounds quaint. One appraisal of the impact of the British school remarks that notions of class are "not central to the current fashion in cultural studies."[41] At best, working-class culture is history—and if E. P. Thompson and the "original" cultural-studies school have a loyal following, it is among labor historians, who want to record the past struggles of the working class. They want to do more than record; they also believe that the working class possessed a distinct vision or "viable labor culture" that challenged a "dreary liberalism."[42]

However, very few argue that a distinct working-class culture still exists in the Western industrial nations.[43] As one labor historian put it: "The fact is that mass culture has won; there is nothing else."[44] This proposition does not derive from a lack of revolutionary rectitude or conceptual rigor; rather, it stems from an observation difficult to challenge, the decay of a working-class movement and the demise of its unique culture. In numbers and proportions factory labor constitutes less and less of the laboring population. Culturally a working class merges with the wider society. Who seriously argues that a working class today represents a distinct cultural entity?

What happens to cultural studies when its original object, working-class culture, vaporizes? If nature does not abhor a vacuum, intellectuals do. Knock-off French theories and instant Gramsci fill up the spaces. The orientation of cultural studies changes from criticizing to interpreting, reading, deconstructing and, increasingly, championing mass culture. "The discipline began to celebrate commercial culture," notes Simon During, a professor of English and cultural studies who approves the shift. It "turned away from the highly theoretical attacks . . . by arguing that at least some popular-cultural products themselves have positive quasi-political effects." He gives an example: an interpretation of Madonna as delivering pleasure and a "feminist-ideology critique" to her fans. To During, "such work is refreshing because it rejects the hierarchies that support monocultures" and "it does not condescend to actual popular-culture practices."[45]

Where does this lead? To an embrace of mass culture. Gorman's *Left Intellectuals and Popular Culture* opens by repudiating those who denounce television. "TV bashing is only the most recent expression of a general bias against mass entertainment that has been held by American intellectuals in the modern era."[46] The newer and younger professors transcend the bias, relishing mass culture. Alan Wolfe summarizes the shift:

> "Roll Over, Beethoven" is the anthem; whatever the literati once denounced, cultural studies will uphold: romance novels, *Star Trek*, heavy metal, Disneyland, punk rock, wrestling, Muzak, *Dallas*.... If shopping centers were for an earlier generation of Marxists symbols of the fetishism of commodities, then contemporary advocates of cultural studies . . . find them "overwhelming and constitutively paradoxical." If Rambo can be seen as little more than a money-maker, he also represents . . . the vulnerability of the American male.[47]

Yet the choices have never been either-or: either celebrate "high" culture or champion mass culture. This is easy to distort or forget, as if proponents of elite culture simply dismissed mass and popular culture. In fact, they have often expounded on the symbiotic relationship between high and popular culture, lamenting the grievous split. Van Wyck Brooks, who popularized the terms "highbrow" and "lowbrow," thought the separation harmful. "Twenty, even ten years ago," he wrote in 1915, "it would have been universally assumed that the only hope for American society lay in somehow lifting the 'Lowbrow' elements in to the level of the 'Highbrow' elements." Now, however, it is "plain" that highbrow culture by itself produces a "a glassy inflexible priggishness . . . which paralyzes life" and that "the lower levels have a certain humanity, flexibility, tangibility." Or, as he put it, "slang has quite as much in store for so-called culture as culture has for slang."[48]

The argument between the exponents of high culture and those of popular culture is often more rhetorical than substantial. At least, the issue may be less the grand theoretical formulations than the cogency of specific studies. On an abstract plane, the propositions that corporations crank out mass culture to make a profit and that people do more than passively receive cultural offerings are both true. Nor can a call advanced by cultural studies for a more nuanced reading of mass culture be rejected. On the contrary, openness should inform any study. To state this more strongly: An argument to take seriously the stuff of everyday life and culture—the icons, rituals, images—is unexceptionable. Conversely, an argument or stance that refuses to consider popular culture sabotages thought.

The problem is not the determination to take popular culture seriously; nor is it the name-dropping prolegomenon with drabs of Barthes, Foucault and Gramsci. Rather, it is the failure to say anything illuminating. The ailment is not the banality of the subject matter, but the banality of the analysis. This is the heart of the matter. The self-satisfied break with old elitism can be tolerated, perhaps even applauded; the incessant repetition of the new academic commonplaces, however, betrays the project. These are not gutsy scholars plowing new ground, but cautious souls trimming their front lawns.

The triteness generally derives from a theoretical jargon that strangles any thought and an insistence on finding subversion or complexity everywhere. These give a fabricated cast to many of the writings on popular culture. The typical essay splices together references to the theoretical masters, defers to the earlier pathbreaking professors—usually just a few years earlier—praises the boldness of the project and, finally reaching the subject at hand, comes up with a string of formulations on paradox, ambiguity and subversion.

Though it is easy to caricature the old critics of mass culture, in fact these cranky elitists took very seriously the stuff of everyday life and entertainment; their essays often crackled with intelligence and insight. From the 1930s in little magazines to the 1960s in *Esquire*, Macdonald wrote about movies with an earthiness that stayed clear of high theory and its pretentions. "The trouble with most film criticism today," he once complained, "is that it isn't criticism. It is, rather, appreciation, celebration, information" by "insiders" who are "able to discourse learnedly" about any aspect of film, but ignore whether it is "good." "The very question must strike them as a little naive and irrelevant."[49]

Macdonald might be known for his attacks on mass culture and "masscult," but his real claim to fame are his essays on specific institutions and subjects like popular novelists (James Gould Cozzens), the Great Books, the new Third (Unabridged) Edition of *Webster's New International Dictionary* and America's love affair with "how-to" books and facts. For instance, a passage from his essay "The Triumph of the Fact" reads:

> Our mass culture—and a good deal of our high, or serious, culture—is dominated by an emphasis on data ... by a frank admiration of the factual and an uneasy contempt for imagination, sensibility, and speculation. We are obsessed with technique, hagridden by Facts, in love with information. Our popular novelists must tell us all about the historical and professional backgrounds of their puppets. ... Our press Lords make millions by giving us this day our daily Fact. ... Our way of "following" a sport is to amass an extraordinary amount of data about batting averages, past performances, yards gained, etc., so that many Americans who can't read without moving their lips have a fund of sports scholarship.[50]

In the same way, the theoretical framework for McLuhan's *Mechanical Bride* might seem simple, but the book itself consists of reflections, brimming with insights, references and wit, on print advertisements. An advertisement for shaving cream that opens with the line "For the One Man in Seven Who Shaves Daily" allowed McLuhan to range widely over the issue of phony and real polls. He pondered the usual appeal that "two out of three people" do this or have bought that. He considered the "close connection between opinion polls and consumer poll surveys." He quoted Gertrude Stein that the "funniest" thing expatriates in Paris discovered about

America after World War II was the Gallup Poll. "When a man can take a poll and tell what everybody is thinking, that means nobody is really thinking anymore." McLuhan reflected that "a political machine wants to have exact knowledge of how to weigh its electoral program" in the same way as big business probes consumers to modify its product. Both call in the scientists. "While it is difficult to obtain a sample of social blood or tissue, it is no exaggeration to say that the pollsters with their questionnaires are out for blood. When they get their sample, they analyze it and turn the results over to their masters, who then decide what sort of shot in the arm the public needs."[51]

Even the uncompromising elitists of the Frankfurt School, which included neo-Marxist scholars like Herbert Marcuse and T. W. Adorno, wrote incisive evaluations of mass-culture phenomena. Siegfried Kracauer, who belonged to its outer circles, viewed the Tiller Girls, synchronized dancers of the 1920s, as a clue to larger social forces. He believed contemporary society could be understood less by studying its philosophers than by scrutinizing "its inconspicuous surface-level expressions" like its fads and fashions. By "virtue of their unconscious nature," these popular phenomena "provide unmediated access to the fundamental substance of the state of things."[52]

He as well as the others in the Frankfurt School took this proposition seriously. Kracauer wrote with warmth and acuity about film, hotel lobbies and best-sellers. "I was still a young boy when I saw my first film," Kracauer wrote in the preface to *Theory of Film*. Its "intoxicating" impression caused the very young Kracauer to set down his thoughts in a piece with a "long-winded title . . . 'Film as the Discoverer of the Marvels of Everyday Life.'"[53] Throughout his career, Kracauer examined popular culture; for instance, in 1925 he published a study of detective novels, which was dedicated to T. W. Adorno.[54]

Adorno himself wrote about television and radio as well as a lengthy consideration of the *Los Angeles Times* astrology column. "Make your appearance more charming early. Then contact co-

workers and make plans for more efficient and harmonious arrangement of future routine chores," cited Adorno from a 1953 "Aries"
forecast. The stars counsel practicality and conformity, according to
Adorno. Although historians have studied astrology, few scholars
have tackled the significance of modern astrology.[55] Yet here is
Adorno, the archetypical elitist, leafing through three months of the
Los Angeles Times to figure out "what astrological publications
mean."[56] Even today, few have followed him.

Leo Lowenthal and Norbert Guterman also wrote about mass culture; they published a book-length study of the speeches of American right-wing propagandists, many of which were aired on radio.[57]
In 1942 Lowenthal analyzed the shifting taste in biographical features that ran in popular magazines. Who were the individuals selected? What characteristics were highlighted and how did they
change over time? "Surprisingly," he noted, "not very much attention has been paid to this phenomenon." He found that compared
to the heroes of business and manufacturing at the turn of the century, the "new heroes" of the early 1940s came from the world of
sports and entertainment.[58]

To be sure, the writings on mass culture by Adorno and his associ-
ates do not always distinguish themselves; they could be heavy-
handed and wrongheaded. A dispute continues to simmer as to why
Adorno misunderstood jazz.[59] Nevertheless, the critics of mass culture did not ignore the phenomena and often wrote provocative
analyses. Conversely, the new populists obsess about mass culture
and revel in banality. The issue is not the overreaching theoretical
framework, but its bearing in particular studies. The new students
are not wrong to take mass culture seriously; the problem is their
findings. Their approaches can be faulted not in general, but in particular. They ring their essays with announcements of audacity and
deliver the academic blather of our time. The examples are endless.

A collection of new television criticism, *Channels of Discourse*,
bruits that it represents "a fundamental departure" from "pre-struc-
turalist or traditional criticism." Traditional approaches looked for
"enduring truths about the world." Contemporary criticism views

meaning as "the product of the engagement of a text by a reader or by groups of readers" and "considers the worlds constructed within the texts."[60] The drift seems clear: The move is away from a familiar denunciation in the name of fixed standards to an appreciation of the complexity of television. Again, though this may be acceptable as a broad formulation, the real weakness surfaces in the particular studies.

The first essay, true to the form, expends the bulk of its pages rephrasing the ideas of various semioticians before demonstrating the power of high-octane theory. "Semiotics allows us to describe the process of connotation, the relationship of signs within a system, and the nature of signs themselves." The author gives an example, a "semiotic analysis of the opening credit sequence for *The Cosby Show*." The sequence lasts one minute, the analysis seven pages. "The *Cosby* sequence has been chosen," writes Ellen Seiter, "because it is something that may have been seen repeatedly, not just by the semiotician, who must go over the text a huge number of times in order to analyze it, but also by the average viewer."

The "huge number of times" Seiter suffered the sequence yielded a chart with observations like the following: "*Signifier*: Computer graphic resembling theatre marquee with neon lights. . . . *Signified*: NBC Logo" or "Close-up; one shot . . . Cosby nods head to music; smiles, eyes raised." She continues for several pages before rehearsing the theory and stating the conclusion. "Semiotics argues," we are informed, "that the meaning of every sign derives in part from its relationship to others with which it is associated in the same sign system. Some of the meaning of this sequence, then, derives from its *difference* from the credit sequences of other TV shows." Seiter boldly concludes, "The syntagmatic structure of the opening credits might be described as a theme and variations, where Cosby is the theme and each child—and his wife—appear as variations."[61]

The other essays follow this formula: lethal theory followed by lame conclusions, and sometimes death. E. Ann Kaplan tells us about Kristeva, Lacan and "pre-Althusserian Marxist feminists" before getting down to the business of MTV. "In the case of MTV, for example, instead of the channel evoking aspects of the Lacanian Mirror Phase Ideal Imago . . . it instead evokes issues of split subjectivity, with the alienation that the mirror-image involves." Freudian theory may not apply, however, since the videos are too short. "There is no possibility within the four-minute segment," Kaplan astutely points out, "for regression to the Freudian Oedipal conflicts."

Yet even Professor Kaplan is not certain what is up or down. "It is often difficult to know precisely what a rock video actually means, because its signifiers are not linked along a coherent, logical chain that produces one unambiguous message." Nevertheless she gives it a try, analyzing a Madonna video, "Material Girl," which is "particularly useful," since it "exemplifies . . . the establishment of a unique kind of intertextual relationship."

She describes the scenes and sequences with commentary like the following: "In Jameson's terms, this lack of criticism [in the video] makes the process pastiche rather than parody and puts it in the postmodern mode. The blurring of the diegetic spaces further suggests postmodernism, as does the following confusion of enunciative stances in the visual track." Moving from the video to the person, Kaplan concludes that Madonna represents postfeminism. "She is neither particularly male- nor female-identified and seems mainly to be out for herself."

Professor Kaplan underlines her breakthrough. "This analysis of 'Material Girl' has shown the ambiguity of enunciative positions within the video that, in turn, is responsible for the ambiguous representations of the female image."[62] Or as John Fiske puts it in another essay on Madonna, "Her image becomes, then, not a model meaning for young girls in patriarchy, but a site of semiotic struggle between the forces of patriarchal control and feminine resistance, of capitalism and the subordinate, of the adult and the young."[63]

The editors of *The Cultural Studies Reader* introduce an essay on shopping malls by calling it "wide-ranging" and an "exemplary instance of contemporary cultural studies." Yet the essay by Meaghan Morris exemplifies only how much jargon, theoretical chit-chat and self-reference can be stuffed into twenty-five pages.

The essay vainly circles about what a study of shopping centers might be. "My difficulty in the shopping-center project will thus be not simply my relation as intellectual to the culture I'm speaking 'about,' but to whom I will imagine that I will be speaking. . . . However, in making that argument, I also evaded the problem of 'other' (rather than 'ordinary') women. I slid from restating the now conventional case that an image of a woman shopping is not a 'real.'. . . First I want to make a detour to consider the second enquiry I've had from 'other' women . . . " In virtually her only specific observation, Morris notes that the benches in the Green Hills shopping center are "brightly coloured," which ratifies the garden motif.

This discovery summons up a reference to Walter Benjamin and the Parisian *flâneur*.

> I want to argue that it is precisely the proclaimed dissolution of public and private on the botanized asphalt of shoppingtown today that makes possible, not a *flâneuse*, since that term becomes anachronistic, but a practice of modernity by women for which it is most important not to begin by identifying heroines and victims (even of conflicts with male paranoia), but a profound ambivalence about shifting roles.

As if this might be too clear or forthright, Morris hurries to add: "Yet here again, I want to differentiate."[64]

Or consider on a very different terrain a semiotic effort to "decode" the American breakfast by looking at it not as a meal, "but rather as a *system*—a collection of units or elements that are structured in some way. . . . There is what might be thought of as a breakfast code." The author rejects temperature, color or shape as the code, before unlocking the door, the transformation from solid to liquid and vice versa. Looking at the typical American breakfast, Professor Arthur Asa Berger finds:

> Orange juice is a solid that becomes a liquid. Coffee is a drink made from a solid, coffee beans. . . . Sugar is a solid that becomes a liquid and then a solid again. Corn flakes is a solid that becomes a liquid and

then made into a solid again. Butter is a liquid that becomes a solid. Eggs are liquid and become solid. The other items—bread, bacon and potatoes—are solids that remain solids, while milk and cream are solids [since cows eat grass] that become liquids.

The conclusion to these observations? Americans eat breakfast in order to transform themselves in the same way as their food is transformed into liquids or solids. "The message of the classic American breakfast is disguise and endless transformation."[65] Professor Berger might want to consider lunch.

Several cultural studies professors argue that video has changed the experience of viewing, encouraging a "mastery over the narrative." Henry Jenkins cites a colleague who states that "video has enabled TV to take on an emphatically Brechtian reflexivity." Jenkins adds that "this new relationship to the broadcast image allows the fans' liminal movement between a relationship of intense proximity and one of more ironic distance." If this is not clear, he quotes a fan of multiple viewings of *Star Wars*: "Each time I see it, a new level or idea about something in it shows itself. As to the complaint that the characters were shallow and there's no background—nitpicky! That's part of the fun." Jenkins concludes that "her understanding of the film has become progressively more elaborate with each new viewing as she made inferences that took her well beyond the information explicitly presented. . . . *Star Wars* fandom may indeed be one of the most extraordinary examples of the productivity of the interpretative process."[66]

The inability of cultural studies scholars to write a sentence is by now a familiar observation; it bears repeating for at least one reason. Half the hoopla about cultural studies derives from its claim to be writing on behalf of the people; its practitioners are breaking with an old elitism that dismissed popular culture. Yet the old elitists like Macdonald wrote in crisp and lucid sentences that any educated person could read. The cultural studies exponents, in general, offer fractured English, jargon and sentences that could bring tears to a

tenth-grade English teacher. They trample the culture they supposedly love. Macdonald's essay on how-to books begins this way:

> The way to deal with ealworm in phlox is to spray with Murphos, a
> paraltrion curb. The way to avoid being slighted by bus drivers, wait-
> ers and salesgirls is to be unselfish, self-confident, thoughtful, enthusi-
> astic and happy. The way to stop a long-winded speaker is for the
> chairman to rise, thank him for his splendid contribution, and lead the
> audience in thunderous applause. The way to resist a male seducer is
> for the lady to sit in an armless straight chair and pop a piece of salt-
> water taffy into her mouth every time he is about to kiss her. . . . The
> above useful information is a dipperful from the great American reser-
> voir of know-how.

Morris on shopping centers opens: "The first thing I want to do is to
cite a definition of modernity. It comes not from recent debates in
feminist theory or aesthetics or cultural studies, but from a paper
called 'Development in the Retail Scene,' given in Perth in 1981 by
John Lennen of Myer Shopping Centers. To begin his talk (to a seminar organized by the Australian Institute of Urban Studies) . . . "[67]
The point hardly needs emphasizing: The stuff that parades its break
with elitism, its subversiveness and its populist commitments reeks
of insularity and conformity.

*   *   *

Arnold deserves attention both for what he has to say and for what
he reveals about current approaches to culture. Although not a professional philosopher, he offers a platform to assess mass culture
that has hardly been bettered. That both left and right misread
Arnold is part of the problem. To put it briefly, Arnold put together
what many contemporary thinkers believe cannot be joined: an uncompromising critique of popular culture with uncompromising
democratic commitments.

Arnold is surely well known. "Arnold was the most influential
critic of his age," stated Lionel Trilling sixty years ago. "The esti-

mate must be as unequivocal as this."[68] For well over a century, few critics have maintained a comparable standing and influence. "No other foreign critic, and perhaps few native ones, have acquired such a reputation and exercised such a palpable influence on American culture," stated one study over thirty years ago.[69] Arnold was "the single most significant disseminator" of the creed of culture, wrote the historian Lawrence Levine a few years ago.[70]

Yet Arnold is also unknown. His life and commitments explode conventional political categories. Conservatives extract from Arnold a single idea, the significance of high culture. Meanwhile they do not breathe a word of Arnold's aggressive defense of public education and social equality or his assault upon the market, all of which sustained his justification of high culture. Conversely, liberals and leftists surrender a vital and radical notion of Arnold's, his criticism of individualism and, implicitly, of mass culture. In dismissing Arnold they gut the utopian vision that sustained his thought.

Except for biographers and historians, Arnold's life and career as an educator, specifically as inspector of schools, passes unnoticed. Conservatives who love to cite Arnold rarely mention it. A basic study, *Matthew Arnold and American Culture*, has no index entry under "schools" or "teaching" or "education." Yet for thirty-five years Arnold was His Majesty's Inspector of Schools—and this was no honorary appointment. Arnold plodded about, examined and questioned; this was his day job—and more: He incessantly addressed education, not simply in regular reports, but in talks, essays and books. Much of his collected works deal with education, including his longest book, *Schools and Universities on the Continent*. Nor were these concerns extraneous to his more widely read cultural writings. On the contrary, his ideas on education infuse his most famous work, *Culture and Anarchy*.[71]

Arnold was not a socialist; nor was he a conservative. In the context of Anglo-American thought he was a radical in this regard: He believed that the state should take responsibility for the education of the people and, indeed, for culture in general. He also believed in egalitarianism and objected to sharp disparities in wealth. These were not separate propositions; for Arnold, a robust public education, a solid social equality and a vibrant culture all went together. To square the real Arnold with the current portrait of him as an elite snob is not possible.

With a notable lack of enthusiasm, in 1851 at the age of twenty-nine Matthew Arnold became a royal inspector of education, charged with examining schools and students and writing regular reports. "Though I am a schoolmaster's son," he stated at his retirement, "I confess that school teaching or school inspecting is not the line of life I should naturally have chosen. I adopted it in order to marry a lady."[72] He also toured European schools several times and wrote up his findings.

His first report after visiting English elementary schools hit on themes he never dropped. He complained that many of the schools in his district supplemented the minimal government support with steep student fees that "generally exclude the children of the very poor." Even when arrangements are made for lower payments for poorer students, the situation does not improve. Teachers respond to those who pay the highest fees. "Those who pay least are to be taught least." Consequently, able poor students are "neglected," while those children who make the highest payments are put into the highest class, "whether fit or not." Arnold remarked that "a plan more calculated to derange and dislocate the instruction of a school would be difficult to imagine."[73]

A commitment to public education in service of national cultivation informed all his work. He took as the epigraph to *Schools and Universities on the Continent* a line from the German humanist Wilhelm von Humboldt: "The thing is not, to let the schools and universities go in a drowsy and impotent routine; the thing is, to raise the culture of the nation ever higher and higher by their means."[74] He rejected throughout his life the attempt to put education on a cash basis. The state must support education to elevate all its citizens.

The democratic and egalitarian thrust of his work surfaced in Arnold's 1861 *The Popular Education in France*, the product of a

European visit sponsored by a royal commission on education. His first chapter opened by citing the basic English credo that the state is inherently despotic and should be entrusted with as little as possible. Arnold disagreed. This approach sufficed when an aristocracy possessed the strength and spirit to run a country, but for England the moment is past. This elite no longer can claim to be a superior class—and cannot stand above the inexorable democratic currents, which Arnold blessed.

"Democracy," wrote Arnold, "is trying *to affirm one's own essence*; meaning by this, to develop one's own existence fully and freely, to have ample light and air, to be neither cramped nor over-shadowed." Phrases like "ample light and air," which would later show up in *Culture and Anarchy*, appear here drenched in a democratic ethos. For Arnold democracy and equality complemented each other, and both invigorated a nation. The proof was France, where democracy and equality had triumphed, giving the common people "a self-respect" and "an enlargement of spirit." "The common people, in France," stated Arnold, "seems to me the soundest part of the French nation."[75]

Arnold never tired of denouncing inequality. If anything, he became increasingly sharp in his criticisms of material and economic inequalities. In the last decade of his life he gave an address to England's largest "working man's college." The fact of the talk itself sits uneasily with the image of Arnold as remote aesthete. He told his working-class audience that three main problems faced England, the first "those immense inequalities of condition and property amongst us."[76]

As he explained in the essay "Equality," almost everyone in England defends equality "before the law." The rub is "social equality," which everyone opposes, since England is the home of the "religion of inequality." The vast inequalities of property, Arnold believed, derived from the "immense inequalities of class and property" of the Middle Ages that are passed along in families; this "freedom of bequest" sanctions the inequalities, and for that reason has been strictly curbed in many European nations, but not in England. Why? In principle the English do not believe in abstract or natural rights of equality. Arnold agreed.

"It cannot be too often repeated: peasants and workmen have no natural rights, not one. Only we ought instantly to add, that kings and nobles have none either." The point is simple: property is "created and maintained by law"; it is not an abstract right. Hence property can be regulated. "That the power of disposal [of property] should be practically *unlimited*, that the inequality should be *enormous*, or that the degree of inequality admitted at one time should be admitted *always*,—this is by no means certain."[77]

Arnold went on to argue that right of bequest or the right to transfer property should be strictly regulated in order to diminish inequality and improve society. First of all, the "well-being of the many" must be pursued—not only for itself, but for the individual, for no one can be truly prosperous, happy or even secure amid misery. It is here where Arnold sidles into his familiar argument:

> It is easy to see that our shortcomings in civilisation are due to our inequality; or in other words, that the great inequality of classes and property, which came to us from the Middle Ages and which we maintain because we have the religion of inequality, that this constitution of things, I say, has the natural and necessary effect, under present circumstances, of materialising our upper class, vulgarising our middle class, and brutalising our lower class. And this is to fail in civilisation.[78]

Here he stated it is "easy to see"; elsewhere he stated it is hard to see, but the point remains the same. "No one in England combines the fact of the defects in our civilisation with the fact of our enormous inequality. People may admit the facts separately; the inequality, indeed, they cannot well deny; but they are not accustomed to combine them."[79]

Arnold combined them: His criticism of the coarseness of culture is driven by his egalitarian sympathies. An impoverished life and circumstances do not allow cultivation and growth. To put this differently, Arnold's criticism of mass culture is grounded in his democratic ethos. To this ethos he appends two closely related propositions, both of which upset conservatives. The state must support education; and individuals by themselves lack the resources to remedy the social ills. Both precepts undermined a voluntarism or subjectivism that informed English Protestantism and life.

Arnold recognized that in defending the right of free opinion and dissent Protestants performed an "invaluable" service. Yet the distrust of the state and the religion of self-help abandons the majority of people. In his address to the "working man's college" Arnold cited a well-wisher who counseled the downtrodden to avoid the state and nourish "self-reliance and self-help." For Arnold, England already suffered from a surfeit of self-reliance and self-help ideology:

> And ever since I was capable of reflexion I have thought that such cautions and exhortations might be wanted elsewhere, but that giving them perpetually in England was indeed carrying coals to Newcastle. The inutility, the profound inutility, of too many of our Liberal politicians, comes from their habit of for ever repeating, like parrots, phrases of this kind. . . . Englishmen are not likely, you may be sure, to let the State encroach too much. . . . Our dangers are all the other way. Our dangers are in exaggerating the blessings of self-will and self-assertion."[80]

The criticism of self-help, individualism and Puritanism formed the backbone of Arnold's cultural criticism. He challenged the idea, today more widespread than ever, that subjective reason is the last court of appeal, that what an individual feels or wants or desires brooks no argument. Arnold understood, as many social thinkers have, that the individual does not drop from the sky; he or she emerges out of social network. The "I want" or "I need" is also a social statement. This may seem obvious, but it also means that critical reason should not stand mute before the whims and wishes of a population.

"The spirit of individualism," he wrote in "Democracy," should not be taken for something it is not. "It is a very great thing to be able to think as you like; but, after all, an important question remains: *what* you think." Here all "the liberty and industry" in the world do not guarantee "high reason and a fine culture." He took this up in *Culture and Anarchy* in a chapter titled "Doing as One Likes": "Our prevalent notion is . . . that it is a most happy and important thing for a man merely to be able to do as he likes. On what he is to do when he is thus free to do as he likes, we do not lay so much stress."

Arnold's insistence that we must consider the ends, and not only the means, constitutes his subversiveness; the issue was not simply the existence of formal freedom, but its content. Addressing the English burgher, Arnold wrote, "You think to cover everything by saying: 'We are free! We are free! Our newspapers can say what they like!'" For Arnold this did not suffice. "Freedom, like Industry, is a very good horse to ride;—but to ride somewhere. You seem to think that you have only got to get on the back of your horse Freedom, or your horse Industry, and to ride away as hard as you can, to be sure of coming to the right destination."

He referred to a British utilitarian's "stock argument for proving the greatness and happiness of England." "May not every man in England say what he likes? Mr. Roebuck perpetually asks; and that, he thinks, is quite sufficient, and when every man may say what he likes, our aspirations ought to be satisfied. But the aspirations of culture . . . are not satisfied, unless what men say, when they may say what they like, is worth saying—has good in it, and more good than bad."

On exactly these grounds, Arnold savaged a middle class that loved wealth and machinery in themselves, with no notion of their ends or purposes:

Your middle-class man thinks it the highest pitch of development and civilisation when his letters are carried twelve times a day from Islington to Camberwell, and from Camberwell to Islington, and if railway-trains run to and from between them every quarter of an hour. He thinks it is nothing that the trains only carry him from an illiberal, dismal life at Islington to an illiberal, dismal life at Camberwell; and the letters only tell him that such is the life there.[81]

The inability to evaluate the ends and the fetish of means characterizes what Arnold called the philistine. Arnold introduced the term *philistines* in an essay on Heine, from whom he adopted the term. "Perhaps we [the English] have not the word because we have so much of the thing." The Philistines, crabbed and limited members of the middle class, were closed to new ideas and experiences; they were "humdrum people, slaves to routine, enemies to light; stupid and oppressive, but at the same time very strong."[82]

Although it might appear that Arnold was defending a spiritualized notion of the good life, it is almost the opposite. He savaged Puritans and ascetics as pinched in spirit and sensation; they were the bane of England. Culture flowered during the Elizabethan era. "A few years afterwards the great English middle class, the kernel of the nation, entered the prison of Puritanism, and had the key turned on its spirit there for two hundred years."[83]

English Puritanism killed pleasure and spirit. Indeed, one of the few things Arnold appreciated about the United States was a "buoyancy, enjoyment, and freedom from constraint" missing in the English middle classes.[84] The point is: Arnold did not defend "sweetness and light" as abstract goods; he defended a bountiful world against a cramped life of money and work. He quoted a doctor who wrote that the prosperous citizens of Liverpool were dying of boredom and atrophy; they lacked excitement. For Arnold this was exactly right: People suffer from an "immense ennui." They need stimuli and passion.

> Health cannot in general be maintained without nervous excitement. . . . Money-making is not enough by itself. Industry is not enough by itself. Seriousness is not enough by itself. . . . The need in man for intellect and knowledge, his desire for beauty, his instinct for society . . . require to have their stimulus felt also, felt and satisfied.[85]

Arnold's ideas on culture are easy to lampoon—as he himself was well aware.[86] By the end of his life he regretted that the phrases he coined were losing their meaning. I am a "nearly worn-out man-of-letters," he stated, "with a frippery of phrases about sweetness and light; seeing things as they really are, knowing the best that has been thought and said in the world, which never had very much solid meaning, and have now quite lost the gloss and charm of novelty."[87] Nevertheless his ideas offer a perspective to judge popular culture.

Undoubtedly, a fear of political unrest surfaces in Arnold's writings, notably in *Culture and Anarchy*. Yet it surfaces, not determines. Arnold was fundamentally a critic of middle-class life and culture. For this reason his importance as a critic only increases today: Middle-class culture has triumphed. He once compared himself to William Cobbett, the English radical and advocate of the working classes whose politics were governed by "one master-thought,—the thought of the evil condition of the English labourer." Arnold's master-thought was "the thought of the bad civilisation of the English middle class."[88]

It is here that Arnold converges with other nineteenth-century liberal thinkers who worried about increasing homogenization and uniformity of a democratic society. Tocqueville noted that many contemporaries dreaded relentless change, but he feared the opposite, the perpetual stagnation in which people become more and more alike in ideas and opinions. Mill agreed, writing to Tocqueville that "the real danger in democracy . . . is not anarchy or love of change, but Chinese stagnation and immobility."[89]

Mill criticized middle-class culture, but did not waver in his democratic and egalitarian sympathies. In discussing Tocqueville's *Democracy in America*, Mill argued that the Frenchman confused "the effects of Democracy" with the effects of "modern commercial society" and its middle class. Mill shared Tocqueville's concern about the "tyranny over the mind" and the "growing insignificance of individuals in comparison with the mass," yet these did not derive simply from democracy. "All the intellectual effects which M. de

Tocqueville ascribes to Democracy are taking place under the Democracy of the middle class."[90]

Like Mill's, Arnold's writings continue to resonate. The democratic criticism of democratic culture gains in import with the decline of radicalism. His objections to the glorification of mass culture in the name of relativism and freedom speak to the present. He stated that "a kind of philosophical theory is widely spread among us to the effect that there is no such thing as a best self and a right reason." Consequently we must accept "the infinite number of ideas" and realize that wisdom consists of "perpetual give and take," with no one right or wrong. For Arnold "the great promoters of these philosophical ideas are our newspapers," trumpeting that England enjoys unparalleled liberties of freedom. "It is no use," quotes Arnold from the *Times*, "for us to attempt to force upon our neighbours our several likings and dislikings. We must take things as they are. Everybody has his own little vision."[91]

Arnold did not accept the intellectual resignation that constitutes this pluralism—a pluralism that today is everywhere. Nor did he defend what many erroneously believe is the opposite of pluralism, authoritarianism or elitism. Rather, Arnold believed that everyone in a democracy could be part of the elite. He rejected the private or individualist solution. Culture must be universal or it is nothing. Culture

> leads us to conceive no perfection as being real which is not a *general* perfection, embracing all our fellow-men with whom we have to do. Such is the sympathy which binds humanity together, that we are indeed, as our religion says, members of one body, and if one member suffer, all members suffer with it. Individual perfection is impossible so long as the rest of mankind are not perfected along with us.[92]

Arnold offered something that has almost been lost, the democratic critique of democratic culture. The treatment of his work signals the atrophy of current political thinking. Conservatives and radicals can no longer grasp a thinker who does not neatly fit contemporary categories. Conservatives avoid Arnold where he champions the state, public education and social equality and where he savages the market. Liberals and leftists see only elitism where Arnold assails individualism and philistinism; they no longer entertain a criticism of mass culture. Yet the old elitists like Arnold and Macdonald kept alive a vision of emancipation that the new critics extinguish in the name of the people.

— 4 —

INTELLECTUALS: FROM UTOPIA TO MYOPIA

Who are intellectuals? If they are defined simply as the educated, intellectuals have existed for millennia as priests, scribes and clerks; and they will continue as teachers, specialists and technicians. "Here are the instruments needed by clerks," stated a thirteenth-century Parisian observer, "books, a desk, an evening lamp with tallow and candle holder, a lantern, and an inkwell with ink, a pen, a lead pencil and ruler for ruling lines, a table, and a ferule, a chair, a blackboard, a pumice stone along with an erasing knife, and chalk." The historian Jacques Le Goff cited this description in his study *Intellectuals in the Middle Ages*. According to Le Goff, intellectuals emerged with the twelfth-century towns.[1]

The expansive definition may mislead, however. The issue may be less how long scholars and clerks have existed than when they coalesced as a group and gained self-awareness—and a name. This is a relatively new development. In a study of "intellectuals" in antiquity, Paul Zanker, a professor of classical archeology, admits they did not exist as a recognized entity. "Neither the Greeks nor the Romans recognized 'intellectuals' as a defined group within society."[2] The term and reality emerge much more recently, in the latter nineteenth century in Europe and Russia. In both countries intellectuals took shape as dissenters and revolutionaries.

The Russian experience is instructive, since it contributed not only a word, the *intelligentsia,* but dense and illuminating discussions. As critics, novelists and revolutionaries the intelligentsia played a key role throughout the nineteenth and early twentieth centuries. One sliver of this history might be helpful: In the wake of the Revolution of 1905, a collection of essays by and on the intelligentsia, titled *Landmarks,* achieved great success.

In the words of its editor, it sought "to tell the Russian intelligentsia the bitter truth about itself."[3] Its contributors grappled with the meaning and role of the intelligentsia. Peter Struve, the liberal or "legal" Marxist, noted that the term had various usages, but stated he had no intention of conflating the intelligentsia and the "educated class." If this were done, "the intelligentsia has existed in Russia for a long time" and "represented nothing remarkable." Rather, for Struve, the Russian intelligentsia distinguished itself by its "ideological and political force" and "its alienation from and hostility towards the state," as well as its "irreligiosity." These characteristics surfaced in the intelligentsia's attraction to anarchism and socialism.[4]

If this was a simplification, in both Russia and France, where the term "intellectuals" emerged during the Dreyfus Affair, intellectuals did appear as critics of state and society, often as socialists and Marxists. The story of the emergence of intellectuals during the Dreyfus Affair has often been told. It gave rise to the *locus classicus* of intellectuals, Émile Zola's open letter, "J'accuse," which appealed to truth and justice and closed with a string of accusations against the state and its agents. "I accuse General Mercier . . . I accuse the three handwriting experts . . . I accuse the offices of War . . . I accuse the first Court Martial . . . I have but one desire, seeing the light, in the name of humanity that has so suffered and that has a right to happiness."[5]

Eric Cahm, a historian of the Affair, summarized:

The Affair thus witnessed the birth of the modern idea of the intellectual committed as a member of a group, made up of writers, artists and those living by their intellect. . . . The committed intellectual is placed . . . outside the power structures of his society, and he gives his opinion in the name of high ethical or intellectual principles, without regard to official truths.[6]

The left inherited this notion of the intellectual; in principle it sympathized with and supported intellectuals, independent dissenters appealing to universal categories. Yet history has not been kind to this model. In the course of the twentieth century, intellectuals have migrated into institutions to became specialists and professors. At the same time, they have turned suspicious of universal categories as unscientific or oppressive. Bernard-Henri Lévy wondered if the following would appear in the (French) dictionaries of the future: "Intellectual, masculine noun, social and cultural category; emerged at Paris during the Dreyfus Affair; died at Paris at the end of the twentieth century."[7]

The fate of a utopian vision is bound up with the fate of intellectuals, for if utopia ever found a home, it was among the independent thinkers and coffee-house patrons. To the degree these no longer exist, the utopian vision flags. To be sure, this is a subject thick with myth and questions. Did intellectuals really ever gather in coffee houses? Did these environs stamp their thought and writing? Is there an affinity between utopia and independent intellectuals? And if intellectuals decamped from old haunts to seminars and conference rooms, what were the gains as well as the losses?

One aspect of this shift may illuminate the eclipse of utopianism among intellectuals. Language and thought register the specific conditions of their gestation. No one completely transcends history. To subsist in the eighteenth century as an independent writer hatching projects affects prose and thought one way; to function in the twentieth century as a professor preparing college lectures and conference papers affects them in another. In his book on Samuel Johnson and "the life of writing," Paul Fussell reflects on the numerous genres that the eighteenth-century critic mastered, including a dictionary, tragedies, essays, travel books, poetry, and sermons. To follow

Johnson's lead today, believes Fussell, and begin a literary career with a narrative poem or travel book "would be to begin no literary career at all. . . . The fact is that no matter what one's ambitions of freedom, one writes essentially what other people are writing."[8]

Fussell may be right, but not only conformity to fashion or expectation limits genres; institutions, the market, forms of leisure and the conditions of work also determine the possibilities. These nourish the limpid essay or opaque book. The timber of prose alters from the essays of Joseph Addison in the eighteenth century to the monographs of professors in the twentieth. The former partake of the openness and informality of the coffee house, the latter of the hierarchy and structure of the university.

"It was said of Socrates," wrote Addison in "The Aim of *The Spectator*," "that he brought Philosophy down from heaven, to inhabit among men; and I shall be ambitious to have it said of me, that I have brought Philosophy out of closets and libraries, schools and colleges, to dwell in clubs and assemblies, at tea-tables, and in coffee-houses."[9] Today not only the ambition, but the cadence of language, and perhaps the texture of thought, has changed. Current academic writing often claims an unprecedented boldness and modernity, but usually betrays deference and insularity, tangled webs of acknowledgments and clichés. *Addison and Steele Are Dead* runs the apt title of a recent criticism of English department jargon and professionalism.[10]

Neither Addison nor Johnson were utopians. Nor can it be maintained that lucidity and utopia are linked, at least directly. For instance, the writings of Charles Fourier, the dazzling and almost unhinged utopian, often baffle readers. Yet many of his passages soar, and an unmatched vision of emancipation animates his work. Utopian thinking may require conceptual and, perhaps, real space, which Fourier, the permanent and perpetual outsider, had in abundance. "From his beginnings as an isolated and unrecognized provincial autodidact to his last years as one of the odder habitués of the cafés and reading rooms of the Palais Royal," writes Fourier's biographer, "he was at pains to separate himself from the ruling ideas and the ruling thinkers."[11]

Without intellectuals or with recast intellectuals, utopia may fade away. Utopia here refers not only to a vision of a future society, but a vision pure and simple, an ability, perhaps willingness, to use expansive concepts to see reality and its possibilities. Mental breathing space might be necessary to sustain these sight lines. As bureaucracies absorb intellectual life, the lines break up into fields and departments; the vision and writing of intellectuals contract; thinking and prose turn cramped and contorted. Intellectuals retreat in the name of progress to narrower turfs and smaller concepts; they disdain lucidity itself, a kin of light and the Enlightenment.

Two books published in the late 1920s, Julien Benda's *The Betrayal of the Intellectuals* and Karl Mannheim's *Ideology and Utopia,* connote a shift in the commitments of intellectuals. Benda's appealed to an intellectual model in eclipse; Mannheim's to one in ascendancy. Benda, who had intervened in the Dreyfus Affair, called for intellectuals to remain loyal to universal ideas of truth and justice, which he saw almost as a spiritual mission. He charged "betrayal" when intellectuals rallied to a specific nation, class or race. These intellectuals "have set out to exalt the will of men to feel conscious of themselves as distinct from others, and to proclaim as contemptible every tendency to establish oneself in a universal." Benda feared a future in which intellectuals, manipulating political passions, would cause "the organized slaughter of nations or classes."[12]

Benda's prescient *Betrayal,* which evoked the *philosophes* of the Enlightenment, might be seen as summarizing a tradition that was ending. He did not quote Voltaire, but might have. Men of letters, wrote Voltaire, are "isolated writers," who have neither "arguified on the benches of the universities nor said things by halves in the academies; and these have nearly all been persecuted." He added that if you write odes to the monarch, "you will be well received. Enlighten men, and you will be crushed."[13] Or Benda could have cited the great utopian Condorcet, who lauded the "class of men" who devoted themselves to "the tracking down of prejudices in the hiding places where the priests, the schools, the governments and all long-established institutions had gathered and protected them." These men took as their "battle cry— *reason, tolerance, humanity.*"[14]

If Benda's book registered the passing of an intellectual type, Mannheim's heralded the new species, the professional beyond ideologies and utopias. Mannheim not only captured the transformation to the postutopian intellectual in his writings, his own life expressed the shifts, which he both celebrated and bemoaned. He belonged to a generation of Hungarian philosophers, poets and Marxists, like Georg Lukács and Arnold Hauser, who gathered in Budapest at the end of World War I searching for a "new culture" to heal the ills of society.[15] The heady days when empires dissolved and revolutions surged did not last. Twice a refugee, from Hungary and Germany, Mannheim ended his career as a professor of education at the University of London, advocating democratic planning.[16]

Ideology and Utopia justified a skepticism about utopia that has since become common coin. Mannheim argued for a scientific approach to ideology and politics in which all knowledge was "partisan and particular," none with a superior purchase on truth. Marxists had confined ideology to the ideas they opposed, assuming their own ideas were true. Mannheim exempted no ideas from the label of ideology. Intellectuals were no longer charged with ferreting out truth and untruth. Rather, they became professional doubters equally distant from ideology and utopia; in the end they mistrusted reason and truth.

*   *   *

The notion that the left forthrightly supported intellectuals distorts the historical reality; it often saw them as elitists and manipulators—and utopians. Anarchists from Bakunin in the nineteenth century to Chomsky in the twentieth century have suspected that intellectuals lacked the discipline, selflessness and humility essential for a serious politics; intellectuals were power-hungry elitists. Marxists hardly differed; they saw intellectuals as shirkers, if not bourgeois sympathizers.

At the turn of the century, a Polish-Russian anarchist, Jan Machajski, believed he had discovered the cause of recent political defeats; intellectuals, to whom workers look for leadership, form a class and seek power for themselves.[17] Machajski developed what might be called a Marxist critique of Marxism. In the name of Marxism intellectuals pursued their own economic interests; they were less revolutionary leaders than self-interested office seekers. In a 1902 May Day appeal, Machajski called upon workers "to abandon the intelligentsia," who use the labor movement to gain "cushy jobs" in the state.[18]

For an obscure radical whose writings have hardly been translated out of Russian (and mainly published in Switzerland), Machajski's idea of intellectuals forming their own class enjoyed amazing success, popping up across the decades. For many anarchists and dissident leftists, Machajski's argument explains what happened to the Russian revolution—intellectuals hijacked it. Critics of Stalinism from Leon Trotsky to the Yugoslavian dissident Milovan Djilas echoed Machajski, arguing that intellectuals constituted a new group of bureaucrats that had captured the state and cast aside the working class.[19] In its more extreme formulation, for instance, as developed by an American follower, Max Nomad, Machajski illuminates what happens to all revolutionary projects—intellectuals manipulate them for their own ends.

Nomad, a marginal figure in New York leftist circles, realized that his argument "may be grist to the mill of reactionaries who take pleasure in disparaging the 'eggheads.'" He protested that a reviewer called one of his previous books "a javelin hurled at the intellectuals."[20] Nomad insisted that he sided with the rebels and dispossessed, but as with many anarchists, his deep suspicion of intellectuals led him into a cul-de-sac, damning his readers and audience as power-hungry and unreliable. His *Skeptic's Political Dictionary and Handbook for the Disenchanted* defined an intellectual as "the descendant of the medicine-man, priest or magician, who has substituted science and literature for the hocus-pocus of his sires." The intellectual is either a "satisfied partner" of power or dreams of "his own enthronement in the seats of power as office-holder or manager."[21]

The acute suspicion of intellectuals remains alive and well in contemporaries like Noam Chomsky, whose political past partakes of the world of Machajski and Nomad, the anarchist left. Chomsky disparages Marxist parties as just "groups of intellectuals."[22] The MIT linguist observes that "for quite understandable reasons" an "antagonism" divides intellectuals and anarchists. "Anarchism offers no position of privilege or power to the intelligentsia. In fact, it undermines that position."[23]

Chomsky's most famous essays, such as "The Responsibility of Intellectuals" and "Objectivity and Liberal Scholarship," chart the betrayal of intellectuals. *American Power and the New Mandarins*, the title of the volume that included these essays, put it concisely: The "new mandarins" are intellectuals, mainly professors, who serve American power. For Chomsky, intellectuals will inevitably adopt an "elitist position," seeking to "manage" and "control" society.[24] A palpable disdain for intellectuals infuses his writings. He refers to intellectuals' "mindless incantation of state propaganda" or to their debased "norms of educated discourse." He writes that intellectuals are "typically the most profoundly indoctrinated and in a deep sense the most ignorant group."[25]

Marxists were rarely more hospitable than the anarchists. They also mistrusted intellectuals as bourgeois sympathizers and elitists who lacked true grit and commitment. In a typical statement, August Bebel, one of the nineteenth-century leaders of the German Social Democrats, advised his party "to take a careful look at every party comrade, but in the case of an academic or an intellectual, don't just look once but twice or three times."[26]

In his informative book on intellectuals subtitled "A History of an Insult," Dietz Bering, a professor of German philology, collects epithets Marxists have used for intellectuals—waverers, opportunists, individualists, vacillators, sell-outs and bourgeois lackeys.[27] Many intellectuals recall the suspicion they provoked within leftist parties.

Christopher Isherwood reported on his interview by a German Communist functionary in Berlin in 1931: "'You have interest for our movement?' His eyes measured me for the first time. No, he was not impressed. Equally, he did not condemn. A young bourgeois intellectual, he thought. Enthusiastic, within certain limits. Educated, within certain limits. . . . Of some small use. . . . I felt myself blushing deeply."[28]

Richard Wright recounted his experience with the Communist Party in Chicago that took place a few years later. "I was shocked to hear that I, who had been only to grammar school, had been classified as an *intellectual*. What was an intellectual?" It connoted unreliability. Some time later, a comrade hinted he should leave the Party. "'Intellectuals don't fit well in the Party, Wright,' he said solemnly, . . . 'We've kept records of the trouble we've had with intellectuals in the past. It's estimated that only 13 percent of them remain in the Party.'" He added ominously, "The Soviet Union has had to shoot a lot of intellectuals."[29]

Or hang them. Milan Kundera's novel *The Book of Laughter and Forgetting*, set decades later in Soviet Czechoslovakia, opens with a historical event, the hanging of leading Czech Communists. Kundera's main character finds himself accused by an old girlfriend of making love "like an intellectual."

> In the political jargon of the day, "intellectual" was an expletive. It designated a person who failed to understand life and was cut off from the people. All Communists hanged at the time by other Communists had that curse bestowed upon them. Unlike people with their feet firmly planted on the ground, they supposedly floated in air. In a sense, then, it was only fair they have the ground pulled out from under them once and for all and be left there hanging slightly above it.[30]

Even Antonio Gramsci, whom Marxists idolize partly because he was one of the few who wrote sympathetically about intellectuals (and partly because he died in one of Mussolini's jails), does not fundamentally differ from other Marxists.[31] He hoped to supplant "traditional" intellectuals of the church and academy with a new type of "organic" intellectuals who were rooted in the proletariat; and like many Marxists, he viewed industrial labor as the basis for a new type of intellectual. "In the modern world, technical education, closely bound to industrial labour . . . must form the basis of the new type of intellectual." This new type will not be defined by "eloquence," but by "active participation in practical life, as constructor, organizer, 'permanent persuader,' . . . "

Moreover, for Gramsci the subordination of intellectuals to the revolutionary party and working class remained primary. "The most interesting question is . . . What is the character of the political party in relation to the problem of intellectuals?" His answer ran: "The political party . . . is precisely the mechanism . . . responsible for welding together the organic intellectuals. . . . The party carries out this function in strict dependence on its basic function."[32] As the historian John Patrick Diggins observes, "However one defines intellectuals—mandarins, scribes, clerks . . . Gramsci's prescriptions tend to reduce them to instruments of organization and persuasion. . . . Gramsci exhorted intellectuals to merge with the masses."[33]

Of course, the left extends beyond the anarchists and Marxists; no single formula can express its relationship to intellectuals. Again, Mannheim might be seen as a typical figure; he viewed himself as defending independent intellectuals. As a refugee, he felt rootless and homeless. "We want to find a home, a world," he wrote, "because we feel that we have no place in this world."[34] Mannheim tried to convert this instability into a virtue; he rejected the standard leftist view that labeled intellectuals as bourgeois. Nor did he believe they could be considered working class. Rather intellectuals are "situated between classes"; they are relatively unattached or "free-floating."[35]

"Hitherto, the negative side of the 'unattachedness' of the intellectuals," Mannheim wrote, has been emphasized, meaning their "instability" and lack of resolution. Intellectuals have sought to escape this precariousness by attaching themselves to a class or party. But for this Jewish-Hungarian refugee, independence was a virtue, not a liability; it might allow intellectuals to glimpse a "total perspective," perhaps "to play the part of watchmen in what otherwise would be a pitch-black night."[36]

Mannheim's defense of independent intellectuals earned him the ire of both left and right. "Virtually nowhere," concludes one study of Mannheim, did he find "support."[37] To Communists, Mannheim's ideas on "the relatively 'unattached intellectuals'" constituted crude "bourgeois apologetics," a pretense that intellectuals did not represent "the ruling, exploiting class."[38] To socialists, Mannheim did not understand that the intelligentsia will escape its homelessness once it cooperates with a socialist organization.[39] To conservatives, Mannheim's ideas expressed a "variant of European nihilism . . . a state of mind, already well described by Nietzsche, of uprooted, modern intellectual strata."[40]

The political hostility has declined, and Mannheim has become a well-known and well-cited reference, but few have followed his analysis of intellectuals as "unattached" and "between classes." Why? The reason may be less the political implications than the sociological realities. Since Mannheim, the structural shifts that affect intellectuals have become so obvious that few can deny them. If Mannheim's analysis of the "free-floating" intellectuals seemed questionable in the late 1920s, eighty years later it is outright impossible. Today intellectuals are increasingly "attached," affiliated or institutionalized. Mannheim can be seen as the last theorist of the independent intellectuals, not the first. After Mannheim, the older vision of intellectuals as independent and rootless makes way for a view of intellectuals as dependent and connected.

Conservatives were hardly more receptive to intellectuals than those on the left. To be sure, the history of intellectuals and conservatism is briefer than that of intellectuals and the left. Fewer intellectuals identified themselves with conservatism, a fact registered in the contemporary scholarship. Hundreds, probably thousands, of books have been written about leftist, Marxist, feminist or socialist intellectuals, but only a handful of books have appeared on conservative intellectuals.

Conservative intellectuals cherish religion or tradition or the state as creations rooted in something deeper than reason. At a certain point they remove the insignia of the intellectual, reason, to wear the colors of church or state or nation—or they risk undermining their own loyalties. From William F. Buckley to Michael Novak, it is not surprising that Catholic intellectuals have led the conservative movement in America.[41] To these thinkers, secular intellectuals appear as dangerous and rootless souls, individuals with no commitments. Consequently, apart from a love of books or learning, conservative intellectuals often nurture an anti-intellectualism. They charge that intellectuals subvert culture and society.

Paul Johnson exemplifies the species. He is a historian, a journalist of great reach and a conservative intellectual. He also has written a book on intellectuals, simply called *Intellectuals*, that must be judged a rant. It catalogs unpaid bills, unhappy companions and misconduct that constituted the lives of intellectuals from Rousseau to Jean-Paul Sartre. Ibsen might have presented himself as a radical and progressive, but did you know (and do you care) that he was actually very cantankerous, hated long banquets, especially when seated next to elderly suffragettes, was afraid of dogs and heights, had an illegitimate child and was anxious about money?

For Johnson, the personal disorder of the lives of intellectuals belies their ideas and writings. On this basis, he rates intellectuals somewhat below any chance gathering of people. Part of his conclusion reads:

> A dozen people picked at random on the street are at least as likely to offer sensible views on moral and political matters as a cross-section of the intelligentsia. But I would go further. One of the principal lessons of our tragic century . . . is—beware intellectuals. Not merely should they be kept well away from the levers of power, they should also be objects of particular suspicion.[42]

*   *   *

Although hardly supported by the left and right, the classic portrayal of isolated intellectuals upholding universal ideas has inspired countless souls over the centuries—and continues to evoke a response. Today the picture looks faded, however. The universal standards are increasingly challenged as the tool of an imperialist West; and the imperatives of professionalization redefine intellectual concerns. To be sure, many intellectuals see themselves in the classic pose as beleaguered outsiders challenging an oppressive state or church. In some parts of the world, this self-image reflects the reality. In contemporary Algeria to be an intellectual is to court assassination.[43] Yet in North America and Western Europe, the situation is very different. Intellectuals are neither endangered nor dangerous. Only a few conservatives continue to rail against intellectuals as subversive. In the main, intellectuals seem hardly revolutionary or marginal.

The image of the ridiculous and inept intellectual or the absent-minded professor, kindred to that of the isolated and useless writer, has also disappeared from popular mythology. Why? Probably because it lacks veracity or resonance. Satire needs to pluck a chord of reality. Intellectuals today are depicted less as bumbling outsiders than smooth insiders. When intellectuals are caricatured, as in the novels of David Lodge, they are presented as operators and hustlers. *The New York Times* magazine regularly features pieces on high-flying professors—their wardrobes, salaries and successes—a genre of journalism almost inconceivable seventy-five years ago.

That most intellectuals do not receive big salaries and fat appointments is not the issue. Over the last fifty years a decisive shift in the place of intellectuals has occurred. Richard Hofstadter's 1963 *Anti-Intellectualism in American Life*, his worried survey of intellectuals, can now be seen as a book of the 1950s. The decisive defeat of Stevenson by Eisenhower in two presidential elections and the longer shadow of McCarthyism prompted his study. Sensing a deep American anti-intellectualism, Hofstadter displayed several "exhibits" as evidence. He quoted a magazine description of an "egghead" as "a person of spurious intellectual pretensions, often a professor . . . a doctrinaire supporter of Middle-European socialism . . . a self-conscious prig."[44] Hofstadter joined other commentators, such as David Riesman and Nathan Glazer, who fretted that America in general and McCarthyism in particular exuded a poisonous anti-intellectualism.[45]

Even as he wrote the book Hofstadter realized something had changed, however. In 1956 *Time* ran a cover story announcing a new spirit traversed the nation. America now embraced intellectuals. "What does it mean to be an intellectual in the U.S.?" asked *Time*. "Is he really in such an unhappy plight . . . the ridiculed double-dome, the egghead, the wild-eyed, absent-minded man who is made to feel an alien in his own country?" According to *Time*, Jacques Barzun, the Columbia University professor and writer, represented a new species, "a growing host of men of ideas who not only have the respect of the nation, but who return the compliment."[46]

The shock of a Soviet satellite in 1957 and the onset of Kennedy's presidency in 1961 redoubled the respect. By the early 1960s intellectuals were welcomed, sometimes honored, in the highest reaches of government. The title of David Halberstam's book on the Kennedy's years, *The Best and the Brightest*, refers partly to the intellectual cream that flowed toward Washington. A "new breed of thinkers-doers, half of academe, half of the nation's thinks tanks" headed to the capital—people like McGeorge Bundy, who was educated at Groton and Yale and had taught at Harvard.[47] The value of knowledge, training and education rose dramatically. "Intellectuals have come to enjoy more acceptance and, in some ways, a more satisfactory position," stated Hofstadter in his conclusion.[48]

Most intellectuals embrace the change, but some affect disaffection, claiming a marginality they do not have. To put this sharply, once intellectuals were outsiders who wanted to be insiders. Now they are insiders who pretend to be outsiders—a claim that can be sustained only by turning marginality into a pose. This is not the whole story, but may be half of it. The other half is the admission, even celebration, of their new insider status as career professionals. These are two responses to the same process. Both signify the eclipse of an older reality, which to be sure was always partly mythic, of the independent intellectual.

The scholarly literature both reflects and analyzes these transformations. In recent decades—to crudely generalize—studies regularly appear analyzing intellectuals as a professional group with professional interests. For instance, a new book on intellectuals concludes that they have moved "from the margins of society towards a more central position"; the terrain of intellectuals has "become more and more institutionalized, professionalized and commercialized."[49] An editor of a book on intellectuals states, "Everyone seems to agree that intellectuals today . . . are bound up in institutional circumstances as never before."[50] Society now requires, concludes another study, "the mass production of academically trained professionals."[51]

A sign of this change is Pierre Bourdieu's *Homo Academicus*, which from its title to its content illustrates how the study of intellectuals and academics has itself become a scientific field or subfield: The place, role and impact of intellectuals can be graphed and dissected. Bourdieu turns the tables on the academic intellectual, trapping the "supreme classifier" in the net of scientific classifications. Among the tools he uses to snare his prey are death notices and home addresses; from these he calculates the clout of intellectuals or what he calls their cultural capital. Obituaries in professional journals, he writes, are "first-rate documents" for revealing group values, "the last judgement made by the group on one of its deceased members." Was the late and lamented professor called "original," "erudite" or merely "diligent"?

The book bristles with scientific graphs with captions like "The space of the arts and social science faculties: analysis of correspondences: plane of the first and second axes of inertia—individuals," "Classification 2: Classificatory machine no. 2: from academic classification to social classification" and "The Morphological Transformations of the Faculties."[52] His book suggests that, willy-nilly, intellectuals have become institutionalized; they constitute a sufficiently coherent object that can be studied by scientifically minded sociologists. The subject of the study, intellectuals, has become an object.[53]

Benda wanted independent intellectuals to defend universal values. Little could be less likely or fashionable. Today intellectuals put a question mark after or quotations around any reference to universal values, signifying their doubts. Oppositional intellectuals prize the specific and local; they prefer words, like "difference," that address what is unique, not what is general. They distrust "metanarratives" of freedom and equality. Zola's appeal to humanity and its right to happiness belongs to a discarded past.

As Jean-François Lyotard puts it, traditional intellectuals appeal to a "universal subject." Today, however, intellectuals can no longer intervene in public affairs in the name of a universal; the only possibilities are "local" and "defensive."[54] "The species of the universal intellectuals is becoming rare or indeed extinct," states M'hammed Sabour, a sociologist.[55] "The 'universal' or 'prophetic' intellectual on the model of Sartre," writes Jeremy Jennings, a political theorist, "has all but disappeared."[56]

The cliché that left and right converge seems accurate. All parties share an aversion to utopian thought and universal concepts, although each is driven by a different logic. One school of conservatism always challenged the abstractions engendered by the Enlightenment and the French Revolution—the talk of rights and equality—and put in its place loyalty to specific traditions and practices. More recently, leftist intellectuals have come to the same position; they tout what is distinct and unique and decry metaphysics, theories that pass beyond the immediate discourse or circumstances. Both right and left revive dubious notions of localism and nativism.

*   *   *

Although the new institutional realities of intellectual life must be recognized, they need not be applauded. Not lamentation, but an appreciation of the losses as well as the gains is necessary. Yet for many observers, the transformation of intellectuals into professionals ratifies the notion of progress. Of course the observers are also those being observed; they not only register the change, they like what they see: themselves. For Bruce Robbins, a Rutgers University English professor, the old-style, "less morally credible" independent intellectuals have been supplanted by professionals with greater legitimacy.[57]

In *Past Imperfect: French Intellectuals 1944–1956,* Tony Judt gives an upbeat report on the decline of French independent intellectuals like Jean-Paul Sartre. For Judt, a New York University history professor, Sartre and company suffered from serious failings that can partly be explained by the fact they existed outside institutionalized restraints. He celebrates their decline and replacement by professors who are much more responsible and careful thinkers. Unlike the preceding generation, the professors are experts writing in specialized journals for specialized audiences, not in newspapers for average citizens.

> This encourages a degree of modesty and care, deriving from the typical professorial sense it is one's colleagues rather than the world whom one has to convince. . . . This marks a distinct change from earlier decades, when the writings of Malraux, Camus, Sartre, Mounier, and their peers, often half-informed, frequently lazy and ignorant, provoked no such rebukes. . . . In the civil society of today's intellectual community, the market operates with reasonable efficiency. . . . Left to their own devices, intellectuals are thus better placed to retain their local influence if they can point to the imprimatur of quality that comes with institutional attachment and disciplinary conventions. The correspondence between the decline of the great public intellectuals and the resurrection of the professors is thus no mere coincidence.[58]

This analysis has the virtue of forthrightness; it celebrates professionalization, the market, disciplinary conventions and institutional attachments as improving the quality of intellectual life, which Judt believes used to be rotten and corrupt.[59] What is striking is not just the buoyancy of the analysis—intellectual life is getting better and better—but how much this position is shared, with different twists, across the political spectrum. Feminists, poststructuralists, deconstructionists, postcolonialists and others cheer the demise of the old intellectuals and rise of the new professionals.

Like Judt, Jonathan Culler, a Cornell University English professor, offers a happy tale of professionalization; he protests "the crisis narratives" that blame professionalization and academization. He stoutly maintains "we must assert the value not just of specialization but of professionalization also, explaining how professionalization makes thought possible."

Culler turns misty-eyed when he writes about the virtues of specialization; it gives rise to "serious" "works of criticism or scholarship," not to be confused with "newspaper articles," "works of popularization" or "especially commentary." It leads to judicious and democratic judgments by peers. "While reducing capriciousness and favoritism in important decisions, this progress in professionalism shifts power from the vertical hierarchy of the institution that employs a critic to a horizontal system of evaluation."[60]

Michael Walzer, the left-leaning political theorist, joins in with a paean to professionalization and, if not conformity, social success and adjustment. He finds that critics in the modern period generally flourish as insiders. Sartre edited the most influential journal in postwar France; Foucault held a chair in the esteemed Collège de France. To consider these people unrecognized outsiders is implausible, writes Walzer. Critics today "are not peculiarly hostile to the societies in which they live; they are not peculiarly alienated from those societies." They write what Walzer calls "mainstream criticism." This pleases Walzer. "The mainstream is better."[61]

He upends the conventional picture of the intellectual as an alienated outsider. Marginality is not "a condition that makes for disinterest, dispassion, open-mindedness, or objectivity." Rather, "disconnected criticism" tends toward "manipulation," what Walzer politely calls "unattractive politics." Walzer, a lifetime member of a research society, the Institute for Advanced Studies, which gathers for weekly lunches in Princeton, offers a better "alternative model" for the intellectual: someone who is member of a learned institute or club, "the local judge, the connected critic, who earns his authority, or fails to do so, by arguing with his fellows." As if there could be some doubt, Walzer notes, "This critic is one of us." And like one of us, the critic is no enemy of society; he or she wants the "major economic and political enterprises" to "go well."[62]

Further to the left, New York University professor Andrew Ross agrees. In *No Respect: Intellectuals and Popular Culture*, he writes that today it is "clear" that the "mantle of opposition no longer rests upon the shoulders of an autonomous avant-garde: neither the elite metropolitan intellectuals . . . nor the romantic neo-bohemians." Rather, it relies on "technical" or "specific" intellectuals and on "professional humanists," who exert a "specialist influence" in areas of "contestation within the academy." In heralding "the achievements of this new specialism," Ross believes he bucks a "reactionary consensus of left and right, each unswervingly loyal to their respective narratives of decline."[63] What reactionary consensus? Ross swims with the current.

Yet the old image of intellectuals as marginalized dissenters who attack injustice does not simply vanish. Many of those who enthusiastically bury this image turn about and coolly announce that they themselves are marginalized intellectuals. Virtually a straight line can be drawn from Voltaire to Edward Said, whose recent *Representations of the Intellectual* advances an idea of the intellectual as a vulnerable critic on the outside. The intellectual, he writes, is "someone whose place it is publicly to raise embarrassing questions, to confront orthodoxy and dogma . . . to be someone who cannot easily be co-opted by governments or corporations." The intellectual, he states, "always has a choice either to side with the weaker, the less well represented, the forgotten or ignored, or to side with the more powerful."

> And there is something fundamentally unsettling about intellectuals who have neither offices to protect nor territory to consolidate and guard; self-irony is therefore more frequent than pomposity, directness more than hemming and hawing. But there is no dodging the inescapable reality that such representations by intellectuals will neither make them friends in high places nor win them official honors. It is a lonely condition.[64]

This is an engaging portrait, but what relationship does it bear to reality? No honors? No hemming and hawing? No offices or territory to defend? Lonely existence, where? Maybe in Egypt or Albania, but hardly in the United States or France. Can we say that Derrida or Said or Henry Louis Gates, Jr., lead unrecognized or marginalized lives? It would be more accurate to state the opposite: They and other oppositional intellectuals hold distinguished positions at major institutions, and they are regularly wined and dined as well as handsomely compensated. Many leading intellectuals, such as Cornel West or Camille Paglia, operate with agents, who arrange fees and schedules for their many speaking engagements. What does this reveal about intellectual life today?

A sign of the times is the exultation of Stanley Fish that intellectual life increasingly mimics corporate practices in establishing conferences and travel as the coin of the realm. "The flourishing of the [conference] circuit has brought with it new sources of extra income, increased opportunities for domestic and foreign travel . . . an ever-growing list of stages on which to showcase one's talents, and geometric increase in the availability of the commodities for which academics yearn, attention, applause, fame." His only regret? The imitation of corporate largesse is only half-hearted and the compensation for professors remains small.[65]

Yet it cannot be stated too forcefully: No link exists between institutional success and intellectual contribution. Good salaries, secure positions and lucrative speaking engagements do not preclude original or subversive work; nor do paltry wages and insecure jobs guarantee revolutionary and critical thought. The notion that an empty larder engenders insight and a full table rationalizations reeks of a debased Puritanism and crude materialism. If suffering gave rise to works of genius, the world would be awash in masterpieces. If misery caused social transformation, paradise would have arrived long ago.

For judging a single individual or one work of art, sociological observations may be a distraction. For surveying large intellectual patterns, however, a consideration of general economic and social trends may illuminate shifts and turns. Here it is relevant to ponder the impact of the institutionalization of intellectuals. How does it affect the way intellectuals think and approach the world? What does it mean, for instance, that many claim to be marginalized? Is it possible to be marginal and successful? Marginal in the mainstream?

If marginalization includes holding unpopular or dissenting opinions, then the label is easy to apply, but loses its meaning. Like *alienation*, a legal and philosophical concept, marginality succumbs to psychology. Alienation once referred to social relations and labor, signifying an objective condition. Later it turned into an irritation or annoyance. "I'm alienated," someone will announce, meaning "I'm unhappy or uncomfortable." *Marginal* reflects the same psychologizing, passing from a term designating an objective condition to one describing an individual's plight; it becomes a buzzword.

Foucault and Derrida nudged the process along; both of them undermined the distinction between margin and center, laying the groundwork for purely subjective definitions. Foucault defined his project as "trying to deploy a dispersion . . . a scattering; . . . it is trying to operate a decentering that leaves no privilege to any centre."[66] One of Derrida's collections, titled *Margins of Philosophy*, "seeks to blur the line which separates a text from its controlled margin." Derrida wants to compel

us not only to reckon with the entire logic of the margin, but also to take an entirely other reckoning: which is doubtless to recall that beyond the philosophical text there is not a blank, virgin, empty margin, but another text, a weave of differences of forces without any present center of reference (everything—"history," "politics," "economy," "sexuality," etc.—said not to be written in books . . .)."[67]

Though Derrida's thought resists summarizing, the implications are obvious—the lines separating margins and center vanish. "Can this text become the margin of a margin?" he asks in his first essay, which is printed as a column parallel to another "marginal" text. Beyond the text, other texts of "politics" and the "economy" subsist. In a world composed of texts, no texts are central. Conversely, if there is no center, anything is marginal to something.

This is music to the ears of many academics, who, no matter how esteemed and established, often claim to be marginalized, victims lacking proper recognition and respect. They see themselves as outsiders, blasting the establishment. Like uptown executives cruising around in pricey jeeps and corporate lawyers in luxurious utility trucks, they pose as rugged souls from the back country; they threaten the seats of power as they glide into their reserved parking spots.

Derrida believes that he himself is an outsider. Many might view him as a consummately successful professor and author who is endlessly cited, discussed and celebrated. However, Derrida considers his own work as "not at present *well received* anywhere"; it lacks a solid institutional or editorial "home." He believes that he has been the object of a vast attack, which "was in fact unleashed against me only in order to get at my work and everything that can be associated with it."[68]

Gayatri Spivak, a chaired professor at Columbia University, a translator of Derrida and a much-lionized speaker at academic conferences, also perceives herself as "marginalized." With no irony she writes of the "explosion of marginality studies" in American universities and her role in it. Although integral to the marginality industry, she has been marginalized by the "deconstructive establishment."[69]

On occasion the irony or at least the difficulty of successful marginality strikes her. She quotes the description of a literary proposal that crossed her desk in which the author viewed American science fiction as "the Third World fiction of the industrialized nations." She asks, "How is the claim to marginality being negotiated here? The radicals of the industrialized nation want to *be* the Third World." Yet she gets only half of it. Spivak is quoting "from a grant proposal written by a brilliant young Marxist academic." That marginal intellectuals are filling out grant applications for American foundations elicits no comment.[70]

Intellectuals often trumpet their marginality, but their marginality is more and more marginal. bell hooks—the lower case bespeaks her nom de guerre—a professor at City College New York and a leading black feminist, recounts grievous tales of marginality. On a plane journey the good professor was outraged because a black friend with a coach ticket could not join her in first class, since the adjacent seat was already taken by a white passenger—an incident of such proportions that it inspired her book *Killing Rage*.

Are these tales of marginality or privilege? She recounts other shocking stories, for instance, a report by a black Harvard graduate student about a seminar in which Professor hooks's own work was read. "Yet the day it was discussed in class the white woman professor declared that no one was really moved by my work . . . this young black woman felt both silenced and victimized."[71] Marginality gets refined to a comment about a comment about a book in a Harvard graduate seminar. The possibilities are endless.

The point is, a sober appraisal of intellectuals in North America and Europe must not simply second or celebrate the classic picture of the vulnerable and independent critic, but consider a newer and different reality. Any analysis must entertain the possibility that marginality is a pose and that the self-defined outsiders are, and are glad to be, consummate insiders. Indeed, Aijaz Ahmad, an Indian scholar, has suggested that the new discipline of "postcolonial literature," which focuses exclusively on marginalized literature, is less a subversive field than a career move for largely upper-class Asian immigrants in American universities.[72] Gerald Early, a professor of African American studies, has pondered whether multiculturalism as an academic field is a strategy for "new intellectuals" to obtain research money, publishing opportunities and patronage.[73]

* * *

In the 1920s Mannheim outlined the prospects for a scientific approach to knowledge and politics in which intellectuals advance from truth to skepticism. Though Mannheim hardly caused the transformation, he accurately anticipated its configurations. Yet one fiber in Mannheim protested against the developments he endorsed. Once he established that knowledge equaled ideology, and once he showed that all ideologies and all utopias deceive intellectuals, Mannheim drew back. How could humankind proceed without any vision of a future and better world?

After debunking ideology and utopia for several hundred pages, Mannheim closed his book with a doubt. He feared his criticism of utopia would prove too damaging. The last sentences of *Ideology and Utopia* run:

> The disappearance of utopia brings about a static state of affairs in which man himself becomes no more than a thing. We would then be faced with the greatest paradox imaginable. . . . After a long, torturous, but heroic development, just at the highest stage of awareness, when history is ceasing to be blind fate, and is becoming more and more man's own creation, with the relinquishment of utopia, man would lose his will to shape history and therewith his ability to understand it.[74]

If any readers made it to the book's conclusion, it hardly mattered. Mannheim's book expressed the Zeitgeist; his concluding words were the vain protestations of the intellectual condemned by the author himself.

— 5 —

THICK AESTHETICISM
AND THIN NATIVISM

Has modern social and philosophical thought ended in doubt and confusion? Has the project of spreading light and liberty retreated to aestheticism and nativism? The roots of the modern critique extend back to Marx, Nietzsche and Freud, who tap earlier figures of the Enlightenment. Its liberating moment has not weakened; in the name of reality the critique gives the lie to talk of equality, justice and universal love. If all men are created equal, why are men enslaved? If justice prevails, why is injustice everywhere? If love is universal, why are some unloved? The claims of equality or justice turned out to be false, ideological camouflage for the powerful.

The goal was to realize the ideas, however, not jettison them, as if injustice improves with cynicism. The notions of equality or universal love were not false in themselves; they were falsified by a reality that required changing. "Criticism has plucked the imaginary flowers from the chain," wrote the young, and still romantic, Marx, "not in order that man shall continue to bear the chain without any fantasy or consolation but so that he shall shake off the chain and cull the living flower."[1]

A generation of thinkers turned the critique against itself, arguing its exponents advanced their own ideology or deceits. The difference between imaginary and real flowers collapsed. Any claim to truth or reality became suspect. The emergence of a new academic field, the sociology of knowledge, worked this out most emphatically. A survey of the discipline is aptly titled *The Road to Suspicion*.[2] Contemporary critics and scholars inherit and redouble the suspicion. The project is not simply to unmask ideological claims as false, but to unmask the unmaskers. All categories deceive; all ideas falsify.

This corrosive skepticism has become the conventional wisdom. Today cynicism, the belief that ideas only serve power and repression, drives intellectual work. Truth is obsolete; appeals to it sound almost embarrassing. "Around 1900," writes Peter Sloterdijk in his suggestive *Critique of Cynical Reason*, "the radical left wing caught up with the right-wing cynicism. . . . Out of the competition . . . arose that twilight characteristic of the present: the mutual spying out of ideologies." For Sloterdijk, this is the real source of the contemporary intellectual "exhaustion." The old ideas of truth stand "at a loss before this cynicism." The new cynicism "presents itself as that state of consciousness that follows" the dissolution of "naive ideologies."[3]

The flight from naïveté into what Sloterdijk calls "ironic, pragmatic, and strategic realisms" can be charted in much liberal and left contemporary thought, for instance, in that of the philosopher Richard Rorty, a self-described ironist. He might be called a post–"end of ideology" thinker—"post" because he surrenders the liberal ideas that the 1950 thinkers championed; even the ghost of utopia dissipates. Rorty may believe in liberal ideas and their future, but his belief lacks conviction. He cites the socialist Raymond Williams, who praised George Orwell as a man who fought for "human dignity, freedom and peace." "I do not think," writes Rorty, "that we liberals *can* now imagine a future of 'human dignity, freedom, and peace.' . . . We have no clear sense of how to get from the actual world to these theoretically possible worlds and thus no clear idea of what to work for."

For Rorty, this state of affairs must be accepted. "It is not something we can remedy by a firmer resolve, or more transparent prose, or better philosophical accounts of man, truth or history. It is just the way things happen to have fallen out."[4]

What remains of the philosophical project for an ironist? Not much. Terms like *just* or *rational* mean little "beyond the language games of one's time." For Rorty, "nothing can serve as a criticism of a final vocabulary save another such vocabulary. . . . Since there is nothing beyond vocabularies which serves as a criterion of choice between them, criticism is a matter of looking on this picture and on that."[5] As one of his harshest critics, Eugene Halton, puts in, "beneath the glamour of 'postmodern chic,' . . . lies . . . a dehumanized world reduced to unreal language conventions."[6]

This may be true, but does not quite capture what Rorty and some other liberal thinkers are up to. Nor does the charge of cynicism stick; this implies that liberals like Rorty and Michael Walzer or Charles Taylor or Clifford Geertz are splenetic debunkers. Yet they appear open, bemused, tolerant and thoughtful—and they are. Insofar as they have severed all links to utopian vision, however, aesthetic criteria come to the fore. Truth recedes before pose. What sounds interesting or feels sensible or looks provocative becomes the criterion. The break from universal and utopian categories leads to "aesthetization," an elevation of paradox, irony and trivia, writes the German critic Hauke Brunkhorst. Interpretations compete on the basis of originality and cleverness.[7]

With half-hearted protests, Rorty and the others say as much. They exchange truth for art appreciation. In *Thick and Thin,* Michael Walzer writes of the eclipse of the "heroic" mode in philosophy, the search for big truths. Rather, Walzer calls for the "minimalist" approach where critics respond "in detail, thickly and idiomatically" to ordinary and local events. He suggests that "we ought to understand this effort less by analogy with what philosophers do than by analogy with what poets, novelists, artists and architects do."[8] Rorty agrees and tells us that the liberal ironist turns away from "social hope" and "social task" toward "private perfection." For this approach, what counts are novels and enthnologies, areas that "specialize in thick descriptions of the private and idiosyncratic."[9]

The references to "thick descriptions" in Walzer and Rorty allude to the work of anthropologist Geertz, who has championed the term. Geertz has had vast influence, not simply in anthropology, but in fields like history and literary theory. Already two decades ago intellectual historians dubbed Geertz their "patron saint" and peppered their writings with references to "thick descriptions."[10] The historian Dominick LaCapra considers Geertz a guiding spirit of intellectual history.[11] Today many studies in cultural history begin with a bow to Geertz and "thick descriptions."

"Thick descriptions" sanctions layered portraits of singular events. It depreciates ambitious theories addressing broad issues, valuing instead modest observations describing small happenings; it encourages immersion in the stuff of everyday life, giving rise to history and anthropology that has more the feel of literature than of cold science. Yet Geertz adopts the term "thick descriptions" from one of the virtuosos of arid theorizing, the Oxford philosopher Gilbert Ryle; and perhaps the concept has the last laugh. "Thick descriptions" nourishes a literary approach; it also suggests the insular ruminations of self-satisfied professors.

In introducing the concept, Geertz cites Ryle's example of three boys, one winking, another with a twitch and a third parodying the winker. For superficial thinkers, these three boys all appear to be winking. For deep thinkers, however, a host of "complexities" emerges. Winker, twitcher and parodist may be embedded in a dense relationship of communications and miscommunications. For instance, the original winker might actually have been fake-winking to mislead others into imagining a conspiracy. As Ryle put it, "The thinnest description of what the rehearsing parodist is doing is, roughly, the same as for the involuntary eyelid twitch; but its thick description is a many-layered sandwich, of which only the bottom slice is catered for by that thinnest description."

Ryle offered other less than compelling examples of thick and thin descriptions like playing tennis, waiting for a train, humming and clearing one's throat. What is a thick description of throat clearing? "I might clear my throat to give the false impression that I was about to sing." A thin description would miss the reference. "This throat-clearing is not a pretence throat-clearing; it is a pretence throat-clearing-in-preparation-for-singing." Or here is Ryle on golfing:

> Strolling across a golf course, we see a lot of pairs and fours of golfers playing one hole after another in a regular sequence. But now we see a single golfer, with six golf balls in front of him, hitting each of them. . . . He then collects the balls . . . and does it again. What is he doing? . . . He is practicing approach-shots. But what distinguishes a practice approach-shot from a real one? . . . Self-training. Training for what? . . . Matches to come. The "thick" description of what he is engaged requires reference to . . . future non-practice approach-shots.[12]

Ryle spent his life meditating on such matters, an effort that Ernest Gellner long ago denounced as "Conspicuous Triviality." The Oxford approach, Gellner stated, was perfect for "gentlemen" philosophers. To those unsettled by ideas or real problems, it gave "something else to do."[13] A student of philosophy at Oxford recalled that inconsequential examples characterized all discussions. "In fact, there seemed some tacit competition to achieve the greatest possible triviality."[14] Nor is it surprising that Ryle's examples are drawn from his everyday Oxford activities. An appreciation of Ryle bestows its highest praise by calling him an eminently "clubbable man."[15]

For Geertz, Ryle's approach opens up many avenues, but the term may not escape its roots in the Oxford clubs. To illustrate its richness, Geertz provides "a not untypical excerpt" from his field journals. His days in the field must have been quite eventful, for this typical selection reports a robbery and two murders with a vast cast of Moroccan Jews, Berbers, French troops and several thousand sheep. The events offer much to chew on. For Geertz they demonstrate that anthropology is an "interpretative activity" akin to literary criticism requiring the classifying of texts. "Here, in our text, such sorting would begin with distinguishing the three unlike frames of interpretation ingredient in the situation, Jewish, Berber and French . . . "

Anthropology, then, is like literature, an act of interpretation, even imagination. "To construct actor-orientated descriptions of the involvements of a Berber chieftain, a Jewish merchant, and a French soldier with one another in 1912 Morocco is clearly an imaginative act, not all that different from constructing similar descriptions of, say, the involvements with one another of a provincial French doctor, his silly, adulterous wife, and her feckless lover in nineteenth-century France." Geertz admits some differences. In *Madame Bovary* the acts may never have happened; in Morocco they are "represented as actual." Nevertheless that is not crucial. "The conditions of their creation, and the point of it . . . differ. But the one is as much a *fictio*—'a making'—as the other."[16]

The difference between fictional representation and actual representation is not crucial for another reason: The Moroccan events may not have happened. At least Geertz evinces no interest in them as facts. His 1968 field report records a story told by a Jewish merchant, who must have been in his eighties, about some events six decades earlier, prior to World War I. Can this account be believed in all respects? Even the greenest investigator would raise questions about a sixty-year-old story of murder, robbery and revenge, but Geertz never inquires whether any other accounts or records confirm these events. Facts are passé. Geertz offers no opinion about the trustworthiness of his informant. For Geertz these questions are immaterial; he has a text ripe for a thick interpretation.

Is this anthropology? Is this history? Historian Carlo Ginzburg has raised the question whether history can be written on the basis of a single witness or text. An account of a fourteenth-century massacre of Jews in southern France comes down to us by way of a few lines left by a lone survivor. Can this report be trusted? Ginzburg argues that history is not like the legal process of indictment, which usually demands at least two witnesses. Sometimes only one witness exists, which the historian must use. "No sensible historian would dismiss this evidence as intrinsically unacceptable."

Yet this does not settle the matter. Ginzburg insists that the question of "proof" or truth does not go away even with a single witness. The historian must verify the sole account. Alluding to those who challenge the existence of Nazi extermination camps, on the one hand, and those who advocate a literary history where fact and fiction merge, on the other, Ginzburg defends "that old notion of 'reality.'" It is unfashionable, he recognizes, to argue for "the connection among proofs, truth, and history." Nevertheless, the historical imperative remains the necessity of confirming the veracity of an account; the difference between history and fiction does not vanish.[17]

For Geertz none of this matters. Yet his own thought hardly suggests cynicism. Like Rorty's, his style exudes a reflective bemusement as he moves from thought as insight to thought as art; he is a modernist content to juggle perspectives and savor texts. "There is no general story to be told, no synoptic picture to be had," Geertz writes in his recent intellectual autobiography. "It is necessary, then, to be satisfied with swirls, confluxions, and inconstant connections; clouds collecting, clouds dispersing." What "recommends" or "disrecommends" his own contributions is "their capacity to lead on to extended accounts which, intersecting other accounts of other matters, widen their implications and deepen their hold."[18]

Geertz writes engaging essays that tell us that the world is complex and the best we can do is talk to our neighbors to figure out what they are up to. He observes that the unitary approach to truth advanced by Matthew Arnold and some utopians has gone the way of "adequate bathtubs and comfortable taxis." He calls for an "ethnography of thought" that reflects the "enormous multiplicity" of modern consciousness. This ethnography "will deepen even further our sense of the radical variousness of the way we think now." His aim is to come up with an "adequate vocabulary" so that "econometricians, epigraphers, cytochemists and iconologists can give a credible account of themselves to one another."[19]

Geertz's forte is describing unique and specific events, yet, pulled out from the larger context, the particular becomes not art, but spectacle, something to gaze upon. His often cited essay, "Deep Play," on cockfighting in Bali, is a small tour de force, but it is as much a dazzling display of self as a penetrating discussion of its subject matter. "Early in April of 1958," begins this essay, "my wife and

I arrived, malarial and diffident, in a Balinese village we intended, as anthropologists, to study." For Geertz cockfighting is a text, "it is a Balinese reading of Balinese experience, a story they tell themselves about themselves," and Geertz, the anthropologist, is straining "to read over the shoulders" of the Balinese.

But what does he find? For this diffident observer everything evokes Shakespeare, poetry and music.

> To call the wind a cripple, as Stevens does, to fix tone and manipulate timbre, as Schoenberg does, or closer to our case, to picture an art critic as a dissolute bear, as Hogarth does, is to cross conceptual wires; the established conjunctions between objects and their qualities are altered, and phenomena—fall weather, melodic shape, or cultural journalism—are clothed in signifiers which normally point to other referents. Similarly, to connect—and connect, and connect—the collision of roosters with the divisiveness of status is to invite a transfer of perception.[20]

An aestheticism drenches everything, a danger Geertz's critics have noted. "Thick description as Geertz actually practices it," writes the anthropologist Aletta Biersack, courts the danger of "aestheticizing all domains."[21] Geertz's semiotics, concludes the historian Ronald G. Walters, risks losing "gritty" experience in elevating it to "literature."[22] Geertz views the anthropologist as an artist who cavorts with perspectives, writes the anthropologist Vincent Crapanzano; "Deep Play" "offers . . . only the constructed understanding of the constructed native's constructed point of view. . . . His constructions of constructions of constructions appear to be little more than projections or blurrings."[23]

To be sure, there is no direct route out of the maze of interpretations; the problem is that Geertz seems happy to wander about. He puts it this way: "The stance of 'well, I, a middle-class, mid-twentieth-century American more or less standard, male, went out to this place, talked to some people I could get to talk to me, and think things are sort of rather this way with them there' is not a retreat, it's an advance."[24]

The advance should not be depreciated. Against a tradition of dreary theorizing, Geertz wandered the byways of Indonesia and Morocco, asking, looking and reflecting. Yet the advance harbored the danger of retreat, the anthropologist content to view and amuse, not fathom. Benedict Anderson, a respectful critic of Geertz, cites a typical passage that begins this way: "I talked to Djojo on the corner the other night about his marvellous grandfather. . . . He said he was able to disappear magically." Anderson comments:

> This was a wholly new voice [in anthropology], and one that was to be widely imitated. The sympathetic, democratic American casually chats up a named individual, Djojo, on a street corner, "the other night," as if he were a neighbor, rather than a scientist or a colonial investigator. He is happy to let Djojo speak about magic, without contradicting him.

Yet in recent years, continues Anderson, the description seems pleased with itself; culture gets reified. Little is explained. Rather, culture turns into art appreciation. He quotes a "marvellous" portrayal of a Javanese celebration, which concludes, "'The Meaning' of all this, just what was being said, and unsaid, by whom, to whom, with what purposes, in this parade of transgressions bracketed with ritualisms, from Marceau's Bip, through Ionesco's 'Language Lessons,' to Lucky's speech in *Godot*, is fairly well obscure. (It is very doubtful that any of the participants had even heard of . . . any of these . . .)."[25]

Some years after Geertz finished his field work in Bali, an unsuccessful Communist coup led to bloody riots in Indonesia with numerous killings. In his piece on Balinese cockfighting only the last footnote alludes to these events; and Geertz's language turns clumsy, as if the grim political facts mangle his aestheticism. His contorted footnote in the penultimate page of his book referring to the coup, riots and deaths begins this way:

> That what the cockfight has to say about Bali is not altogether without perceptions and the disquiet it expresses about the general pattern of

Balinese life is not wholly without reason is attested by the fact that in two weeks of December 1965, during the upheavals following the unsuccessful coup in Djakarta, between forty and eighty thousand Balinese . . . were killed, largely by one another.[26]

Geertz's other work, which tackled problems of Indonesian agriculture and state development, also tends to etherealize reality.[27] His notion of the Bali state as a "theatre state" more devoted to spectacle than power encourages a literary approach. As a Dutch scholar of Bali notes, Geertz's "concept of the theatre state leaves little room for the conflicts and the violence inherent in Balinese society." According to this anthropologist, H. Schulte Nordholt, the Princeton professor underrates power and leadership.[28]

Yet the point is not to wield the hammer of political reality against efforts to look at small chunks of the world. The tiniest fragment can yield the sharpest insights; conversely, the most expansive overview can yield the most banal platitudes. Indeed, the categories of small and large deceive, as if important thoughts derive from important subjects and little ideas come from little subjects. It is not the size of the canvas that is at issue with Geertz or Rorty, but what they do with it. They are satisfied to sketch and paint, proposing minimal ideas about interpretation, diversity and communication; their pose is increasingly aesthetic.

With and without the appeal to "thick descriptions," literary and aesthetic modes enjoy vast popularity in the social sciences and humanities. In anthropology, history and English the talk is of tapestries of interpretations, imaginations of texts, the author as subject and poet, dialogic approaches. James Clifford, an anthropologist, writes that a literary and "dialogical" ethnology removes stability and objectivity. Subjectivity is the name of the game. The anthropologist's voice "pervades and situates the analysis, and objective, distancing rhetoric is renounced."[29] The anthropologist does not simply enunciate, but, as a writer, participates in the discourse about representation.

Ernest Gellner, the late Cambridge University anthropologist, looked upon this with undisguised horror. Clifford, according to

Gellner, has renounced studying other societies and cultures. "Clifford is not interested in the Navajo or Nuer or the Trobianders, he is interested in what anthropologists say about them." From there it is a small step to study "what Clifford says about what others say," to analyze the representation of the representation of the represented; and, as Gellner notes, the step has been taken. For Gellner, this all makes for narcissistic, cloudy and deficient anthropology. "What it means in literature does not concern me."[30]

What it means in literature is pertinent, however. The claim to be literary or poetic entails a renunciation of scientistic truths. In return, the piece of work turns literary. Yet how do "thick" descriptions, instability or multiple perspectives turn something into art or literature? Can art be reduced to the strategies and formulas these postmodernists claim? Do thick descriptions characterize Kafka's writings? Is Joyce dialogic? Even if some of the terms fit, they do not apprehend the essence of art.

To put this differently, literary anthropology or history is not literature—and does not read like literature. In fact, the postmodern scholars are usually less readable than the more scientific predecessors they disdain. Nor should "readability" be understood simplistically. Works of literature are not always easy to read. Yet no one can confuse Faulkner or Joyce with literary postmodernism, which is unreadable in a precise sense: jargon-filled and half-written. These writings signal not the affirmation, but the demise of literature.

The issue, however, is not simply one of style; it concerns the categories of truth. Art too has its truth, but this is ignored. The new literary scholars extol an artistic approach that yields neither literature nor rigorous thinking about literature. The practitioners of a literary mode aestheticize reality. Art devolves into theories about art. Anthropologists become literary, historians imaginative. However, this is not art, but its debased form, a pretense to be artistic, as if multiple perspectives and self-referential writing constitute art. Literary postmodernism is to literature as a postcard of a church is to religion.

The new literary professors abandon truth for art, and art for art appreciation. In their rebellion against scientism they alter the values, but accept the terms. Objective is bad; subjective is good. In the name of subversion, they consign art to the reservation called subjectivity, in which it has long been imprisoned. Yet art is not simply subjectivity, multiple perspectives and thick descriptions; it also partakes of truth, and hints of freedom and happiness. For this reason, poets like Wordsworth protested the casual talk of art as a taste, as if poetry did not also partake of truth and insight. "It is the language of men who speak of what they do not understand," wrote Wordsworth in the preface to *Lyrical Ballads*, "who talk of Poetry as a matter of amusement and idle pleasure; who will converse with us as gravely about a *taste* for Poetry, as they express it, as if it were a thing as indifferent as a taste for Rope-dancing."

Wordsworth does not speak for all poets or artists or for Art itself. Yet he addressed a characteristic of art that the exponents of literary approaches hardly mention: its truth. The object of poetry, he stated, "is truth, not individual and local, but general, and operative; not standing upon external testimony, but carried alive into the heart by passion; truth which is its own testimony, which gives strength and divinity to the tribunal to which it appeals."[31]

* * *

Many scholars and academics have not only prospered in the marginality business, they have unloaded old, slow-selling stock. In the close-out sale, they drastically mark down concepts that hint of old-world Enlightenment or out-of-the-world utopia. The new lines dispense with balky universals and one-size-fits-all engineering. Designed for local markets, the new items are smaller, easier to handle, neater.

A preference for the local and the specific is benign, even salutary. What is wrong with favoring the unique and distrusting universals? In the short run, nothing. Yet over time the suspicion of universals takes its revenge. Despite a rhetoric of subversion, it leads intellectuals down the path of acquiescence. Without an emphatic idea of freedom and happiness, a better society can scarcely be envisioned; utopia withers. Those who celebrate difference and discredit universals cannot think beyond the limited possibilities tossed up by history; at best, they appreciate anything unique or non-Western; at worst, they mythologize questionable practices.

They also relinquish the willingness to judge. Divested of a resolute idea of truth, political thinking turns murky. The new professors brag of their theoretical daring, but revel in unclarity; they confuse profundity and complexity. Proponents of cutting-edge theories do not acknowledge complexity as a stage in the process of thinking or recognize ambiguities as constituent of life and society. These become the goal or conclusion, proof of theoretical acumen.

To be sure, the issues preclude a brief discussion. All philosophy attends to the relationship of universals and particulars, which no formula can govern. In the domain of morality and politics the problems are no less dense. Do universal codes of justice and rights exist? And if they do, should they be used to criticize specific practices and acts? A case like that of Salman Rushdie, the English-Indian author, focuses the theoretical issues inasmuch as it seems to set a universal idea of human rights against the particular beliefs of several Islamic nations. His 1988 novel, *Satanic Verses*, provoked riots in India and censorship in several countries.

Iran's leader, Ayatollah Khomeini, issued a death sentence to Rushdie "and all those involved in" the publication of the book. "I call on all zealous Muslims to execute them quickly, wherever they may be found, so that no one else will dare to insult the Muslim sanctities." To encourage the deed, heavenly defenders of the faith offered a secular million dollars to the successful assassin or assassins.[32] Since then, Rushdie has lived in seclusion with armed bodyguards, which has done little to curb the casualties among his translators and editors. "In Japan a translator was murdered, in Italy a translator received life-threatening injuries and in Turkey thirty-seven people were killed . . . in a terrorist incendiary attack on an editor who published *The Satanic Verses* in his newspaper," reports William Nygaard, Rushdie's Norwegian publisher, who himself was seriously wounded in an assassination attempt.[33]

If the Rushdie affair were a test, however, many Western intellectuals would flunk.[34] As Robert Hughes has stated, "American academics failed to collectively protest," and he supposed this neglect was due to a politically correct relativism, the argument that "what they do in the Middle East is 'their culture.'"[35] This may be unfair, yet the writings on Rushdie by leftist academics are cautious to a fault. Confronted with sharply etched conflict, militant intellectuals with supercharged concepts reach for jargon and platitudes. The point is not that intellectuals come out on the wrong side in the Rushdie affair; they come out on no side.[36]

This is even true for some of the best and most lucid thinkers, like Charles Taylor, who frets that a Western standard of liberty may be inappropriate in the Rushdie dispute. "It goes without saying that there should be full freedom of publication," Taylor forthrightly states and forthrightly retracts. "That applies to us," meaning North Americans and Europeans. In India, Iran and elsewhere, other imperatives intrude. Perhaps no "abstract principle" of freedom applies. Diverse societies judge diversely what defines blasphemy and heinous insults. To stand above and outside "local conditions" with a single criteria implicitly endorses "the superiority of the West."

"I believe it is misguided to claim to identify culture-independent criteria of harm," he states. Where do these judicious thoughts lead Taylor? Nowhere. Since there is no "universal definition of freedom of expression," he argues, "we are going to have to live with this pluralism. . . . That means accepting solutions for one country which don't apply in others." Faced with a state-sponsored plan to assassinate a novelist, this stalwart liberal philosopher calls for acceptance and "some degree of understanding." He closes his reflections on Rushdie with mind-numbing clichés: "To live in this difficult world, the western liberal mind will have to learn to reach out more."[37]

If the best say little, the others say less. In a brief overview of the controversy about *Satanic Verses* Vijay Mishra and Bob Hodge, two professors of literature, summarize a half dozen discussions of Rushdie and reach the ringing conclusion: "Here is the crux of the matter. The moment the dominant culture itself begins to draw generic lines (fiction, history; politics and postmodern play), the text gets transformed into distinct objects, with distinct effects and meanings. In political terms *The Satanic Verses* ceases to be post-colonial and becomes postmodern." Even this statement seems too audacious and the authors retreat, noting that another stalwart theorist "in a suggestive essay" shows how the book is "postmodern and post-colonial at the same time."[38]

Jim McGuigan raises the issue of how the "left-liberal intelligentsia" did and should respond to the Rushdie affair. After surveying the principal players, he gets no further than calling for dialogue. This is especially urgent since Rushdie's "own formation, predominantly within Western elite culture, did indeed separate him rather sharply from the popular culture of Islamic communities in Britain and elsewhere." As McGuigan sees it, Rushdie failed to communicate. "The fact of the matter is that *The Satanic Verses* was never addressed to ordinary British Muslims," as if a novel needs popular ratification or its author should be executed. McGuigan caps his discussion with postmodern homilies, calling for "self-consciousness about the interpretative project itself."[39]

Gayatri C. Spivak devotes an essay to the Rushdie affair that nimbly avoids any lucidity. In her inimitable style she cites her inimitable style. "Faced with the case of Salman Rushdie, how are we to read . . . ? I have often said, and said again in Chapter Two, that the (tragic) theater of the (sometimes farcically self-indulgent) script of poststructuralism is 'the other side.'" To nail down these statements she throws into the Rushdie controversy an account of Shahbano, a divorced Indian Muslim woman who sued for financial support from her ex-husband. To Hindu applause, the Indian Supreme Court found in her favor, but Shahbano in a change of heart protested the verdict in the name of Islam. To Spivak, this involuted case illuminates the Rushdie affair:

Once again I emphasize the implausible connection-by-reversal—the simulated Khomeini as Author and the dissimulated Shahbano mark-

ing the place of the effaced trace at the origin: an invocation of a collective support projecting a singular agent filled with divine intention;
an invocation of collective resistance displacing a censor patient as
cross-hatched by discursivities.

She adds, as if these sentences were not already sufficiently incisive,
"It is only if we recognize that we cannot not want freedom of expression as well as those other normative and privative rational abstractions that we on the other side can see how they work as alibis.
It is only then that we can recode the conflict as Racism versus Fun-
damentalism, demonizing versus disavowal."[40]

The inability to write a sentence and the inability to make a frank
political judgment might be related. This surfaces not simply in major conflicts like that of Rushdie, but also in small matters. Wendy
Brown, a feminist political theorist, recounts that in her very liberal
university town (Santa Cruz, California), the governing council considered a new ordinance banning discrimination on the basis of
"sexual orientation, transsexuality, age, height, weight, personal appearance, physical characteristics, race, color, creed, religion, national origin, ancestry, disability, marital status, sex, or gender."
This would seem to cover all bases, but the law drives Brown into a
theoretical rage—not because it evidences liberalism amok but domination unleashed.

The soapy-headed denizens of Santa Cruz forgot their Foucault,
according to Professor Brown. The law reduces people to empirical
traits, "as if their existence were intrinsic and factual, rather than effects of discursive and institutional power." Did the lawmakers do
their theoretical homework? "Here is a perfect instance of how the
language of recognition becomes the language of unfreedom, how
articulation in language, in the context of liberal and disciplinary
discourse, becomes a vehicle of subordination."

This bold thinker finds a disaster in Santa Cruz: "This ordinance,
I want to suggest . . . is symptomatic of a feature of politicized identity's *desire* within liberal-bureaucratic regimes, its foreclosure of its
own freedom, its impulse to inscribe in the law and in other political

registers its historical and present pain rather than conjure an imagined future of power to make itself."[41]

*   *   *

A flight from universals, driven by simplistic notions of power and
history, cripples political thinking. At the end of the twentieth century, vanguard thinkers hawk the most elementary ideas as revolutionary breakthroughs. The notion that history is complex is
presented as late news; the idea that many perspectives constitute
the world is discovered afresh.

All this is written up in the clotted language of the new academics,
who often deride coherency as inescapably repressive. "The demand
for coherence," write a feminist theorist, "requires the exclusion of
any elements—such as ambiguity, conflict, and contradiction—which
threaten coherence," as if Marx or Hegel did not discuss conflict co-
herently. Janet R. Jakobsen, who teaches women's studies, continues
in the famous style of postcoherent thinkers, illustrating her point:

> I am not simply inciting a discourse which somehow focuses on all dif-
> ferences simultaneously, a move with universalizing tendencies that
> can reinstate a singular discourse by subsuming multiple sites of strug-
> gle; rather, I am suggesting that by reading for multiplicity and ambi-
> valence it might be possible to articulate the "intersectionality" of
> differences—the points at which multiple processes of social differenti-
> ation come together to form nexuses of oppressions, as well as spaces
> in between the chasms of differentiation.[42]

Leftist thinkers monomaniacally extend the truism that power is
powerful to the proposition that power is everything, as if this were
a subversive notion. "In this book," goes a typical sentence by two
cultural-studies practitioners, "we make the scandalous claim:
everything in social and cultural life is fundamentally to do with
power. Power is at the centre of cultural politics. . . . We are either
active subjects . . . or we are subjected to . . . others."[43]

Scandalous claim? This is the wisdom of executive suites and
abandoned streets. "Money talks." "The bottom line is . . . "

"You're either with us or against us." "It's who you know . . . " The belief engenders a vision of the world of insiders and outsiders, those on top and those on bottom, all beyond good and evil. If history were only the story of contending power cliques, then every chapter would begin with a power struggle and end in blood, which is almost the case. Those out of power offer the same program as those in power, except that they list different individuals to be shot or imprisoned. That this is a recurring tale does not transform a truth into a critique.

Foucault redoubled the cynicism with his idea of total, not partial, power. Those who follow Foucault scrap as too limited notions of power and politics defined by the state; rather, power expands to encompass all domains, including concepts, rules, representations and categories. Power and politics saturate everything. Truth itself is a function of power. "Truth is what counts as true with the system of rules for a particular discourse," write several exponents of "postcolonial" literature. "Power is that which annexes, determines, and verifies truth. Truth is never outside power." [44]

"To say that 'everything is political,'" stated Foucault, "is to affirm this ubiquity of relations of force. . . . To the vast new techniques of power correlated with multinational economies and bureaucratic States, one must oppose a politicization which will take new forms." [45] In this approach, utopia is another name for domination. "Historians of ideas usually attribute the dream of a perfect society to philosophers and jurists of the eighteenth century," wrote Foucault, "but there was also a military dream of society," of "meticulously subordinated cogs of a machine." [46]

The search for omnipresent power inspires some original research; it also opens the floodgates to demi-scholarship that endlessly rediscovers power. Traditionally, political thinking began, not ended, with the recognition of power. Now the fact of power appears as a dazzling insight. The third chapter of Rousseau's *Social Contract* questioned the "right of the strongest." As Rousseau put it, the phrase is nonsense. "To yield to force is an act of necessity." No arguments need be adduced to make you hand over your purse to pistol-packing robbers, but where is the right? "If force creates right, the effect changes with the cause: every force that is greater than the first succeeds to its right. . . . But what kind of right is that which perishes when force fails?"[47]

The ability to distinguish what is and what should be, the *sine qua non* of political thinking, dwindles; the reality of a multifarious domination stuns liberal and leftist thinkers into reiterating the platitude that all categories deceive. A political theorist derides impartiality as a cloak for power. "The idea of impartiality," writes Iris M. Young, "legitimates hierarchal decisionmaking and allows the standpoint of the privileged to appear as universal."[48] Inasmuch as impartiality is rarely impartial, it never is and should be shelved. All universal categories serve as tools of power in history; since they are not uniformly realized, they are false.

Banal ideas of history supplement banal ideas of power. Critics incessantly observe that global intellectual diversity proves no idea is truer than any other, as if the fact of slavery justified its practice. The late bourgeois mind, Adorno proclaimed, is unable to comprehend validity and genesis in their simultaneous unity and difference.[49] To put this more crudely, the reality that all thought originates somewhere (genesis) does not constitute an argument for its falseness (validity). Nor is something invalid because it is not generally recognized—or because it is misused. This may seem obvious, but left-leaning scholars regularly argue that global power and complexity disprove universals.

"The concept of universalism," state the editors of an anthology of a marginalized literature, excludes the colonialized peoples. "The myth of universality is thus a primary strategy of imperial control. . . . The assumption of universalism is a fundamental feature of the construction of colonial power because the 'universal' features of humanity are the characteristics of those who occupy positions of political dominance."[50]

The ideas fall upon receptive ears. These same editors anthologize an essay of the Nigerian novelist Chinua Achebe in which he angrily charges that Western literature is often considered "universal," while African literature is not. "I should like to see the word 'universal' banned altogether from discussions of African literature until such a time as people cease to use it as a synonym for the narrow, self-serving parochialism of Europe."[51] In regard to music or poetry or fiction these sentiments could be easily multiplied; artists or writers of South America or Africa or Asia rightly object to being considered less than universal.

The extension of this criticism from art to politics, philosophy and science is questionable, however. Although music or poetry may be culturally specific, this is less true for scientific axioms and philosophic principles. Are human rights invalid because they are violated or ignored—or unknown? If they are not recognized, does this makes them false? "The truth is also valid for those who contradict it, ignore it, or declare it unimportant," stated Max Horkheimer on behalf of a notion almost obsolete.[52]

To the modern academic, empirical diversity signifies multiple truths; imperialism spawns "universal" truths. Human rights, states an anthropologist, Ann-Belinda S. Preis, are "culturally constructed." Observer and observed participate in a complex reality. What does this mean? "There is no objective position from which human rights can be truly measured." And the conclusion? "This ought to fundamentally challenge the current practice of establishing 'human rights records' of particular states (by organizations such as Human Rights Watch, Amnesty International, and the International Commission of Jurists) because such evaluations are always inherently partial, committed and incomplete."[53]

One vigilant anti-imperialistic scholar attacks "Western mathematics" as "the secret weapon of cultural imperialism." The reasoning is familiar. Though it claims universalism, Western mathematics is really a tool of domination and control. "With the assumptions of universality and cultural neutrality," Western mathematics has been "imposed on the indigenous cultures." However, the world has produced other, equally valid systems of computation.

"All cultures have generated mathematical ideas, just as all cultures have generated language, religion, morals, customs and kinship systems." According to Alan Bishop, a professor of education, "alternative mathematical systems" exist; for instance, in Papua New Guinea some six hundred systems of counting have been reported, including finger counting, body pointing, knotted strings, beads and so on. This suggests we should recognize "ethno-mathematics" as a "more localised and specific set of mathematical ideas" outside or against mainstream mathematics.[54]

Another adherent of "ethnomathematics" denounces the "Euro-centric" approach with its pretense of universality. Marcelo C. Borba, a mathematics educator, writes that European mathematics is "an historical construction" representing "the codes and under-standings" of Western academics. In fact, "only a small percentage" of the world's population uses it. "Therefore, 'academic mathematics' is not universal." Much better is "ethnomathematics" developed by diverse cultures; local arithmetic surpasses academic mathematics "because the ethnomathematics developed by a given culture group is linked to the obstacles which have emerged in this group."[55]

Empirical observations of diverse mathematical and scientific practices across the globe can hardly be challenged. The conclusion that each society can and should have its own unique mathematics does not follow; and the notion that local obstacles inexorably yield effective solutions is delusional. Meera Nanda, a science writer, protests the intellectual and political consequences of this position. It undermines cosmopolitanism and encourages dubious politics. She cites Abdus Salam, the Pakistani Nobel Laureate in physics, affirming the universality of science. "There is no such thing as Islamic science, just as there is no Hindu science, no Jewish science, no Confucian science . . . nor indeed, 'Western' science."[56]

Nanda, who is from India, finds that the criticism of scientific universalism reinforces the most retrograde tendencies and groups. Hindu nationalism "in my native India has definitely benefited from the cultural climate in which even supposedly Left-inclined intellectuals and activists tend to treat all liberal and modern ideas as 'Western,' unauthentic, and thus inappropriate for India." She notes "the sad irony" of "the most 'radical,' cutting-edge thinkers in the West giving intellectual ammunition to our nativists."[57]

From here it is a small jump to the Sokal brouhaha, an intellectual event that fed or fed off of the idea of science as less than universal. In 1996 a New York University physicist published in a leading journal of cultural studies, *Social Text*, a long article that called for a new mathematics and physics. With great panache and learning, Alan Sokal attacked the "dogma" still prevalent among scientists that "there exists an external world" whose properties can be codified in universal laws. Instead, he proposed a postmodern science that recognizes multiple truths and approaches.

"A simple criterion for science to qualify as postmodern," wrote Sokal, citing another authority, "is that it be free from any dependence on the concept of objective truth." Like art and philosophy, he argued, all science is historical, yet few scientists admit this fact. "Rather, they cling to the dogma imposed by the post-Enlightenment hegemony over the Western intellectual," in which "there exists an external world, whose properties are independent of any individual human being." Unfortunately scientists still believe that "human beings can obtain reliable" knowledge of this world through "objective procedures."

After quoting Derrida on Einstein, the author gave an example of the historical approach: any "space-time point" can be transformed into any other, eroding "the distinction between observer and observed"; "the π of Euclid and the G of Newton, formerly thought to be constant and universal, are now perceived in their ineluctable historicity." Sokal closed by calling for a new "emancipatory mathematics," seconding those feminist thinkers who have denounced Western mathematics as "capitalist, patriarchal and militaristic."[58]

The piece was a hoax. As a leftist and a physicist, Sokal wanted to expose the nonsense that much of the literary left believed about science, in particular its lax notions about how scientific knowledge was historical. To this end he contrived a patently inane essay that hailed the cultural-studies muck-a-mucks. "I structured the article,"

Sokal explained to the *New York Times*, "around the silliest quotes about mathematics and physics from the most prominent [cultural-studies] academics, and I invented an argument praising them and linking them together." He added that this was easy to do, for he ignored "standards of evidence and logic."[59] *Social Text* loved it.

Afterward, editors and other supporters scrambled to make the best of the situation. They denounced Sokal, claimed he was "half-educated" or simply blustered. The editors of *Social Text*, Bruce Robbins and Andrew Ross, who in publishing the piece demonstrated they know nothing about science, charged that Sokal is "threatened" by cultural studies, as if the threat were the denunciation of shabby scholarship, not the shabby scholarship itself.[60] "In my view, the hoax cathected such intense feelings of resentful glee precisely because it crystallized a large, important fault line in the 'postsocialist' condition," stated Nancy Fraser, as if this illuminated anything.[61] "Sokal's hoax is a form of 'acting out,'" opined Homi K. Bhabha. "I detect in Sokal's essay—in his rhetorical strategies, in his linguistic constructions—a displaced anxiety about the contested 'autonomy' of science."[62]

Stanley Fish, executor director of Duke University Press, which publishes *Social Text*, defended his editors; they all believe in the real world and its historical context in the same way they view baseball as both real and historical.[63] Who could doubt that baseball is a historical construct, but are the laws of physics that sustain it also historical, even imperialist? "It is almost as if Fish were to astound everyone," grumbled Martin Gardner, a science writer, "by declaring that fish are not part of nature but only cultural constructs. Pressed for clarification of such a bizarre view he would then clear the air by explaining that he wasn't referring to 'real' fish out there in real water, but only to the word 'fish.'"[64]

With deep misgivings about universals, an unwillingness to judge on the basis of them and a trite notion of history, leftist intellectuals drift into a major current of conservatism that includes Burkean traditionalism, German romanticism and American regionalism. All repudiate abstract and uniform systems of thought, usually associated with the French Enlightenment, and champion the particular and the different.

To classify these currents simply as conservative would be inaccurate; a suspicion of universals has been embraced by various schools of thought, including liberal American pragmatism and English empiricism.[65] William James's 1909 lectures, titled *A Pluralistic Universe*, offered three hundred pages defending the particular and unique from an all-embracing monism. Pluralism means that "things are 'with' one another in many ways, but nothing includes everything, or dominates over everything."[66]

The progressive and regressive elements of this orientation intermingle. Inasmuch as the individual is defended against an oppressive totality the approach breathes of liberation, which surfaced in romanticism. A bracing protest at the subordination, and often sacrifice, of the individual to the wider system infused eighteenth-century romanticism. "In the entire history of thought," wrote Arthur O. Lovejoy in his classic *The Great Chain of Being*, there have "been few changes of standards of value more profound and more momentous" than romanticism.

Lovejoy cited the eighteenth-century theologian Friedrich Schleiermacher to illustrate the new sensibility, a disdain for homogeneity and an appreciation of individuality. "Why . . . does this pitiable uniformity prevail, which seeks to bring the highest human life within the compass of a single lifeless formula?" asked Schleiermacher. "How can this ever have come into vogue, except in consequence of a radical lack of feeling for the fundamental characteristic of living Nature, which everywhere aims at diversity and individuality?"[67]

With his attack on "the dogmatizing love of system which . . . excludes all difference" Schleiermacher sounds intellectually up to date; he intuited that the drive to uniformity feeds violence.

This miserable love of system rejects what is strange . . . because were it to receive a place, the closed ranks would be destroyed and the beautiful coherence disturbed. . . . The system mania is the seat of the art and love of strife. War must be carried on, and persecution.. These systematizers, therefore, have caused it all . . . The adherents of the dead letter . . . have filled the world with clamor and turmoil.[68]

Yet Lovejoy, who applauded the new appreciation of individual diversity, also registered the danger, where the radical elements turn suspect. Praise of a prolific multiplicity was "not selective" and "the revolt against standardization of life easily becomes a revolt against the whole conception of standards." The love of diversity, he wrote in the early 1930s, "has lent itself all too easily to the service of man's egotism, and especially—in the political and social sphere—of a kind of collective vanity which is nationalism or racialism."[69] Exactly.

The flat rejection of the universal leads to the rote affirmation of the unique and specific. History becomes the great excuse. This train of thought inexorably becomes conservative inasmuch as it sabotages the general propositions required to judge. Once writers and scholars isolate local conditions from universal categories, they lose the ability to evaluate them. They become cheerleaders, nationalists and chauvinists. With equal enthusiasm Rajani K. Kanth, in *Breaking with the Enlightenment,* denounces the fraud of Western univer-alism and touts non-Western localism. In "Eurocapitalist societies" people demonize each other with broad categories. In the non-Western world, "people tied to each other by kinship, affinity, and affection (as, for instance, in tribal forms) are incapable, and unwilling, to abstractly demonize their fellows."[70] Does this prevent them from murdering each other? That war, violence, slavery and caste are not Western monopolies and that they do not improve when rooted in local situations do not seem to occur to Kanth.

Scholars often point to German historicism as a classic case of a tradition that began scorning universals and ended upholding a virulent nationalism. The title of an essay by Justus Möser, an eighteenth-century historicist, concisely captures the approach: "The Modern Taste for General Laws and Decrees Is a Danger to Our

Common Liberty."[71] From Möser to the twentieth-century nationalists, historicists claimed that universals violated the complexity and
variety of the German reality; they defended a unique German reality against the universalism of Western Europe.[72] For instance, in the
midst of World War I, Ernst Troeltsch, an esteemed theologian, rallied to the cause, contrasting German distinctiveness to the European "abstraction of a universal and equal humanity."[73]

The same distrust of universals pervaded American regionalists
and conservatives. It is not by chance that American slavery became
known by its defenders as "the peculiar institution"—peculiar inasmuch as it diverged from the universal rights established elsewhere.[74]
Similar reasoning surfaced in exponents of American regionalism,
for instance, the Agrarians, who defended a Southern life against in-
dustrialism and progressivism in their 1930 classic book, *I'll Take
My Stand*.[75]

Recent regionalists return to the same principles, upholding local
and perhaps unjust realities against the abstract universals. "Unlike
the America of the New World Order," runs a statement by the
Southern League, a conservative group headquartered in Tuscaloosa,
Alabama, the League is "wedded, not to a universal proposition:
democracy, or the rights of man, but to a real past of place and kin."
The League "supports a return to a political and social system based
on allegiance to kith and kin rather than to an impersonal state wedded to the idea of the universal rights of man."[76] A particularism that
scorns universals inevitably ends by celebrating blood and race.

The Dreyfus case, again, offers the classic example. Maurice Barrès, an anti-Dreyfusard, denounced intellectuals as "logicians of the
absolute." He considered them "deracinated" internationalists who
trade in abstractions like "Justice" and "Truth" and "who no longer
spontaneously feel any rapport" with the nation. The next step
seemed obvious. Dreyfus was Jewish; many of his supporters were
Jewish. Deracinated Jews and intellectuals trade in abstractions.
"For us," stated Barrès, "the nation is our soil and our ancestors; it
is the land of our dead." For the Jewish intellectuals, on the other
hand, nationalism is an "idea" or a "prejudice to destroy."[77]

The same sentiment animated German reactionaries like Ernst von Salomon, who assassinated the Jewish industrialist Rathenau in the first years of the Weimar Republic. "The intellectual speaks and writes 'I.' He feels no connectedness. He causes disintegration. . . . The emphatic 'we' of the new generation is a clear renunciation of intellectualism. The 'we' of the young, nationalist generation . . . is tied to blood."[78]

Vanguard thinkers return to primal ideas, doubting any concepts that go beyond blood and place. Truth becomes "truth"; reason becomes "reason"; human rights "human rights." The quotation marks signify the subjective quality—as said by. Context is everything; truth is nothing. Today few could speak the language of the Enlightenment: "We hold these Truths to be self-evident . . . " For today's scholars these words hide as much as they state. No truths are self-evident; they are constructed and invented. They emerge at specific times and places; these are "truths" of eighteenth-century Europe and America. And who is the "We"? A bunch of white patricians?

All "the constituting notions of Enlightenment metanarratives have been exposed," writes a feminist political thinker, Jane Flax, referring to concepts like reason and history. "True and false" are themselves obsolete, since "truth is always contextual."[79] These platitudes enjoy great success. As Luc Ferry and Alain Renaut write of recent French philosophy, "If the truth must be shattered, if there are no facts but only interpretations, if all references to universal norms are inevitably catastrophic," then what remains but "authenticity . . . whatever its content may be?"[80]

Yet it must be insisted upon: The universal also has its claims. Even, or exactly, the protest of the individual against a political system taps into universal rights and equalities. Without these universals, which weaken in the face of appeals to localism and authenticity, the opposition crumbles. In the name of universals, the protest not only protests, but affirms a world beyond degradation and unhappiness; it hints of utopia.

Herbert Marcuse's most visionary work, his 1955 *Eros and Civilization*, brought out the links between utopia, protest and universal categories. During the 1960s Marcuse championed what he dubbed "the absolute refusal," a call to individuals to refuse cooperation with a deadly economic and social system.[81] Despite its political and activist accents, the term *absolute refusal* originated in his philosophical work *Eros and Civilization*, where Marcuse explored the utopian dimensions of art and imagination.

Drawing upon the surrealists, Marcuse argued that in repudiating a narrow realism imagination and fantasy nurtured their own truths. "In its refusal to accept . . . final limitations" to freedom and happiness and its "refusal to forget what *can be*, lies the critical function of phantasy." Imagination transcends the limited reality to glimpse its latent possibilities; it "comprehends reality more fully" than realism. Conversely, on behalf of a constricted reality imagination is damned as untrue.

Marcuse compressed his analysis into what he called the "great refusal." "This Great Refusal is the protest against unnecessary repression, the struggle for the ultimate form of freedom—'to live without anxiety.' But this idea could be formulated without punishment only in the language of art." In "realistic" philosophy and politics, the idea of life without anxiety would be "defamed as utopia."[82]

Marcuse derived the phrase "the great refusal," which simultaneously invoked protest and utopia, from a discussion of universals by Alfred North Whitehead. The English-American philosopher held that universals in art and criticism transcend their particular cases. His language is a bit sticky, but the argument is clear. "Every actual occurrence" must be set within an abstract realm that transcends it. "To be abstract is to transcend particular concrete occasions of actual happening." To transcend does not mean to be disconnected; indeed, the exact relationship of the universal and concrete is crucial. Any particular "red" flower falls short of the universal "red" by which we judge it. Yet the universal is not false.

The truth that some proposition respecting an actual occasion is untrue may express the vital truth as to the aesthetic achievement. It ex-

presses the "great refusal," which is its primary characteristic. An event is decisive in proportion to the importance (for it) of its untrue propositions. . . . These transcendent entities have been termed "universals."[83]

The logic sticks in the craw of empiricists, postmodernists and most leftists. Metaphysical universals inhere in the world, but transcend it. An individual event may be "untrue" in that it is contradicted by reality, but this untruth expresses its achievement or different truth, its basis in metaphysical principles.

To shift to political philosophy, the argument parallels the logic of the opening of Rousseau's *Social Contract*. "Man is born free and everywhere is in chains." To conventional logic and leftists, these statements are wildly contradictory, untrue or meaningless. How could man be metaphysically free and empirically unfree? As the skeptic in Alexander Herzen's *From the Other Shore* commented, the proposition shows "contempt for the facts." "Why do all things exist as they should, while man alone does not?" Rousseau might well have said fish are born to fly, but everywhere swim under water.[84]

Yet the logic in Whitehead and Rousseau bespeaks the logic of negativity: Although the first statement, the universal, is contradicted by the reality of the second—by the domain of empirical reality—it retains its truth. From here it is not a great leap to everyday politics and protest. Those who know nothing of the argument of the "great refusal" often instinctively accept it as the historic basis of protest. In refusing cooperation with this society, the "great refusal" contains an affirmation of a better one. Conversely, despite the political posture of subversiveness, a casual rejection of universals as imperialist undermines the drive for a different world.

Eugene Genovese, the historian, reminds us how "Fourth of July" celebrations caused problems in the slave South. During these events the glaring disjuncture between the idiom of universal freedom found in the Declaration of Independence and the fact of slavery gave rise to uneasiness.[85] In the North abolitionists and ex-slaves appealed to its principles and daily violation. "Once, every year, in this land of the free, on Freedom's Natal day," stated a black petitioner to the Boston Legislature in 1853, "the people assemble in public convocation, and in intonations loud and long, proclaim to the despotism of the world, 'We hold these truths to be self-evident . . . '" But, continued William J. Watkins, "Your laws are founded in caste, conceived in caste, born in caste. Caste in the God whom this great Nation delights to honor." He thundered, "*Give us our rights.*. . . Treat us like men; carry out the principles of your immortal declaration."[86]

It was and is tempting to dismiss the festivities and its principles as bogus. "What, to the American slave, is your Fourth of July?" thundered Frederick Douglass in his 1852 speech, "The Meaning of July Fourth for the Negro." "I answer: a day that reveals to him, more than all other days in the year, the gross injustice and cruelty to which he is the constant victim. To him, your celebration is a sham, your boasted liberty, an unholy license . . . your shouts of liberty and equality hollow mockery."

This might sound very modern, a ringing attack on "Western" universals as frauds. On closer inspection, however, it is almost the opposite, a denunciation of the reality in the name of the ideas. Douglass damns slavery for betraying the ideas of liberty, not the ideas for betraying African Americans. The denunciation of the Fourth of July as hypocrisy appeals to the idea of equality; it bemoans the gap between the claim and reality.[87]

Like other abolitionists, Douglass drew "encouragement" from "the great principles" of the Declaration of Independence, and he saw them spreading throughout the world. No longer can "established customs of hurtful character . . . do their evil with social impunity. . . . No abuse, no outrage whether in taste, sport or avarice, can now hide itself from the all-pervading light."[88] Fifty years later Émile Zola stated, "I have but one desire . . . seeing the light, in the name of humanity . . . " All this sounds naive. What light? What principles? What humanity? Today the new generation of critics sees through this stuff; they also see less.

— 6 —

RETAIL SANITY AND
WHOLESALE MADNESS

In 1918 the poet Aleksandr A. Blok ecstatically greeted the Russian Revolution. The aim of the revolution, he wrote, is *"to make every-thing over . . .* to make everything different, to change our false, filthy, boring, hideous life into a just, clean, gay, and beautiful life."

> The sweep of the Russian Revolution, which wants to engulf the whole world . . . is such that it hopes to raise a world-wide cyclone, which will carry warm winds and the sweet scent of orange groves to snow-covered lands, moisten the sun-scorched steps of the South with cool northern rain. . . . "Peace and the brotherhood of nations" is the sign under which the Russian Revolution runs its course.[1]

Blok's was hardly the last outburst of utopian élan in the twenti-eth century. However, with each decade the enthusiasm waned. The reasons are not hard to see. Some writers and activists concluded that utopian hopes ended in the 1950s, but for others World War I, Stalinism and Nazism had already delivered the news. Blok himself died disenchanted in 1921.

If the nineteenth century gave rise to utopias, the twentieth cen-tury spurred anti-utopias. Since the beginning of the century with Karl Kraus's *The Last Days of Mankind* and Otto Spengler's *The Decline of the West,* the mood has been of collapse and decay. "The formative period of anti-utopianism," writes the historian Eugen

Weber, "lies in the years following the First World War, when the high hopes . . . culminating in 1917 and 1918, were seen to be left unfulfilled."[2] The utopias that speak to this century are dystopias like Zamyatin's *We*, Huxley's *Brave New World* and Orwell's *1984*, which envision a world of control and domination.

The West "won" the cold war, a victory that momentarily fed optimism and hope; for an instant a weak utopian breeze wafted across the globe. The fear of world communism had prompted the wealthy nations to spend billions on bombs, defense and missiles. With the demise of the Soviet Union, talk of a "peace dividend" could be heard; monies freed from military spending would flow toward education, health and community needs. For the first time in many decades, the rich Western countries could focus on global needs unhampered by Communist subversion.

What happened? Little has changed. Savage local, territorial and religious wars regularly break out. "There are more regional conflicts and civil wars than at any time this century," notes a survey of global conflicts.[3] Military spending has barely diminished. A few commentators, recalling the promises of 1989, ask "What happened to the peace dividend?"[4] "Hopes for a better and saner world raised by the end of the Cold War," concludes a somber study of world violence, "have largely evaporated."[5]

The world threat to the Western democracies has lifted; communism has virtually disappeared; the globe seems ready for a celebration, but the temper remains dark and foreboding. A succession of books raises the specter of global decline and anarchy. Things have gotten worse, not better. Stewart Lansley, a British economist, begins his book *After the Gold Rush* with a chapter outlining the prospects: "War and recession in Europe. Famine in a third of Africa. Growing and unsustainable migration. A deteriorating global environment. The erosion of political and economic stability throughout the West."[6]

One might think that a veteran anticommunist like Zbigniew Brzezinski would exult in the disappearance of Soviet communism. Not so. He titles his reflections on the post–cold war era *Out of*

Control. He sees the intensification of regional wars, the proliferation of weapons of mass destruction and a foundering United States. "The crisis in the postcommunist world," he writes, "could deepen," leading to "the reappearance of millennial demagogy" and wars between the nations of the North and South. "A new coalition of the poorer nations against the rich—perhaps led by China—might then emerge."[7]

Samuel Huntington, another veteran cold warrior, parts with Brzezinski's script, but also forecasts bloodletting and decline. "The moment of euphoria at the end of the Cold War," he states in *The Clash of Civilizations and the Remaking of World Order*, "generated an illusion of harmony." This grave Harvard professor foresees an "emerging world of ethnic conflict and civilizational clash." He sketches out a world war between the United States and China leading to nuclear devastation and, unaccountably, to a new Hispanic leadership in the United States, who blame the WASP elite for the destruction. Meanwhile "hordes" of Africans pick through the European wreckage. If war is evaded, Huntington ponders whether the ailing West, beset by "moral decline, cultural suicide, and political disunity," will succumb to Islamic and Asian nations. The future looks grim. "Can the West renew itself or will sustained internal rot simply accelerate its end?"[8]

The contemporary mood might be best captured in the writings of the journalist Robert D. Kaplan. *The Ends of the Earth*, his report on worldwide anarchy and disintegration, concludes: "We are not in control." Europe and North America have come through two world wars and the cold war to find themselves swamped by "disease pandemics like AIDS, environmental catastrophes, organized crime, . . . failed states" and global overpopulation. Intensifying disasters throughout the world threaten to engulf the precarious affluence and freedoms of the West. "The banal truth" is that the future will be "cruel, painful, violent and uneven."[9]

More recently Kaplan has argued that democracy itself is a dubious prospect for much of the world. "The post–Cold War effort" to force democracy has not been reasonable, he writes. We "put a gun to the head of peoples of the developing world and say, in effect, 'Behave as if you had experienced the Western Enlightenment. . . . Behave as if 95 percent of your population were literate. Behave as if you had no bloody ethnic or regional disputes." He offers examples galore. "Look at Haiti," where 22,000 American troops sought to restore "democracy" in 1994, where 5 percent of those eligible voted in the last election and where famine and crises continuously threaten.[10] To Kaplan and many observers, the victory of the Western democracies in the cold war has brought nothing but gloom.

The grimness is not confined to commentators on the world situation. From the outlook of college students to that of the most advanced academic theories, cynicism advances and utopianism retreats. The name of the game is realism and practicality. For students and the young, the vast shift to practical concerns is obvious, justifiable and inexplicable. It is obvious because the simplest probing finds that careers and jobs are paramount for students. It is justifiable because earning a living, and a desire for earning a good living, can hardly be belittled.

It is also inexplicable inasmuch as the economic situation is not dramatically worse than it was twenty or thirty years ago, when a buffer seemed to exist—at least for some—providing a momentary protective space from crushing economic imperatives. The danger that the good sons and daughters of the middle and upper middle class will end up homeless may keep people on a narrow career path, but has little basis. What has led to a jump in careerism and practicality among students is not the collapse of the economy, which has not collapsed, but the collapse of a belief in a future that might be different. The conviction that the future will replicate the present stifles utopian longings.

*   *   *

Of course, the twentieth century is not an unbroken story of a declining utopian vision. In the wake of the Russian Revolution, in the 1920s around the Surrealists and again in the 1960s, utopian ideas flared up—and burned out. However, today almost everyone has become realistic; the guiding ideas are limited policies and programs for specific ills. Although scholarly studies of utopianism persist, across the land a utopian spirit is dead or dismissed.[11]

The distance between today and the most recent utopian eruptions of the 1960s might be measured in centuries. The gap can perhaps be grasped by glancing not at the emphatic utopians of the 1960s, but at those resistant to excess, liberal thinkers. In the 1960s even sober liberals pondered the possibilities of a completely transformed society. Though not blind to economic and racial inequalities, they entertained the prospects of a widespread affluence and freedom. The problem became less how to reach the new society, which appeared to be around the corner, than how to organize it. "We too can have a society of abundance in the rich countries before the end of the twentieth century," wrote Robert Theobald in his 1961 *The Challenge of Abundance*. Every individual, including "the student, the writer, the artist, the visionary, the dissenter" would receive the "necessities of life."[12]

In the same spirit David Riesman pondered the prospects of general affluence in his 1963 *Abundance for What?* "No other society has ever been in the same position as ours," he wrote, "of coming close to fulfilling the age-old dream of freedom from want, the dream of plenty." Capitalism has outstripped even its "most optimistic boosters." Previous thinkers are useless as guides. We cannot "discover much wisdom in earlier prophets of abundance, for very few of them foresaw the actual cornucopia." Edward Bellamy's utopia "envisaged an amiable and genteel level of living, long since attained in amount throughout a large middle-income belt." For Riesman the problem was what to do with this affluence. "It is extraordinary how little we have anticipated the problems of the bountiful future."[13]

In 1963 another liberal thinker, George Kateb, published *Utopia and Its Enemies*, which was a moderate defense of utopias. Though the book hardly breathed of 1960s rebelliousness, its frame and terms suggest how much has changed. Kateb responded to familiar arguments against utopias, for instance, that their establishment would require violence; however, his main concern lay in reassuring those challenging, not the means, but the goals. The doubts were pressing because the goals were within sight. The real prospects motivated critics who were asking, in effect, what will we do in this future society?

"These attacks stem from the belief," Kateb wrote, "that the world sometime soon (unbearably soon) will have at its disposal—if it wishes them—the material presuppositions of a way of life commonly described as 'utopian.'" With technological and scientific development, the past "dreams and visions of a life of fullness and harmony for the whole race, have now, and for the first time, acquired plausibility." As this possibility emerges, the critics recoil, finding utopia tedious and insufferable. Kateb wanted to convince the skeptics that utopia would not be boring or distressing.[14]

It need hardly be underlined that the danger of universal prosperity no longer keeps anyone awake at night. Liberal thinkers are not agonizing about what to do in the affluent society. Jumpy citizens need no comforting as to how to keep occupied if freed from labor and drudgery. No society on the horizon promises a world beyond work.

If anything, the opposite has become the conventional wisdom and painful reality: Affluence calls for additional work and longer hours. Families with one wage earner become families with two; high-school and college students increasingly hold jobs. Work expands, not contracts. Moreover, today almost everyone believes that affluence must be temporary or circumscribed. Any apprehension over endless prosperity would be misplaced because it will not last; nor can there be too much. Books and articles address the "end of affluence" or accelerating inequalities between the rich and poor, but not the dangers of widespread wealth, which no one anticipates or fears.

Yet not all utopias have disappeared. Millenarian groups, devotees of science fiction and a few ecologists retain a utopian vision. Among the remaining utopians the most significant today are undoubtedly the "futurists," those presenting visions of the future heavily based on technological advances. They are utopian in their belief that a very different, and very superior, society is possible, even imminent. They envision a new industrial civilization based on a transformed existence.

Are they really utopians? They diverge from traditional utopians, partly because they do not set their societies in the distant past, distant future or distant islands. Yet it is not the shift in space or place that signals their break with classical utopias; it is the thinness of vision. Thomas More dreamed of a utopia without war, money, violence or inequality. Five centuries later the most imaginative futurists foresee a utopia with war, money, violence and inequality. Their future looks very much like the affluent enclaves of today, only more pleasant and commodious. They paint a picture not very different from contemporary luxury suburbs, grassy subdivisions with homes and computer and work stations set off from a larger terrain of violence and injustice. The futurists are utopians in an anti-utopian age.

For instance, Newt Gingrich in an introduction to a book by two futurists, Alvin and Heidi Toffler's *Creating a New Civilization*, tells us that their model of the "third-wave" civilization has been very useful to the American army. "The new army doctrine led to a more flexible, fast-paced, decentralized, information-rich system which assessed the battlefield, focused resources and utilized well-trained but very decentralized leadership to overwhelm an industrial-era opponent." The Tofflers themselves dream of a world in which the United States would "sell . . . military protection based on its command of superior Third Wave forces."

To be sure, their vision goes beyond selling arms to selling goods. The Tofflers exult that "the shift toward smart flex-tech promotes diversity and feeds consumer choice to the point that a Wal-Mart store can offer the buyer nearly 110,000 products in various types, sizes, models and colors to choose among." Yet Wal-Mart remains a traditional mass merchandiser that will be left behind by new types of micro-marketers. "Specialty stores, boutiques, superstores, TV home-shopping systems, computer-based buying, direct mail and other systems provide a growing diversity of channels through which producers can distribute their wares." With cable and interactive television, they enthuse, "sellers will be able to target buyers with even greater precision."

Lest this vision of utopia as marketing heaven seem too impractical, they offer some suggestions to galvanize support for a new civilization. They believe a broad constituency could coalesce around one issue: "liberation." Once upon a time liberation meant emancipation from work and oppression. For the new millennium it means "liberation from all the old Second Wave" regulations. The Tofflers give an example of the old regime—tax codes. "Depreciation tax schedules lobbied into being by the old manufacturing interests presuppose that machines and products last for many years." For the "fast-changing high-tech industries" of the future, machines might only last months or weeks. The old tax codes hamper emancipation. When the old regulations are set aside, "a new and dramatically different America will rise."[15]

Michael L. Dertouzos, of the MIT Laboratory for Computer Science, set forth his utopian vision in a book with the confident title *What Will Be.* Perhaps he is confident because what will be is more or less what is. In a foreword Bill Gates, the head of Microsoft, writes that he does not agree with Professor Dertouzos in all respects, but they do share a radiant vision: "New businesses will be created and new fortunes will be made." Dertouzos describes a new world centered about what he calls the Information Marketplace, a new way to shop, work and relax.

He provides examples of a better life. A citizen of the future would wake up to music that is not limited to his or her dreary collection of compact disks. Every piece of music ever recorded will be cataloged and, for a small daily fee, music will be piped in based on a personal profile. No more drudgery sifting through your disks. Sound too confining? "Of course, you need not stay shackled to this setup. If you are adventurous, you can always ask for surprises and the system will comply by randomly searching for different, even totally 'opposite' profiles." Dertouzos patters on about this and that change, but nothing suggests any fundamental transformation—or any spontaneity. Freedom corrodes to random computer options.

Dertouzos knows he is addressing the rich nations and holds out little prospect that his utopian Information Market will encompass everyone; in fact, he indicates it might aggravate inequalities, since much of the world lacks the requisite technological infrastructure. Although movies-on-demand are almost a reality in the industrialized nations, "only 2 percent of the homes owned by blacks in South Africa have a telephone." He suggests that the wealthy nations assist poor nations by forming a "Virtual Compassion Corps" that would operate through the Information Marketplace. How would this function? Devoted souls would put in long hours slogging through knowledge networks like the Internet, matching up those in need with those who have services or supplies. This would be a two-way street. He gives an example:

> Imagine a Sri Lankan doctor who earns very modest fees . . . who could offer health care to Americans who cannot afford the high cost of care in their own country. They could plug themselves in monitoring devices on medical kiosks at their neighborhood clinic and the Sri Lankan doctor could observe . . . and instruct a nurse to administer much-needed care, all for a minuscule fee, which might be paid by a benefactor or a welfare organization. Imagine being able to offer this kind of service to the poor and homeless of America who now go without health care.[16]

"Dread" might be a more appropriate word than "imagine." The notion that the United States, which has transferred much of its manufacturing to low-wage countries, will dump its unprofitable medical cases onto poorly paid Third World doctors, who will pony up at computer terminals to dispense expertise to remote patients, summons up not a glowing but a grim future.

A less ambitious utopianism surfaces in the plans to link all classrooms to the Internet for the cost of several billion dollars. As Vicepresident Al Gore put it, "By doubling our investment in education technology . . . we will meet our goal of connecting every classroom and library to the information superhighway by the year 2000. That's how we must prepare our children for the 21st century, with the full promise of the information age at their fingertips."[17] While few want to be called Luddites, the proposal mythologizes technology; the future will arrive by way of improved wires and electrical connections.

The hope is not new, nor are the problems. Will more computers and instant information alter learning, if the human environment remains deficient? Can computers compensate for the lack of teachers? According to an association of school principals, few studies demonstrate a link between computers and achievement; this group wondered if the billions earmarked for computers entails the sacrifice of "less 'exciting'" teachers of music or art.[18] They might have added, less exciting and old-fashioned books. One month after a series on the introduction of computers to classrooms, *The Los Angeles Times* ran an article noting that half of California's students needed textbooks, and that many teachers believe much time is lost in reading aloud to make up for their absence.[19] Meanwhile the construction of the "information superhighway" continues.

The belief a new media will transform the cultural terrain is trotted out every generation. Yet each new medium—radio, film or television—quickly gets integrated into the culture. The Internet and "cyberspace" are hardly different. "Advertisers are not just supporting online content," reports one critic, "they are shaping much of the virtual landscape for children." This means that entertainment, advertising and information will be "blended." It also means that children become consumers. "The new interactive media are being designed to compile personal profiles on each child to help in developing individually tailored advertising known as 'microtargeting' or 'one-to-one marketing.'"[20]

The Center for Media Education petitioned the Federal Trade Commission to block these practices and gave an example of an Internet Web site that calls itself a "playground for kids ages 4 to 15." In order to access the various activities, children first respond to a query, "Who Do You Wanna Be?" which includes questions about their address, age, birthday, favorite activities, as well as information about other family members. The company that runs the site takes and sells this information. "When it comes to children's attitudes and opinions," states this company in a marketing brochure, "KidsCom can provide answers. If you're introducing a new product ... KidsCom offers a fast, efficient way to conduct your research."[21]

At its best the technological model of learning is inspired by visions of facts and information. Its enthusiasts assume that the world will improve if more people have easier access to knowledge. Is the problem the availability of knowledge, however? Will additional information alter the nature of learning? Or is something else missing, a desire to learn and imagine? Do we lack facts or comprehension, the ability to think about information? American culture has always tilted toward amassing facts. Yet the delivery of information progresses, while social relations regress. "A friend of mine complained to her eight-year-old child's teacher that fairy tales, myths, and other kinds of imaginative literature had been almost eliminated from the curriculum in favor of handbooks of information."

This was Dwight Macdonald in 1957, protesting the "triumph of the fact," the American attitude that facts are gold. He worried that facts will swamp reflection. The problem is how "to elude the voracious demands on one's attention enough to think a little."[22] He was writing in the age of fat almanacs and multivolume encyclopedias. What would Macdonald have said about the banks of statistics and information available almost instantly at computer terminals? What would he have thought of the plans to "plug" students into the vast data warehouses?

Some critics worry that "meaning" is lagging behind information. Technology can rapidly deliver vast amounts of material, but thoughtful assimilation takes time and effort. Pondering a subject, writes the sociologist Orrin E. Klapp, is "inherently slow, as suggested by synonyms like brooding, contemplating, meditating, deliberating, mulling things over." We end up with "a growing mountain of information about which people do not know what to think."[23]

In the spirit of Macdonald, the writer Sven Birkerts frets that instant information drowns understanding and a larger vision. We have exchanged thinking about a problem for amassing information.

> The explosion of data . . . has all but destroyed the premise of understandability. Inundated by perspectives, lateral vistas of information that stretch endlessly in every direction, we no longer accept the possibility of assembling a complete picture. Instead . . . we direct our energies to managing information.

We are losing the time and leisure to figure out what the facts mean. "Where the electronic impulse rules, where the psyche is conditioned to work with data, the experience of deep time is impossible. No deep time, no resonance; no resonance, no wisdom."[24]

*   *   *

In the twentieth century utopia has had bad press, often for good reasons. The traditional criticism that utopias lack any pertinence has not abated. If anything, it has intensified. "In everyday language the adjective 'utopian' means mainly 'over-the-top,' 'unrealistic,' and 'eccentric.'" To call individuals utopian suggests they possess no sense of reality; their projects or ideas must fail for ignoring the concrete possibilities.[25] This criticism, however, does not damn utopians as malicious or dangerous; they are viewed as, at best, benign or, at worst, irrelevant.

The criticism of utopia, however, hardly stops here. The notion, first advanced by conservatives, has nowadays been accepted by virtually everyone: armed with blueprints and floor plans, utopians would wreak havoc to establish their private vision—and they have: The horrors of the modern world can be attributed to utopians. The statement seems plausible, but misses the mark. The bloodbaths of the twentieth century can be as much attributed to anti-utopians—to bureaucrats, technicians, nationalists and religious sectarians with a narrow vision of the future.

Hannah Arendt's 1963 *Eichmann in Jerusalem* continues to spark controversy, but her subtitle "A Report on the Banality of Evil," rings of truth. Her book considered the Israeli case against Karl Eichmann, who was instrumental in Jewish deportation and mass death during World War II. To Arendt no utopian element could be detected in the minds of Eichmann or the Nazis. "Except for an extraordinary diligence in looking out for his personal advancement," Arendt wrote of Eichmann, "he had no motives at all." Even with the greatest effort, she added, "one cannot extract any diabolical or demonic profundity from Eichmann."[26]

More recently, the historian Christopher Browning studied the practices of a World War II German police battalion, composed largely of "middle-aged family men of working- and lower-middle class background," who were sent to Poland to murder Jews. He did not find them unique in any way. They were not marked by passion or hatred or utopian dreams. They acted "not out of frenzy, bitterness, and frustration, but with calculation." The police battalion was made up of regular guys or, as Browning puts it in the title of his book, *Ordinary Men.*[27]

These studies illuminate twentieth-century violence better than casual reference to savage utopians. More blood has been shed in the twentieth century on behalf of bureaucratic calculation, racial purity, ethnic solidarity, nationalism, religious sectarianism and revenge than utopia.[28] To confirm this statement requires entering the dark world of the dead and their numbers. Though many ponder the uniqueness of Nazi extermination, the issues shift with a different framework, mass violence of all kinds. Here the problem is not simply state-sponsored murder of a group, but mass deaths from world wars and civil wars, and how utopia connects to this violence.

The assassination of an archduke in the name of Serbian nationalism set in motion a war that can scarcely be explained by utopian categories; and, it could be reasonably argued, World War I not only brought about the Russian Revolution, but set the stage for World War II. The sentence of the great French historian Élie Halévy captured the sequence: "The era of tyrannies dates from August 1914."[29] How are the two world wars related to utopianism?

The aftermath of the partition of India led to about a million deaths among Hindus and Muslims; this might be more characteristic of modern violence than Soviet repression. "The most recent large-scale genocide," wrote two political scientists in the late 1970s, "was that incident to the . . . secession of Bangladesh," in which they estimate a million lives were lost.[30] Or consider the Spanish Civil War, where executions and reprisal killings outnumbered battle deaths. According to Gabriel Jackson, the Nationalists "liquidated 300,000 to 400,000 of their compatriots."[31]

Very few have sought to calculate and categorize the total number of those killed in wars of all types. Gil Elliot's neglected *Twentieth Century Book of the Dead* stands almost alone. His opening sentence reads: "The number of man-made deaths in the twentieth century is about one hundred million." The major terrains of violence he considers include World War I, China (mainly the Sino-Japanese war), Russian civil war, the Soviet state, Jews of Europe, World War II.[32] Without evaluating these numbers,[33] it seems evident that only one portion could be attributed to utopians.

Elliot was writing in the early 1970s, and today casualties in Cambodia, Rwanda, Bosnia, Sri Lanka, Algeria and elsewhere would have to be added to the tally. However, they do not fundamentally change the picture. Even if the violence in Cambodia might be due to a demented utopianism, this does not generally hold true elsewhere. National, ethnic and religious violence fills reservoirs with blood. "Within a few short months of the Cold War's end, old aggressive nationalist habits reasserted themselves with Iraq's invasion of Kuwait," states a Carnegie report on world violence. "The war in the Gulf was soon followed by bloody conflict in the Balkans and the Horn of Africa, and outright genocide in Bosnia and Rwanda." The commission estimates that over four million have been killed in "violent conflicts" since 1989, over a half million in Rwanda alone.[34] Where are the utopians?

This is not to deny their sanguinary role. Distinctions must be made, nevertheless. Who is likely to be violent—and who has been most violent? Religious sectarians? Fervid nationalists? Angry racists? Ardent utopians? To tar all utopians with the brush of violence is imprecise and unjust. In his book on utopia and violence, Julien Freund linked them as cause and effect, but this French sociologist only focused on revolutionary terrorism from Robespierre to Lenin.[35] Fair enough, but what does this say about the benign utopianism of a Charles Fourier or a William Morris? Nothing.

What does talk about violence and utopians have to do with Edward Bellamy and his vision of vegetarianism? "The sentiment of brotherhood, the feeling of solidarity," wrote Bellamy of his utopia, "asserted itself not merely towards men and women, but likewise toward the humbler companions of our life on earth . . . the animals." The good doctor points out to his nineteenth-century visitor, "'Do you not see, Julian, how the prevalence of this new view might soon have led people to regard the eating of the fellow-animals as a revolting practice, almost akin to cannibalism?'"[36]

Nevertheless, conventional wisdom links utopia and violence. Ironically refugees from Nazism like Popper and Talmon, more bewitched by the failures of Marxism than the nature of Nazism, successfully argued that utopians have bloodied the world.[37] The factual basis of this proposition remains slender. The notion that utopians are violent and that realists are benign belongs to the mythology of our time.

Other criticisms of utopia derive from psychology. In an age of debunking, many view utopias as reflecting the urge of their inventors to dominate and control; the future societies are defined by discipline and routine. Detailed plans of utopias often seem autocratic and repressive—and utopians themselves appear authoritarian. Lewis Mumford in his history of utopia wrote that the "authoritarian discipline" and "dictatorial tendencies" of many utopias repelled him. The utopians generally "sought to impose a monolithic discipline upon all the varied activities . . . by creating an order too inflexible, and a system of government too centralized and too absolute."[38]

Without doubt many utopias confirm these charges. In *Christianopolis*, Johann Valentin Andreae described the clothing women wear in a seventeenth-century utopia: they "have only two suits of clothes, one for their work, one for the holidays; and for all classes they are made alike. Sex and age are shown by the form of dress . . . the color for all is white or ashen grey."[39] Several centuries later Edward Bellamy divided the "industrial army" of his utopia into three grades with each grade subdivided into two classes. Each worker sports a badge indicating industry and rank; "the badge of third grade is iron, that of the second grade is silver, and that of the first is gilt."[40]

These utopias appear constricted and oppressive; and the authors themselves are easy game for psychological debunking. Sometimes they admit their failings. "For inasmuch as other people (and I myself also) do not like to be corrected," wrote Andreae in 1619, "I have built this city for myself where I may exercise the dictatorship."[41] If Bellamy did not confess his foibles, his critics found and savored them. His authoritarianism, writes historian Arthur Lipow, "expressed a deep need in Bellamy's psychological make-up"; he was a "deeply troubled and lonely person."[42]

Yet these arguments do not close the case. Psychological debunking is sometimes illuminating, but it is a game all can play. Are the realists, cynics and anti-utopians—those whom C. Wright Mills called "the crack-pot realists"—more balanced and less lonely and troubled? Unlikely. The notion that the psychological fitness of artists or poets or utopians (or actors or politicians) speaks to the value of their work reveals a crude reductionist approach. The dreariness of many utopias is another matter. Here things are not so simple.

The drabness may derive less from utopianism than its absence, a failure to think boldly. During a trip to Europe, Bellamy was much impressed by the German army; he obviously used it as a model for his future. The detailed plans and routines that infect many utopians may come from generalizing dubious aspects of contemporary reality. For this reason, Marx and those who followed him remained silent about the future; they believed the free society could not be foreordained. Utopia could only plan itself. In any event, the cheerless dimension of utopias is hardly the whole story. If it were, utopians would merit little attention.

After listing the faults, Mumford's book on utopia did not end on page 3. He continued since he found in utopias something he found nowhere else; utopias treated society as a dynamic unity, the opposite of the prevailing "partiality, provinciality, specialism." Utopias address the "reservoir of potentialities" to which no society is "fully awake." And he discovered that even "the most simpleminded" utopia "possesses notably human qualities" that skeptics fail to recognize. "Utopian idealists who have overestimated the power of the idea are plainly much more fully in possession of their sense and more closely linked to human realities than the scientific and military 'realists.'"[43]

To demonstrate this risks a problem. As Krishan Kumar remarks, books on utopia "generally have all the interest of a telephone directory. A string of names—of books and authors—unfolds, accompanied by capsule summaries of the books' contents."[44] Nevertheless, even a brief glimpse of classic utopias substantiates Mumford's view. Andreae might have wanted women to dress in greys and whites, but his society would shame more modern ones. His utopia established "three good qualities of man: equality, the desire for peace, and the contempt for riches, as the world is tortured primarily with the opposite of these." His community has an armory, but the inhabitants show it to visitors with great disapproval. "For while the world especially glories in war-engines, catapults, and other machines and weapons of war, these people look with horror upon all kinds of deadly and death-dealing instruments, collected in such numbers."[45]

Though it is easy to lampoon Bellamy, consider one exchange between Mr. West, the nineteenth-century visitor to utopia, and his guide, Doctor Leete. West inquires what happens to individuals too

sick or disabled to work, and Leete explains that in a complex society all are enmeshed with all, and all are taken care of.

> "That may all be so," I replied, "but it does not touch the case of
> those who are unable to contribute anything to the products of indus-
> try."
> "Surely I told you this morning . . . " replied Doctor Leete, "that the
> right of a man to maintenance at the nation's table depends on the fact
> that he is a man and not on the amount of health and strength he may
> have. . . . "
> "You said so," I answered, "but I supposed the rule applied only to
> workers of different ability. Does it also hold of those who can do
> nothing at all?"
> "Are these not also men?"
> "I am to understand, then, that the lame, the blind, the sick, and the
> impotent, are as well off as the most efficient, and have the same in-
> come?"
> "Certainly," was the reply. . . . "If you had a sick brother at home
> . . . unable to work, would you feed him on less dainty food, and lodge
> and clothe him more poorly, than yourself? More likely, you would
> give the preference."
> "Of course," I replied, "but the cases are not parallel . . . this gen-
> eral sort of brotherhood is not to be compared . . . to the brotherhood
> of blood. . . . "
> "There speaks the nineteenth century!" exclaimed Doctor Leete. . . .
> "If I were to give you, in one sentence, a key to what may seem the
> mysteries of our civilization as compared with that of your age, I
> should say that it is the fact that the solidarity of the race and the
> brotherhood of man, which, to you were but fine phrases, are, to our
> thinking and feeling, as real and as vital as physical fraternity."[46]

The term itself, *utopia,* derives from Thomas More's 1516 *Utopia*;
and little in that work would validate the conventional denunciation
of utopias. Melvin J. Lasky in his book on utopia compares Popper's
strictures about utopia with More's ideas. Popper insisted that the
idea of utopia is dangerous and violent, a notion, wrote Lasky, that
"would have perplexed Thomas More," who hardly considered his

utopia either dangerous or violent. Popper believed that utopians would crush their opponents. "Thomas More would indeed have been puzzled." Popper thought that utopians would be opposed to reason. Thomas More would have found it "strange that the humane attempt to work out an arrangement of reasonable institutions for men in society should ever be accounted unreasonable."[47]

Like all utopias, More's spoke to his time, addressing the problems of the age. "He bases his construction," wrote the historian J. H. Hexter, "on a diagnosis of the maladies of the European polities of the early sixteenth century."[48] Like all utopias as well, More's looked beyond his time. His sketch of a future, now almost five centuries old, still stands light-years ahead of advanced industrial civilization. In *Utopia,* he wrote, all effort is directed towards the public.

> In all other places, regardless of the prosperity of the country, unless the individual takes care of his own needs, starvation will be his fate. Thus self-preservation has priority over the common good. Here . . . no one ever lacks anything. There is no begrudging the distribution of goods, poverty and begging are unknown, although possessing nothing, all men are rich. For who is richer than he who lives a happy and tranquil live free from the anxieties of job holding and domestic troubles?[49]

*   *   *

The first, and sometimes the last, charge against the utopian vision is its impracticality and irrelevance. In a capacious essay Thomas Macaulay, the prolific nineteenth-century historian, formulated an unsurpassed indictment of the uselessness of utopia; he was assessing the contribution of Francis Bacon, the seventeenth-century philosopher and statesman. Referring to Bacon's conviction for corruption, Macaulay judged him the blackest of blackguards, a man who perverted government office for private gain. Yet this was only "one-half" of Bacon. Macaulay also celebrated Bacon's insistence that philosophy be judged by its "fruit," or practical consequences, its ability to ameliorate the living conditions. With this criterion Bacon broke with traditional philosophers happier to spin conceptual wheels than employ real ones.

As Macaulay saw it, ancient and traditional philosophy devoted itself to intellectual sparring, Bacon's to improving man's lot. Bacon had no "fine theories," but he knew that "philosophers as well as other men, do actually love life, health, comfort, honour, security, the society of friends and do actually dislike death, sickness, pain, poverty, disgrace, danger." Bacon did not accept the conventional philosophical approach of refining categories, but ignoring reality; he did not understand the "wisdom there could be in changing names, where it was impossible to change things; in denying that blindness, hunger, the gout, the rack, were evils."

"We have sometimes thought," wrote Macaulay, of an "amusing fiction" in which a follower of Epictetus, the Greek Stoic, and a follower of Bacon were traveling together.

> They come to a village where the small-pox has just begun to rage, and find houses shut up, intercourse suspended, the sick abandoned, mothers weeping in terror over their children. The Stoic assures the dismayed population that there is nothing bad in small-pox, and that to a wise man disease, deformity, death, the loss of friends, are not evils. The Baconian takes out a lancet and begins to vaccinate.

For Macaulay, following Bacon, a chasm separates "the philosophy of words and the philosophy of works." The boast of ancient philosophy to improve the mind or morals has not been met. The ancient thinkers "promised what was impracticable; they despised what was practical; they filled the world with long words and long beards; and they left it as wicked and ignorant as they found it." Macaulay continued:

> An acre in Middlesex is better than a principality in Utopia. The smallest actual good is better than the most magnificent promises of impossibilities. The wise man of the Stoics would, no doubt, be a grander object than a steam-engine. But there are steam engines. And the wise

man of the Stoics is yet to be born. A philosophy which should enable a man to feel perfectly happy while in agonies of pain would be better than a philosophy which assuages pain. But we know there are remedies which will assuage pain; and we know that the ancient sages like the toothache just as little as their neighbor.[50]

This is so well put and persuasive that objections seem tiresome. "An acre in Middlesex is better than a principality in Utopia." Who can argue with that? Its good sense silences talk of utopias. Or does it? Macaulay's words and sentiments correspond so closely to the contemporary mind-set that we should be on guard.

For starters, it could be noted that the utilitarian Bacon himself sketched out a utopia in "New Atlantis"; and several scholars find a utopianism infusing all his work.[51] Benjamin Farrington considers Thomas More and Bacon both utopians, but judges Bacon "much more radical." He sought "not the subdivision of poverty, but the creation of plenty."

The texts of Bacon that Farrington presents reveal an exuberant, almost utopian thinker. "What I propose," Bacon says to a fictional disciple, "is to unite you with *things themselves* . . . and from this association you will secure an increase beyond all the hopes and prayers of ordinary marriages, to wit, a blessed race of Heroes or Supermen who will overcome the immeasurable helplessness and poverty of the human race." In another essay, Bacon wrote, "Shake off the chains which oppress you and be masters of yourself. . . . Not for nothing have we opposed our modern 'There is more beyond' to the 'Thus far and no further' of antiquity."[52]

Yet Bacon's own utopianism may be as irrelevant as his questionable life. As John Henry Newman, the nineteenth-century English churchman, commented, Bacon "aimed low," but "fulfilled" his aim. "Moral virtue was not the line in which he undertook to instruct men."[53] What was the line? Does a hearty practicality brook no criticism? Emerson also pondered Bacon's writings, noting that the Englishman would have achieved little if he had remained as close to utility as Macaulay supposed. "It is because he had imagination, the leisures of the spirit, and basked in an element of contemplation out of all modern English atmospheric gauges, that he is impressive."

Emerson challenged the "English cant of the practical" he found in Macaulay's Bacon, the belief that "to convince the reason, to touch the conscience, is romantic pretension." To Emerson, Macaulay extolled the philistine, who knows only crude materialism: The "*good* means good to eat, good to wear, material commodity." For Macaulay "the glory of modern philosophy is its direction or 'fruit'; to yield economical inventions; and that its merit is to avoid ideas, and avoid morals." From this vantage point,

> The eminent benefit of astronomy is the better navigation it creates to enable the fruit-ships to bring home their lemons and wine to the London grocer. It was a curious result, in which the civility and religion of England for a thousand years, ends, in denying morals, and reducing the intellect to a sauce-pan.

According to Emerson, Macaulay and other English Victorians crippled art and philosophy. "Squalid contentment with conventions, satire at the names of philosophy and religion, parochial and shop-till politics . . . betray the ebb of life and spirit . . . 'The fact is,' say they over their wine, 'all that about liberty, and so forth, is gone by; it won't do any longer.'"[54]

This cuts closer to the bone, the charge that thought is reduced to convention and utility. An acre in Middlesex is better than an estate in utopia, but is a dreary flat in Middlesex the goal of life? Is it worth surrendering all desires—"all that about liberty, and so forth"—that go beyond the immediate possibilities? A materialism that values the here and now may be beyond reproach, but a utilitarianism that swallows imagination may not be.

With different phrases, arguments espousing utilitarianism are as fresh as yesterday; they express a pragmatism and materialism perennially in fashion. The opposite is true as well: To some critics utilitarianism always undermines spirit or culture. Yet the strengths of utilitarianism, especially in its Victorian format, must be acknowledged.[55] Victorian utilitarianism exuded a robustness and earthiness: What mattered above all was making one's way in the world. It challenged vague concepts of "the good," reminding us, as one Victorian thinker put it, that "The happiness of a people is made up of the happiness of single persons."[56]

It also risked shrinking life to a calculus of the immediate options; the future collapses into the present. The nineteenth-century historian James Froude defended the utilitarian ethos in an address to students: "Lord Broughham once said he hoped a time would come when every man in England would read Bacon." Froude, for his part would be content "if a time came when every man in England would eat bacon." Practical achievements and skills are paramount. In the competition for a place, "history, poetry, logic, moral philosophy, classical literature are excellent as ornament," but nothing more. "The only reasonable guide to choice in such matters is utility."[57]

In a classic statement of a Victorian practicality, the chaplain to Queen Victoria, Charles Kingsley, stated:

> In an industrial country like this, the practical utility of any study must needs be always thrown into the scale. . . . "What money will it earn for a man in after life?" is a question which will be asked; and which it is folly to despise. For if the only answer be: "None at all," a man has a right to rejoin: "Then let me take up some pursuit which will train and refresh my mind . . . and yet be of pecuniary benefit to me."[58]

Where does this lead? In the famous fifth chapter of his autobiography, John Stuart Mill, meticulously educated by his exacting father, told of his crisis. The father, James Mill, followed the teachings of his friend, the utilitarian Jeremy Bentham, who depreciated feelings and poetry. "Bentham frankly objected to poetry in general," wrote the nineteenth-century critic Leslie Stephen. "It proved nothing. The true Utilitarian was the man who held on to fact. . . . Poetry . . . came within the sweep of his denunciations of 'sentimentalism' and 'vague generalities.'"[59]

James Mill sought to mold his son into a good utilitarian. Like Bentham, the father disparaged emotions. "For passionate emotions of all sorts," wrote the son, "he professed the greatest contempt. He regarded them as a form of madness." The elder Mill fed the boy a heavy diet of classics, history and logic. "Of children's books, any more than of playthings, I had scarcely any." The father raised a very educated, very focused and very self-confident student.

He also raised a young man who lacked passion and a self. One day Mill woke up frightened, aware of his crippled emotional life. His father's careful procedures left the son dry, analytic, cold. He approached everything as a means to an end, but the goal "had ceased to charm. . . . I seemed to have nothing left to live for. . . . I was thus . . . left stranded at the commencement of my voyage, with a well-equipped ship and rudder, but no sail; without any real desire." Mill contemplated suicide.

Mill's discovery of art and poetry, which had little place in Bentham's system, helped lift the darkness. To balance his previous extreme intellectualism, "the cultivation of feelings" became one of Mill's "cardinal points." He turned to music and Wordsworth's poetry. He was also led, partly under the influence of his newly found love, Harriet Taylor, to rethink his Benthamism. If Bentham's utilitarianism aimed for limited reforms within an unjust economic order, Mill and Taylor now saw "all existing institutions and social arrangements as being . . . 'merely provisional'"; they welcomed socialist and cooperative "experiments."[60] As Mill came to realize, a calculating utilitarianism flattens experience and life. Mill called Bentham a "one-eyed" thinker with little depth. "We have a large tolerance for one-eyed men," wrote Mill, "provided their one eye is penetrating." Yet they offer, at best, "fractional truths."[61]

This may be the weakness of the-acre-in-Middlesex argument; it is a partial truth. The utilitarian ethos is not wrong; it is incomplete. We need to keep an eye on what is under foot, but also what is on the horizon. In principle this is feasible. The utopian vision does not slight everyday life. The glance at the possible need not diminish the pleasure in the probable. Herbert Marcuse's most utopian work, *Eros and Civilization*, broached concepts like the arrest of time and the conquest of death; it also used as an epigraph a passage from

Sean O'Casey that celebrates the sweetness of everyday life. In the midst of an encomium for George Bernard Shaw, O'Casey, who himself was a socialist, wrote:

> What time has been wasted during man's destiny in the struggle to decide what man's next world will be like! The keener the effort to find out, the less he knows about the present one he lived in. The one lovely world he knew, lived in, that gave him all he had, was, according to preacher and prelate, the one to be least in his thoughts. He was recommended, ordered, from the day of his birth to bid goodbye to it. Oh, we have had enough of the abuse of this fair earth! It is no sad truth that this should be our home. Were it but to give us simple shelter, simple clothing, simple food, adding the lily and the rose, the apple and the pear, it would be a fit home for mortal or immortal men.[62]

Utilitarianism not only constricts life, it sanctions conformity by shrinking reason to evaluating options. Leo Strauss, the conservative political thinker, evinced little interest in utopias. Yet he forcefully outlined the danger of utilitarian minimalism—it forsakes reason or the effort to glimpse the whole reality and celebrates technique. It renounces thinking about goals, while perfecting the means to reach them. For Strauss this philosophy led to intellectual suicide. We become "wise in all matters of secondary importance" that address the best mechanism, but "we have to be resigned to utter ignorance in the most important respect . . . the ultimate principles." For Strauss, the result was paradoxical: "We are then in the position of beings who are sane and sober when engaged in trivial business and who gamble like madmen when confronted with serious issues—retail sanity and wholesale madness."[63]

*   *   *

Yet the most compelling arguments for utopianism do not suffice today. World events and the Zeitgeist militate against a utopian spirit—and have for decades. If not murderous, utopianism seems unfashionable, impractical and pointless. Its sources in imagination and hope have withered. The demise of radicalism affects even the unpolitical and the unconcerned, who viscerally register a confirmation of what they always intuited: This society is the only possible one. Those who resist the inference do so with little conviction or consequence. Success and its insignias become the goal for the best and wisest youth—and who can begrudge them, since they are simply drawing conclusions from what they see? Politics devolves into scandals or, at best, policy, ways to tinker with the ship of state. No one even pretends to believe in a different future.

Little seems more quixotic or irrelevant than defending the utopian impulse. The path, however, is not without its honor and heroes. Nor should it be forgotten that many utopian thinkers from Tommaso Campanella to the Marquis de Condorcet were not persecutors, as foes of totalitarianism might suppose, but were persecuted. To be sure, with the best will or courage, utopian thought cannot jump out of history. However, it must vault beyond the immediate prospects or surrender its raison d'être.

Dreams and imagination have always sustained the utopian vision. "Let us endeavor to render this life tolerable; or, if that be too much, let us at least dream that it is so," wrote Sébastien Mercier in his utopian *Mémoires de l'An 2440* from 1770.[64] From the Surrealists of the 1920s to the cultural rebels of the 1960s, twentieth-century utopians sought to replenish these energies. The devotion to imagination set them apart from conventional leftists, who were planning centralized kitchens and laundries. "To reduce the imagination to a state of slavery," wrote André Breton, in the first manifesto of Surrealism, "is to betray all sense of absolute justice within oneself. Imagination alone offers me some intimation of what *can be.*"[65]

On the walls of Paris in 1968 "All Power to the Imagination!" expressed the utopian impulse filtered through the Surrealists and Situationists.[66] Throughout the 1960s the celebration of drugs, dreams and imagination sought to blast a stifling reality into smithereens.[67] What was achieved? The record is mixed and can hardly be discussed in brief. In the plus column many enduring political and cul-

tural accomplishments could be listed. The utopian moment, however, vanished without a trace.

Yet in an era of political resignation and fatigue the utopian spirit
remains more necessary than ever. It evokes neither prisons nor programs, but an idea of human solidarity and happiness. "Something's
missing." Ernst Bloch cited this sentence from Bertolt Brecht's *Mahagonny* as a clue to the utopian impulse.[68] Something *is* missing. A
light has gone out. The world stripped of anticipation turns cold and
grey.

What is to be done? The question, routinely addressed to all critics, insists on a practicality inimical to utopianism. Nothing is to be
done. Yet that does not mean nothing is to be thought or imagined
or dreamed. On the contrary. The effort to envision other possibilities of life and society remains urgent and constitutes the essential
precondition for doing something. We must, to follow T. W.
Adorno, "contemplate all things as they would present themselves
from the standpoint of redemption." That means viewing the world
"as it will appear one day in the messianic light."[69]

That day is more distant than ever. Or is it? History outwits even
its most diligent students. No one foresaw the rapid demise of the
Soviet system in 1989; careful scholars believed that its deadly empire would last another fifty years. The 1960s exploded with almost
no advance notice; most observers had dubbed the 1950s an age of
conformity and apathy and expected more of the same. Who can say
if the future holds similar surprises?

NOTES

Preface

1. "Population Implosion Worries a Graying Europe," *New York Times*, July 10, 1998, A1.

2. *Dialectic of Defeat: Contours of Western Marxism* (New York: Cambridge University Press, 1981), p. 4.

3. *Collected Letters of Samuel Taylor Coleridge*, ed. E. L. Griggs, vol. 1, 1785–1800 (Oxford: Clarendon, 1956), p. 289 (undated, circa September 10, 1799).

Chapter One

1. Edward Shils, "Letter from Milan: The End of Ideology?" *Encounter* 5, no. 5 (November 1955): 54. The conference was sponsored by the Congress for Cultural Freedom; much later, it was discovered that the congress and some its publications, such as *Encounter*, were receiving funds from the CIA in its efforts to support liberal anticommunists. See, generally, Peter Coleman, *The Liberal Conspiracy: The Congress for Cultural Freedom and the Struggle for the Mind of Postwar Europe* (New York: Free Press, 1989).

2. Raymond Aron, "Nations and Ideologies," in *The Future of Freedom*, Papers from the International Conference on the Future on Freedom convened by the Congress for Cultural Freedom in Milan, 1955 (Bombay: Indian Committee for Cultural Freedom, n.d.), pp. 20–21.

3. "Khrushchev's Secret Report," in Bertram D. Wolfe, *Khrushchev and Stalin's Ghost* (New York: Praeger, 1957), pp. 102, 124, 222.

4. *Bertolt Brecht Poems*, ed. J. Willett and R. Mannheim (London: Methuen, 1979), p. 440.

5. See, generally, Robert Colquhoun, *Raymond Aron*, vol. 1 (Beverly Hills, Calif.: Sage, 1986), pp. 453–494.

6. Raymond Aron, *The Opium of the Intellectuals* (New York: Norton, 1962), pp. 309, xiii, xv.

7. Albert Camus, "The Confusion of Socialists" (November 21, 1946), in Camus, *Between Hell and Reason: Essays from the Resistance Newspaper Combat, 1944–1947*, ed. A. de Gramont (Hanover, N.H.: Wesleyan University Press, 1991), pp. 124–125. To be sure, a series of writings by Aron from the middle 1940s broached the idea of the end of ideology; for instance, in 1944 he remarked that the end of the war, unlike World War I, was not likely to see a rebirth of ideology. "The present phase could be characterized by the decline of dogma" (Aron, "L'avenir des religions séculières" [1944], reprinted in *Commentaire* 29–29 [1985]: 379).

8. H. Stuart Hughes, "The End of Political Ideology," *Measure* 2, no. 2 (1951): 146–158.

9. Judith N. Shklar, *After Utopia: The Decline of Political Faith* (Princeton: Princeton University Press, 1957), pp. 219, 256.

10. Seymour Martin Lipset, *Political Man: The Social Bases of Politics* (1960; Garden City, N.Y.: Anchor, 1963), pp. 442–443.

11. Daniel Bell, *The End of Ideology: On the Political Exhaustion of Political Ideas in the Fifties* (New York: Free Press, 1960), pp. 369–373.

12. Daniel Bell, *The End of Ideology*, pp. 374–375.

13. Bell, *The End of Ideology* (Revised Edition) (New York: Free Press, 1962), p. 405.

14. Todd Gitlin, *The Sixties: Years of Hope, Days of Rage* (New York: Bantam, 1987), p. 87.

15. C. Wright Mills, "The New Left" (1960), in *Power, Politics and People*, ed. I. L. Horowitz (New York: Ballantine, n.d.), pp. 248, 251, 254.

16. Donald Clark Hodges, "The End of the 'The End of Ideology,'" *American Journal of Economics and Sociology* 26, no. 2 (1967): 135.

17. Steven Kelman, "The Feud Among the Radicals," in *The End of Ideology Debate*, ed. C. I. Waxman (New York: Funk & Wagnalls, 1968), p. 372.

18. Michael Novak, "The Student Movement and the End of the 'End of Ideology,'" in *Decline of Ideology*, ed. M. Rejai (Chicago: Aldine Atherton, 1971), p. 302.

19. Christopher Lasch, "The Revival of Political Controversy in the Sixties," in *The Agony of the American Left* (New York: Vintage, 1969), pp. 172–175.

20. "We Are All Totalitarians," *Times Literary Supplement*, May 5, 1972, as cited in Seymour Martin Lipset, "The End of Ideology and the Ideology of the Intellectuals," in *Culture and Its Creators: Essays in Honor of Edward Shils*, ed. J. Ben-David and T. N. Clark (Chicago: University of Chicago Press, 1977), pp. 15–16. See this essay and Lipset's "A Concept and Its History: The End of Ideology" (in Lipset, *Consensus and Conflict: Essays in Political Sociology* [New Brunswick, N.J.: Transaction, 1985], pp. 81–109) for other references and a reprise of the debate.

21. Honecker, cited in Patrick Brogan, *The Captive Nations: Eastern Europe, 1945–1990* (New York: Avon, 1990), p. 30.

22. Paul Lauter, "'Political Correctness' and the Attack on American Colleges," in *Higher Education Under Fire: Politics, Economics, and the Crisis of the Humanities*, ed. M. Bérubé and C. Nelson (New York: Routledge, 1995), p. 83.

23. The connection is taken up in Frank Fürdi, "The Enthronement of Low Expectations: Fukuyama's Ideological Compromise for Our Time," in *Has History Ended? Fukuyama, Marx, Modernity*, ed. C. Bertram and A. Chitty (Aldershot, England: Avebury, 1994), pp. 31–45.

24. See Philip T. Grier's convincing argument that neither Kojève nor Fukuyama got Hegel right, "The End of History and the Return of History," in *The Hegel Myths and Legends*, ed. J. Stewart (Evanston, Ill.: Northwestern University Press, 1996), pp. 183–198.

25. Francis Fukuyama, *Have We Reached the End of History?* (Santa Monica, Calif.: Rand Corporation, 1989), p. 2.

26. Fukuyama, *Have We Reached the End of History?* p. 1.

27. Fukuyama, *Have We Reached the End of History?* pp. 22–23.

28. For a summary of Marxist critiques, see Jules Townshend, *The Politics of Marxism: The Critical Debates* (London: Leicester University Press, 1996), pp. 256–259.

29. Francis Fukuyama, *The End of History and the Last Man* (New York: Avon, 1993), p. 46.

30. Robert Steigerwald, *Anti-Communist Myths in Left Disguise* (New York: International, 1977).

31. Paul Berman, *A Tale of Two Utopias: The Political Journey of the Generation of 1968* (New York: Norton, 1996), p. 16.

32. Adam Michnik, "Gray Is Beautiful," *Dissent* (Spring 1997): 15–16.

33. Berman, *Tale of Two Utopias*, pp. 201, 195–253.

34. Timothy Garton Ash, *The Magic Lantern: The Revolution of '89* (New York: Random House, 1990), p. 151.

35. H. Bruce Franklin, ed., *The Essential Stalin* (Garden City, N.Y.: Anchor, 1972), pp. 1, 38.

36. One effort is Alex Callinicos, *The Revenge of History: Marxism and the East European Revolutions* (Cambridge: Polity Press, 1991). "The East European revolutions . . . are thus the vindication, rather than the refutation, of the classical Marxist tradition" (p. 20).

37. André Gorz, *Capitalism, Socialism, Ecology*, trans. C. Turner (London: Verso, 1994), p. 4.

38. Eric Hobsbawm, "Goodbye to All That," in *After the Fall: The Failure of Communism and the Future of Socialism*, ed. R. Blackburn (London: Verso, 1991), pp. 117, 122–123.

39. Robin Blackburn, "*Fin de Siècle*: Socialism After the Crash," in Hobsbawm, *After the Fall*, p. 173.

40. Jorge E. Castañeda, *Utopia Unarmed: The Latin American Left After the Cold War* (New York: Vintage, 1994), pp. 240–241.

41. Ash, *The Magic Lantern*, p. 151.

42. Michnik, "Gray Is Beautiful," p. 16.

43. Ernest Gellner, *Conditions of Liberty: Civil Society and Its Rivals* (New York: Penguin, 1996), p. 38.

44. Misha Glenny, *The Rebirth of History: Eastern Europe in the Age of Democracy* (New York: Penguin, 1993), p. 232.

45. Gale Stokes, *The Walls Came Tumbling Down: The Collapse of Communism in Eastern Europe* (New York: Oxford University Press, 1993), p. 101.

46. David Marquand, "Against Socialism," in *The End of 'Isms'? Reflections on the Fate of Ideological Politics After Communism's Collapse*, ed. A. Shtromas (Oxford: Blackwell, 1994), p. 46.

47. Glenny, *Rebirth of History*, pp. 200, 235.

48. Douglas Kellner, "The Obsolescence of Marxism?" in *Whither Marxism? Global Crises in International Perspectives*, ed. B. Magnus and S. Cullenberg (New York: Routledge, 1995), p. 25.

49. Norman Birnbaum, "Socialism Reconsidered—Yet Again," *World Policy Journal* 13, no. 3 (Fall 1996): 50–51.

50. Stanley Aronowitz, *The Death and Rebirth of American Radicalism* (New York: Routledge, 1996), p. 91.

51. Perry Anderson, "The Ends of History," in his *A Zone of Engagement* (London: Verso, 1992), pp. 358–359.

52. Richard Rorty, *Contingency, Irony, and Solidarity* (Cambridge: Cambridge University Press, 1989), pp. 181–182.

53. Richard Rorty, "The End of Leninism and History as Comic Frame," in *History and the Idea of Progress*, ed. A. M. Melzer et al. (Ithaca: Cornell University Press, 1995), pp. 212–214.

54. Michael J. Sandel, *Democracy's Discontent: America in Search of a Public Philosophy* (Cambridge, Mass.: Harvard University Press, 1996), pp. 203, 324, 335, 338.

55. Thomas A. Spragens, Jr., "Communitarian Liberalism," in *New Communitarian Thinking: Persons, Virtues, Institutions, and Communities*, ed. A. Etzioni (Charlottesville: University Press of Virginia, 1995), pp. 49–50.

56. On the ongoing debate as to the depth of Mill's socialism, see Oskar Kurer's cogent overview and argument, "J. S. Mill and Utopian Socialism," *The Economic Record* 68, no. 202 (1992): 222–232. See also Richard K. P. Pankhurst, *The Saint Simonians, Mill and Carlyle* (London: Sidgwick & Jackson, 1957), pp. 6–28.

57. John Stuart Mill, *Principles of Political Economy*, ed. D. Winch (Middlesex: Penguin, 1970), p. 384 (Book 2, chap. 2, sec. 6).

58. Jeffrey C. Alexander, *Fin de Siècle Social Theory* (New York: Verso, 1995), pp. 8, 32–33.

59. Michael Tomasky, *Left for Dead: The Life, Death and Possible Resurrection of Progressive Politics in America* (New York: Free Press, 1966), p. 35.

60. Tomasky, *Left for Dead,* pp. 196–197.

61. Robert Kuttner, *Everything for Sale: The Virtue and Limits of Markets* (New York: Knopf, 1997), pp. 3, 5–6, 109–109, 351.

62. Paul Starr, "Liberalism After Socialism," *American Prospect* 7 (Fall 1991): 70–80.

63. Ralph Miliband, *Socialism for a Skeptical Age* (London: Verso, 1994), p. 123.

64. Ira Katznelson, *Liberalism's Crooked Circle* (Princeton: Princeton University Press, 1996), p. 73.

65. Bogdan Denitch, *After the Flood: World Politics and Democracy in the Wake of Communism* (Hanover, N.H.: Wesleyan University Press, 1992), p. 125.

66. Charles Derber et al., *What's Left: Radical Politics in the Postcommunist Era* (Amherst: University of Massachusetts Press, 1995), pp. 177–185. Many collections have appeared that seek to salvage socialism by resuscitating a civic ideal or a market orientation; for instance, see Michael Crozier and Peter Murphy, "Introduction: Searching for the Civic Center," in *The Left in Search of a Center*, ed. M. Crozier and P. Murphy (Urbana: University of Illinois Press, 1996); and Konrad H. Jarausch, "Towards a Postsocialist Politics?" in *The Crisis of Socialism in Europe*, ed. C. Lemke and G. Marks (Durham, N.C.: Duke University Press, 1992).

67. Erik Olin Wright, "Rethinking Socialism: Introduction," *Politics and Society* 22, no. 4 (December 1994): 447–448.

68. John E. Roemer, *A Future for Socialism* (Cambridge, Mass.: Harvard University Press, 1994), p. 68.

69. Roemer, *A Future for Socialism*, pp. 133–143.

70. Roemer, *A Future for Socialism*, p. 54.

71. James A. Yunker, *Socialism Revised and Modernized: The Case for Pragmatic Market Socialism* (New York: Praeger, 1992), pp. 67–69.

72. Donald Weiss, *The Specter of Capitalism and the Promise of a Classless Society* (Atlantic Highlands, N.J.: Humanities Press International, 1993), pp. 2, 141, 150–153.

73. Michael Albert, *Thinking Forward* (Winnipeg: Arbeiter Ring, 1997), pp. 173, 180, 184.

74. William Wolman and Anne Colamosca, *The Judas Economy: The Triumph of Capital and the Betrayal of Work* (Reading, Mass.: Addison-Wesley, 1997), pp. 19, 167–168, 206–208.

75. "Something's Missing: A Discussion Between Ernst Bloch and Theodor W. Adorno on the Contradictions of Utopian Longing," in Ernst Bloch, *Utopian Function of Art and Literature* (Cambridge, Mass.: MIT Press, 1988), pp. 12–13.

76. The standard source for Marx's anti-utopianism is Frederick Engels's *Socialism: Utopian and Scientific* (Peking: Foreign Language Press, 1975), which dispatched the utopian ideas as nothing more than a "mish-

mash" lacking a real basis in history (pp. 61–62). A more exact rendering of its German title, "Socialism from Utopia to Science," better captures Engels's argument. Engels championed "scientific" socialism as dislodging a "utopian" socialism that failed to understand the vector of history and the working class. In *The Dictionary of Marxist Epithets* (Orthodox Ed.) "utopian," means ill-founded, foggy and diversionary. Yet Marx himself reproved the utopian socialists less for their hope for the future than their inability to understand how to reach it; they did not comprehend that political activity replaced utopian blueprints. Marx's object was not to destroy, but realize the visions. In his address on the Paris Commune, he had stated that the working classes have "no ready-made utopias to introduce. . . . They have no ideals to realize, but to set free the elements of the new society with which old collapsing bourgeois society itself is pregnant." In a draft of that address Marx was more precise and detailed: Although utopian socialists "in their criticism of present society clearly described the goal of the social movement," they failed to understand the means, mainly because the working class itself was not sufficiently developed. The utopians "tried to compensate for the historical conditions of the movement by fantastic pictures and plans of a new society in whose propaganda they saw the true means of salvation." He continued: "From the moment the working men's class movement became real the fantastic utopias evanesced—not because the working class had given up the end aimed at by these Utopians, but because they had found the real means to realize them"(Karl Marx and Frederick Engels, *On the Paris Commune* [Moscow: Progress Publishers, 1971], pp. 76, 166). See, generally, Vincent Geoghegan, *Utopianism and Marxism* (London: Methuen, 1987). Even the blunt realism of Lenin sometimes breathed of utopianism. "We are not utopians," he stoutly maintained in *The State and Revolution* (Peking: Foreign Languages Press, 1976), but not many pages later he defended Marxist utopianism against bourgeois philistinism (pp. 60, 117–118, 121). In his practical guide *What Is to Be Done?* Lenin whipped himself up to an enthusiastic vision of a revolutionary upsurge, concluding that this is "what we ought to be dreaming about." He then parodied the response of somber Marxists to his exuberant visions: "'We ought to dream!' I wrote these words and then got scared." He formulated the objections of a dreary comrade: "'I ask, has a Marxist any right at all to dream, knowing that according to Marx, man always sets himself achievable tasks and that tactics is a process . . . which grow together with the party?'" Lenin responded by citing the novelist Pisarev, who affirmed that without dreaming no one would devote him- or herself to politics or art or science. Lenin added, "Now of this kind of dreaming there is unfortunately too little in our movement. And those most responsible for this are the ones who boast of their sober views, their 'closeness' to the 'concrete'" (V. I. Lenin, *What Is to Be Done?* [New York: International, 1943], pp. 158–159).

77. Paul Lafargue, *The Right to Be Lazy* (1883; Chicago: Kerr, 1975), pp. 35, 49, 66.

78. "Theses on the Philosophy of History," in Walter Benjamin, *Illuminations*, ed. H. Arendt (New York: Schocken, 1969), pp. 258–261.

79. Jonathan Beecher, *Charles Fourier: The Visionary and His World* (Berkeley and Los Angeles: University of California Press, 1986), pp. 251–253.

80. Charles Fourier, *The Theory of the Four Movements*, ed. G. S. Jones and I. Patterson (New York: Cambridge University Press, 1966), p. 269.

81. Georg Lukács, "The Old Culture and the New Culture" (1920), *Telos* 5 (Spring 1970): 30.

Chapter Two

1. O. B. Hardison, Jr., *Entering the Maze: Identity and Change in Modern Culture* (New York: Oxford University Press, 1981), pp. 4–5.

2. Monroe E. Deutsch, "E Pluribus Unum," *The Classical Journal* 18 (1922–1923): 387–407. See also Richard Patterson and Richardson Dougall, *The Eagle and the Shield: A History of the Great Seal of the United States* (Washington, D.C.: Office of the Historian, Bureau of Public Affairs, Department of State, 1978), pp. 6–84; Frank H. Sommer, "Emblem and Device: The Origin of the Great Seal of the United States," *Art Quarterly* 24, no. 1 (Spring 1961): 57–76; Meyer Reinhold, *Classica Americana: The Greek and Roman Heritage in the United States* (Detroit: Wayne State University Press, 1984), p. 247.

3. The title page and first page of *The Gentleman's Magazine* are reproduced in Howard P. Arnold, *Historic Side-Lights* (New York: Harper & Brothers, 1899), after p. 288.

4. Cited in and see for Cave and his magazine, C. Lennart Carlson, *The First Magazine: A History of The Gentleman's Magazine* (Providence, R.I.: Brown University, 1938), (pp. 65–66).

5. For instance, Cave was party to the fake speech of Polly Baker that Benjamin Franklin wrote. See Max Hall, *Benjamin Franklin and Polly Baker: The History of Literary Deception* (Pittsburgh: University of Pittsburgh Press, 1990).

6. Robert N. Cunningham, *Peter Anthony Montteux, 1663–1718* (Oxford: Blackwell, 1933), pp. 190–194.

7. Arnold, *Historic Side-Lights*, pp. 311–312, 315.

8. Several paragraphs and references in this chapter are adapted from my "The Myth of Multiculturalism" (*New Left Review* [November-December 1994]: 121–126) and from Chapter 5 of my *Dogmatic Wisdom: How the Culture Wars Divert Education and Distract America* (New York: Doubleday, 1994).

9. *Sources: Diversity Initiatives in Higher Education: A Directory of Programs, Projects, and Services for African Americans, Asian Americans, Hispanic Americans, and Native Americans in Higher Education*, ed. Suzanné D. Mintz (Washington, D.C.: Office of Minorities in Higher Education, American Council on Education, 1993).

10. *Diversity: A Critical Journal of Race and Culture* 1, no. 1 (October-November 1991). This was published by the Madison Center for Educational Affairs, a conservative foundation.

11. Lawrence W. Levine, *The Opening of the American Mind: Canons, Culture, and History* (Boston: Beacon, 1996), p. 139. See my review in *Dissent*, Winter 1997: 115–119.

12. Horace M. Kallen, *Culture and Democracy in the United States* (New York: Bone and Liveright, 1924), pp. 11, 43.

13. Nathan Glazer, *We Are All Multiculturalists Now* (Cambridge, Mass.: Harvard University Press, 1997), pp. 7, 160.

14. David A. Hollinger, *Postethnic America: Beyond Multiculturalism* (New York: Basic Books, 1995), p. 101.

15. Christopher Newfield and Avery F. Gordon, "Multiculturalism's Unfinished Business," in *Mapping Multiculturalism*, ed. A. F. Gordon and C. Newfield (Minneapolis: University of Minnesota Press, 1966), p. 104.

16. Glazer, *We Are All Multiculturalists Now*, p. 75.

17. William James, *Pragmatism* (New York: Meridian, 1955), pp. 102, 107.

18. John Browning and Curt Gentry, *John M. Browning: American Gunmaker* (Garden City, N.Y.: Doubleday, 1964), pp. 180, 288. "By 1909 500,000 [of the new pistols] had been produced. Since F.N. [Fabrique Nationale d'Armes de Guerre] had chosen to designate the pistol by the name Browning, very soon the Browning name was better-known in Europe than in the United States" (p. 184).

19. *Hanns Johst's Nazi Drama Schlageter*, translated with an introduction by Ford B. Parkes-Perret (Stuttgart: Akademischer Verlag Hans-Dieter Heinz, 1984), p. 89; Hanns Johst, *Schlageter* (Munich: Albert Langen, 1933), p. 26. See, generally, Helmut F. Pfanner, *Hanns Johst: Vom Expressionismus zum Nationalsozialismus* (The Hague: Mouton, 1970), esp. pp. 252–258.

20. Frantz Fanon, *The Wretched of the Earth* (New York: Grove, 1965), p. 43.

21. Both quoted in Matthew Arnold, *Culture and Anarchy and Other Writings*, ed. S. Collini (Cambridge: Cambridge University Press, 1993), p. 55.

22. Moses Mendelssohn, "On the Question: What Is the Enlightenment?" in *What Is Enlightenment: Eighteenth-Century Answers and Twentieth-Century Questions*, ed. J. Schmidt (Berkeley and Los Angeles: University of California Press, 1996), p. 53.

23. Immanuel Kant, *Anthropology from a Pragmatic Point of View* (1798), ed. Hans J. Rudnick (Carbondale: Southern Illinois University Press, 1978), pp. 3, 240.

24. Cited in and see the detailed discussion "Zivilisation, Kultur," in *Geschichtliche Grundbegriffe*, ed. O. Brunner, W. Conze and R. Koselleck, vol. 7 (Stuttgart: Klett-Cotta, 1992), pp. 679–774.

25. A. L. Kroeber and Clyde Kluckhohn, *Culture: A Critical Review of Concepts and Definitions* (New York: Vintage, n.d.), pp. 66–67. This book was originally published in 1952 as vol. 47 of the Papers of the Peabody Museum of American Archaeology and Ethnology, Harvard University.

26. Kroeber and Kluckhohn, *Culture*, pp. 68–69.

27. Margaret M. Caffrey, *Ruth Benedict: Stranger in this Land* (Austin: University of Texas Press, 1989), pp. 213–214. See Christopher Shannon, *Conspicuous Criticism: Tradition, the Individual, and Culture in American*

Social Thought from Veblen to Mills (Baltimore: Johns Hopkins University Press, 1996), pp. 87–104.

28. Ruth Benedict, *Patterns of Culture* (New York: Mentor, 1959), p. 239.

29. Margaret Mead, "A New Preface," in Ruth Benedict, *Patterns of Culture* (New York: Mentor, 1959), p. v.

30. See the smart essay by Christopher Shannon, "A World Made Safe for Differences: Ruth Benedict's *The Chrysanthemum and the Sword*," *American Quarterly* 47, no. 4 (December 1995): 659–680.

31. Werner Jaeger, *Paideia: The Ideas of Greek Culture*, vol. 1, 2d ed. (New York: Oxford University Press, 1965); and Werner Jaeger, *Humanistische Reden und Vorträge*, zweite erweiterte Auflage (Berlin: Walter de Gruyter, 1960), pp. 117–124.

32. S. Freud, *The Future of an Illusion*, ed. James Strachey (New York: Norton, 1961), p. 6.

33. Franz Boas, "The Outlook for the American Negro" (1906), in *The Shaping of American Anthropology 1883–1911: A Franz Boas Reader*, ed. G. W. Stocking, Jr. (New York: Basic Books, 1974), pp. 313–314. See David L. Lewis, *W. E. B. Du Bois, 1868–1919* (New York: Holt, 1993), pp. 351–352.

34. Carl N. Degler, *In Search of Human Nature: The Decline and Revival of Darwinism in American Social Thought* (New York: Oxford University Press, 1991), pp. 61–83.

35. Clifford Geertz, "Common Sense as a Cultural System," in his *Local Knowledge* (New York: Basic Books, 1983), pp. 73–93.

36. Kroeber and Kluckhohn, *Culture*, p. 367.

37. I borrowed several of these sentences from my "Wither Marxism," *Transition* 69 (Spring 1996): 100–115.

38. Stanley Aronowitz, *The Death and Rebirth of American Radicalism* (New York: Routledge, 1996), p. 121.

39. David Bromwich, "Anti-Intellectualism," *Raritan* (Spring 1996): 27.

40. Abbott Gleason, in *Totalitarianism: The Inner History of the Cold War* (New York: Oxford University Press, 1995), rebuts the notion that totalitarianism was applied to the Soviet Union only after 1939 (pp. 29–50). However, the material he offers only qualifies, but does not negate, the point.

41. Herbert Heaton, "Discussion of Totalitarianism," in *Symposium on the Totalitarian State*, Proceedings of the American Philosophical Society,

February 23, 1940, vol. 82, no. 1, p. 89. The symposium took place in November 1939.

42. Gleason, *Totalitarianism*, p. 51.

43. Thomas Woody, "Principles of Totalitarian Education," in *Symposium on the Totalitarian State*, p. 44.

44. "Immigrant social scientists remained at the forefront of the development of the concept of totalitarianism" (Thomas E. Lifka, *The Concept of "Totalitarianism" and American Foreign Policy 1933–1949* [New York: Garland, 1988], p. 14).

45. Andrzej Walicki, *Marxism and the Leap to the Kingdom of Freedom: The Rise and Fall of the Communist Utopia* (Stanford: Stanford University Press, 1995), p. 509. Walicki is critical of this lax use. On the other hand, in his lengthy discussions of the meaning, significance and evolution of the term *totalitarian*, he evinces no interest in its application to Nazism or fascism.

46. J. L. Talmon, *The Unique and the Universal* (London: Secker & Warburg, 1965), p. 9.

47. J. L. Talmon, *The Origins of Totalitarian Democracy* (New York: Norton, 1970), p. 1.

48. Yehoshua Arieli, "Jacob Talmon—An Intellectual Portrait," in *Totalitarian Democracy and After: International Colloquium in Memory of Jacob L. Talmon* (Jerusalem: Magnes Press, 1984), p. 18.

49. Friedrich A. Hayek, *The Road to Serfdom* (Chicago: University of Chicago Press, 1972), pp. iii, 27.

50. Karl R. Popper, *The Open Society and Its Enemies*, 2 vols. (New York: Harper & Row, 1963), vol. 1, pp. 158–159; vol. 2, p. 396.

51. Hannah Arendt, *The Origins of Totalitarianism* (New York: World, 1958), p. 470.

52. Isaiah Berlin, "Political Ideas in the Twentieth Century" (1949), in *Four Essays on Liberty* (Oxford: Oxford University Press, 1969), pp. 29, 39.

53. Isaiah Berlin, "Two Concepts of Liberty," in *Four Essays on Liberty*, pp. 118–172.

54. Stanislaw Ehrlich, *Pluralism On and Off Course* (Oxford: Pergamon, 1982), p. xi.

55. See Claude J. Galipeau, *Isaiah Berlin's Liberalism* (Oxford: Oxford University Press, 1994), p. 134. For this judgment, among other things, Galipeau is drawing upon several unpublished interviews with Berlin.

56. Isaiah Berlin, in *Authors Take Sides on Vietnam*, ed. C. Woolfe and J. Bagguley (London: Peter Owen, 1967), pp. 60–61.

57. Alfred G. Meyer, "Coming to Terms with the Past . . . And with One's Older Colleagues," *Russian Review* 45 (1986): 402.

58. Gleason, *Totalitarianism*, pp. 4, 131.

59. Preface, *Power and Community: Dissenting Essays in Political Science*, ed. P. Green and S. Levinson (New York: Vintage, 1970), p. ix. For another 1960s criticism of pluralism, see *The Bias of Pluralism*, ed. W. E. Connolly (New York: Atherton, 1969). See also Oliver C. Cox, "The Question of Pluralism," *Race* 12, no. 4 (April 1971): 385–400. The entire issue is devoted to "Race and Pluralism."

60. Henry S. Kariel, *The Decline of American Pluralism* (Stanford: Stanford University Press, 1961).

61. Michael P. Rogin, *The Intellectuals and McCarthy: The Radical Specter* (Cambridge, Mass.: MIT Press, 1967), p. 9.

62. John Higham, *Send These to Me: Immigrants in Urban America*, rev. ed. (Baltimore: Johns Hopkins University Press, 1984), p. 198.

63. Marcus Lee Hansen, *The Problem of the Third Generation Immigrant*, intro. P. Kivisto and O. Handlin (Rock Island, Ill.: Swenson Swedish Immigration Research Center, 1987), pp. 14–19. This famous essay was originally delivered as an address in 1937.

64. See, generally, *American Immigrants and Their Generations: Studies and Commentaries on the Hansen Thesis After Fifty Years*, ed. P. Kivisto and D. Blanck (Urbana: University of Illinois Press, 1990).

65. Nathan Glazer and Daniel P. Moynihan, *Beyond the Melting Pot* (Cambridge, Mass.: MIT Press, 1963), p. v.

66. Milton M. Gordon, *Assimilation in American Life: The Role of Race, Religion, and National Origins* (New York: Oxford University Press, 1964), p. 110.

67. Gordon, *Assimilation in American Life*, p. 158.

68. Stephen Steinberg, *The Ethnic Myth* (1981; New York: Beacon, 1989), pp. 51, 58.

69. Steinberg, Preface to the Updated Edition, *The Ethnic Myth*, p. ix.

70. See Richard D. Alba, "Assimilation's Quiet Tide," *Public Interest* no. 119 (Spring 1995): 3–19.

71. Geoffrey Nunberg, "Lingo Jingo: English-Only and the New Nativism," *American Prospect* 33 (July-August 1997): 42.

72. Clifford Adelman, *Tourists in Our Own Land: Cultural Literacies and the College Curriculum* (Washington, D.C.: U.S. Department of Education, 1992), pp. 37–38.

73. See, in general, Susan M. Rigdon, *The Cultural Façade: Art, Science and Politics in the Work of Oscar Lewis* (Urbana: University of Illinois Press, 1988), p. 55.

74. Charles A. Valentine, *Culture and Poverty: Critique and Counter-Proposals* (Chicago: University of Chicago Press, 1968), pp. 98–120.

75. Carl H. Nightingale, *On the Edge: A History of Poor Black Children and Their American Dreams* (New York: Basic Books, 1993), pp. 135–165.

76. Sterling Stuckey, *Slave Culture: Nationalist Theory and the Foundations of Black America* (New York: Oxford University Press, 1987); Melville J. Herskovits, *The Myth of the Negro Past* (1941; Boston: Beacon, 1990).

77. Donald B. Kraybill, *The Riddle of Amish Culture* (Baltimore: Johns Hopkins University Press, 1989), pp. 254–255.

78. Randy-Michael Testa, *After the Fire: The Destruction of the Lancaster County Amish* (Hanover, N.H.: University Press of New England, 1992), p. 176.

79. Horace M. Kallen, as cited from letters in Sarah Schmidt, *Horace M. Kallen: Prophet of American Zionism* (Brooklyn, N.Y.: Carlson, 1995), pp. 20–21.

80. T. W. Adorno, *The Jargon of Authenticity* (Evanston, Ill.: Northwestern University Press, 1973), pp. 126–128.

81. E. J. Hobsbawm, *Nations and Nationalism Since 1780: Programme, Myth, Reality* (New York: Cambridge University Press, 1991), pp. 59, 103.

82. Leigh Eric Schmidt, *Consumer Rites: The Buying and Selling of American Holidays* (Princeton: Princeton University Press, 1995), p. 134.

83. See Andrew R. Heinze, *Adapting to Abundance: Jewish Immigrants, Mass Consumption, and the Search for American Identity* (New York: Columbia University Press, 1990), pp. 74–76.

84. See the reflections of Gerald Early, "Dreaming of a Black Christmas," *Harper's* (January 1997): 55–61.

85. Charles Taylor, "The Politics of Recognition," in *Multiculturalism*, ed. Amy Gutmann (Princeton: Princeton University Press, 1994), pp. 25–73.

86. Homi K. Bhabha, *The Location of Culture* (New York: Routledge, 1994), p. 162.

87. Christopher Newfield and Avery F. Gordon, "Multiculturalism's Unfinished Business," in Gordon and Newfield, eds., *Mapping Multiculturalism*, pp. 102–109.

88. I borrow these sentences from my review of Paul Berman, ed., *Debating P.C.* (New York: Dell, 1992), in *The Nation* (March 9, 1992): 307–309.

89. Karl Galinsky, *Classical and Modern Interactions* (Austin: University of Texas Press, 1992), p. 116.

90. Ted Gordon and Wahneema Lubiano, "The Statement of the Black Faculty Caucus," in Berman, ed., *Debating P.C.*, pp. 249–257.

91. Wahneema Lubiano, "Like Being Mugged by a Metaphor," in Gordon and Newfield, eds., *Mapping Multiculturalism*, p. 70.

92. M. Annette Jaimes Guerrero, "Academic Apartheid: American Indian Studies and 'Multiculturalism,'" in Gordon and Newfield, eds., *Mapping Multiculturalism*, pp. 57–59.

93. Nancy Fraser, *Justice Interruptus: Critical Reflections on the "Postsocialist" Condition* (New York: Routledge, 1997), pp. 11–31.

Chapter Three

1. Matthew Arnold, *Mixed Essays, Irish Essays and Others* (New York: Macmillan, 1883), p. 8. "Democracy" and "Equality" are the lead essays in this volume, although both had been published earlier.

2. Roger Kimball, *Tenured Radicals: How Politics Has Corrupted Our Higher Education* (New York: Harper & Row, 1990), p. xiii.

3. Nicholas Murray, *A Life of Matthew Arnold* (New York: St. Martin's, 1997), p. 243.

4. John C. Olin, "More, Montaigne, and Matthew Arnold: Thoughts on the Utopian Vision," in his *Erasmus, Utopia and the Jesuits* (New York: Fordham University Press, 1994), pp. 80–81.

5. Todd Gitlin, who quotes Rubin, believes the new left had no coherent ideas, much less strategy, about the mass media. See his *The Whole World Is Watching: Mass Media in the Making and Unmaking of the New Left*

(Berkeley and Los Angeles: University of California Press, 1980). Rubin is cited on p. 175.

6. Hans Magnus Enzensberger, "Constituents of a Theory of the Media," in *The Consciousness Industry* (New York: Seabury, 1974), pp. 102–103.

7. Robert C. Allen, "Introduction," in *To Be Continued . . . Soap Operas Around the World*, ed. R. C. Allen (London: Routledge, 1995), p. 12. See also Charlotte Brunsdon, "The Role of Soap Opera in the Development of Feminist Television Scholarship," in Allen, ed., *To Be Continued*, pp. 49–65.

8. Marshall McLuhan, *The Mechanical Bride: Folklore of Industrial Man* (1951; Boston: Beacon, 1967), p. v.

9. Marshall McLuhan, "Sight, Sound and the Fury" (1954), reprinted in *Mass Culture: The Popular Arts in America*, ed. B. Rosenberg and D. M. White (New York: Free Press, 1957), p. 495.

10. Cited in and see the discussion in Judith Stamps, *Unthinking Modernity: Innis, McLuhan, and the Frankfurt School* (Montreal: McGill-Queen's University Press, 1995), pp. 97–121.

11. Andrew Ross, *No Respect: Intellectuals and Popular Culture* (New York: Routledge, 1989), p. 11.

12. James B. Twitchell, *Carnival Culture: The Trashing of Taste in America* (New York: Columbia University Press, 1992), pp. 194–195.

13. David Marc, *Bonfires of the Humanities: Television, Subliteracy and Long-term Memory Loss* (Syracuse, N.Y.: Syracuse University Press, 1995), pp. 44, 90–91.

14. Herbert J. Gans, *Popular Culture and High Culture* (New York: Basic Books, 1974), pp. 53–54.

15. Edward Shils, "Daydreams and Nightmares: Reflections on the Criticism of Mass Culture" (1957), in his *The Intellectuals and the Powers and Other Essays* (Chicago: University of Chicago Press, 1972), pp. 248–264. For a response, see Lewis A. Coser, "Nightmares, Daydreams, and Prof. Shils," *Dissent* 5 (1958): 268–273.

16. John Fisher, "The Masses and the Arts," *The Yale Review* 47 (1957–1958): 114–115.

17. George Cotkin, "Post-war American Intellectuals and Mass Culture," in *Intellectuals in Politics: From the Dreyfus Affair to Salman Rushdie*, ed. J. Jennings and A. Kemp-Welch (London: Routledge, 1997), pp. 249–250.

18. For a discussion of Macdonald and mass culture criticism, see Lou Anne Bulik, *Mass Culture Criticism and Dissent* (Bern: Peter Lang, 1993).

19. See Stephen J. Whitfield, *A Critical American: The Politics of Dwight Macdonald* (Hamden, Conn.: Archon, 1984), p. 125.

20. Dwight Macdonald, "A Theory of Mass Culture," in *Mass Culture*, ed. B. Rosenberg and D. M. White (New York: Free Press, 1975), p. 59. See Thomas S. Edwards, "The Pursuit of the Ideal: Mass Culture and Mass Politics in the Works of Dwight Macdonald" (Ph.D. diss., Bowling Green State University, 1989), p. 110.

21. Dwight Macdonald, "Masscult and Midcult," in his *Against the American Grain* (New York: Da Capo, 1983), p. 10; "A Theory of Mass Culture," p. 60.

22. Dwight Macdonald, *The Root Is Man: Two Essays in Politics* (Alhambra, Calif.: Cunningham, 1953), p. 52.

23. Macdonald, "Masscult and Midcult," pp. 10, 64–65.

24. Paul R. Gorman, *Left Intellectuals and Popular Culture in Twentieth-Century America* (Chapel Hill: University of North Carolina Press, 1996), pp. 190–192. Another historian determines that the leftist cultural studies breaks with Macdonald in looking at culture "from the point of view of the user" (Barry D. Riccio, "Popular Culture and High Culture: Dwight Macdonald, His Critics and the Ideal of Cultural Hierarchy in Modern America," *Journal of American Culture* 16, no. 4 [Winter 1993]: 15).

25. Patrick Brantlinger, *Bread and Circuses: Theories of Mass Culture and Social Decay* (Ithaca: Cornell University Press, 1983), pp. 30–31.

26. J. B. S. Hardman, "Masses," *Encyclopaedia of the Social Sciences* (New York: Macmillan, 1935), vol. 10, p. 195. See Edward Shils, "The Theory of Mass Society," in his *Center and Periphery: Essays in Macrosociology* (Chicago: University of Chicago Press, 1975), pp. 91–107.

27. To be sure, for many decades socialists and Communists used the term *masses* in a positive sense—for the same reason conservatives and liberals rejected it. For the leftists, the masses represented the revolutionary people. A classic American magazine of radical art and politics was called *The Masses*, and this was followed by a less distinguished Communist journal called *The New Masses* (see Eugene E. Leach, "The Radicals of *The Masses*," in *1915, The Cultural Moment*, ed. A. Heller and L. Rudnick [New Brunswick, N.J.: Rutgers University Press, 1991], pp. 27–47;

and *Echoes of Revolt: The Masses 1911–1917*, ed. W. L. O'Neill [Chicago: Ivan R. Dee, 1989]). A typical pronouncement by a Communist functionary of the 1930s called for a "red mass novel." "In the struggle for the masses," stated this apparatchik, "the party must repel" sticky romantic and patriotic literature and write what he called the "the *red mass novel*." "Instead of depicting personal conflicts and private passions," the mass novel will "give shape to the conflicts of our time and the *struggle of the masses*"(Otto Biha, "The Proletarian Mass Novel" [1930], in *The Weimar Republic Source Book*, ed. A. Kaes, M. Jay and E. Dimendberg [Berkeley and Los Angeles: University of California Press, 1994], p. 240). With the decline of orthodox Marxism, however, this positive reading of masses has declined as well, although it is still surfaces in Communist sectarians.

28. Matthew Arnold, *Culture and Anarchy and Other Writings*, ed. Stefan Collini (Cambridge: Cambridge University Press, 1993), p. 79.

29. David Horowitz, cited in Lawrence Levine, *Highbrow/Lowbrow: The Emergence of Cultural Hierarchy in America* (Cambridge, Mass.: Harvard University Press, 1988), p. 217.

30. Dissenting leftists and Marxists never accepted the idea of distinct proletarian culture—any more than they accepted the idea of unique proletarian science. "There is no proletarian culture and . . . there never will be and in fact there is no reason to regret this," stated Trotsky. "The proletariat acquires power for the purpose of doing away forever with class culture and to make way for human culture"(Leon Trotsky, *Literature and Revolution* [Ann Arbor: University of Michigan Press, 1960], pp. 186–187). The affinity between Trotskyism and vanguard intellectuals, especially in France and the United States, derives from this position of Trotsky. For instance, André Breton and the French surrealists were drawn to Trotsky because they shared a rejection of "socialist realism" and Stalinism; see "Visit with Leon Trotsky" (1938) and "Manifesto for an Independent Revolutionary Art" (1938), in André Breton, *What Is Surrealism? Selected Writings*, ed. F. Rosemont (New York: Monad, 1978), pp. 173–187.

31. Editorial in *Proletarian Culture* (1918), cited in Lynn Mally, *Culture of the Future: The Proletkult Movement in Revolutionary Russia* (Berkeley and Los Angeles: University of California Press, 1990), p. 38.

32. "Introduction to the Soviet Pavilion, the World's Fair, 1939," reprinted in *The Aesthetic Arsenal: Socialist Realism Under Stalin* (New York: Institute for Contemporary Art, 1993), p. 11.

33. Simon During, "Introduction," *The Cultural Studies Reader*, ed. S. During (New York: Routledge, 1993), p. 3.

34. Richard Hoggart, *The Uses of Literacy: Changing Patterns in English Mass Culture* (Boston: Beacon, 1961), pp. 277–278.

35. E. P. Thompson, *The Making of the English Working Class* (London: Victory Gollancz, 1965), pp. 194–195.

36. Raymond Williams, *Politics and Letters: Interviews with New Left Review* (London: NLB, 1970), pp. 73–74.

37. John McIlroy, "Border Country: Raymond Williams in Adult Education," in *Border Country: Raymond Williams in Adult Education*, ed. J. McIlroy and S. Westwood (Leicester: National Institute of Adult Continuing Education, 1993), p. 273. This volume consists mainly of material by Williams on adult education.

38. Raymond Williams, "The Future of Cultural Studies," in *The Politics of Modernism*, ed. T. Pinkney (London: Verso, 1989), p. 154.

39. Tom Steele, *The Emergence of Cultural Studies: Adult Education, Cultural Politics and the "English Question"* (London: Lawrence & Wishart, 1997), pp. 15, 204–205. See also Graeme Turner, *British Cultural Studies: An Introduction* (Boston: Unwin Hyman, 1990), pp. 44–45; and Stuart Laing, *Representations of Working-Class Life 1957–1964* (London: Macmillan, 1986), pp. 196–198.

40. Cited in Steele, *Emergence of Cultural Studies*, p. 15. Steele footnotes as the source Raymond Williams, "The Future of Cultural Studies," p. 162. However, those words do not seem to appear in that lecture, although something very similar does; see Williams, "The Future of Cultural Studies," in his *The Politics of Modernism*, p. 154.

41. Jean Lave, Paul Duguid and Nadine Fernandez, "Coming of Age in Birmingham: Cultural Studies and Conceptions of Subjectivity," *Annual Review of Anthropology* 21 (1992): 258.

42. For a recent statement about this issue, see Leon Fink, "New Labor History and Historical Pessimism," with responses, in his *In Search of the Working Class* (Urbana: University of Illinois Press, 1994), pp. 89–143.

43. For a German discussion, see *Arbeiterkultur seit 1945—Ende oder Veränderung?* ed. W. Kaschuba, G. Korff and B. J. Warneken (Tübingen: Tübingen Vereinigung für Volkskunde, 1991).

44. Michael Denning, "The End of Mass Culture," with responses, in *International Labor and Working-Class History*, no. 37 (Spring 1990): 4–40; and Michael Denning, "The Ends of Ending Mass Culture," in *International Labor and Working-Class History*, no. 38 (Fall 1990): 63–67.

45. During, "Introduction," pp. 17–18.

46. Gorman, *Left Intellectuals and Popular Culture*, p. 1. As proof that denunciation of television has no merit, Gorman appeals to a 1988 Department of Education study by Daniel R. Anderson and Patricia A. Collins, *The Impact on Children's Education: Television's Influence on Cognitive Development* (U.S. Department of Education, 1988). According to Gorman, "The study found that most research had been designed to support the foreordained conclusion that television was necessarily dangerous." This is not accurate. The authors are very disdainful of journalistic and popular accounts of the harmfulness of television, but their careful review of the literature comes forcefully to no conclusion. For these social scientists none of the research is up to snuff; they find no "important or even reliable cognitive effects of television viewing." They are reluctant to conclude, however, that television has no effect beyond a shadow of doubt, for this would put them out of business (p. 72). "For a number of reasons, however, it is difficult to conclude that television has no major effects" (p. 5). Carefully read, their report does admit more than they might wish; for instance: "There are also consistent indications that organized outdoor activities (especially sports) may be displaced by television. There is little consistent evidence that television viewing displaces leisure time reading (other than comic books) or homework." To this they add the surprising statement: "There is little reading done by children anyway" (p. 65). Maybe their kids.

47. Alan Wolfe, *Marginalized in the Middle* (Chicago: University of Chicago Press, 1996), p. 28.

48. Van Wyck Brooks, *America's Coming-of-Age* (New York: Huebsch, 1915), p. 29. On the origins of the terms *highbrow* and *lowbrow,* see Levine, *Highbrow/Lowbrow*, pp. 221–222.

49. Dwight Macdonald, *On Movies* (New York: Berkeley Medallion, 1971), p. 513.

50. Dwight Macdonald, "The Triumph of the Fact," in *Against the American Grain*, pp. 393–394.

51. McLuhan, *Mechanical Bride*, pp. 46–47.

52. Siegfried Kracauer, "The Mass Ornament" (1927), in *The Mass Ornament: Weimar Essays*, ed. T. Y. Levin (Cambridge, Mass.: Harvard University Press, 1995), p. 75.

53. Siegfried Kracauer, *Theory of Film: The Redemption of Physical Reality* (London: Oxford University Press, 1965), p. xi.

54. Siegfried Kracauer, "Der Detektiv-Roman" (1925), in his *Schriften I* (Frankfurt: Suhrkamp, 1971). To be sure, Kracauer and Adorno differed on much; see Dagmar Barnouw, *Critical Realism: History, Photography, and the Work of Siegfried Kracauer* (Baltimore: Johns Hopkins University Press, 1994).

55. The revival of astrology in the twentieth century has frequently been noted, but little investigated. F. Saxl, of the Warburg Institute, wrote an essay about it in 1936, but except for its first several sentences his concern lay with the early history; see F. Saxl, "The Revival of Late Antique Astrology," in his *Lectures I* (London: Warburg Institute, 1957), pp. 73–84. See also Ellic Howe, *Urania's Children: The Strange World of Astrologers* (London: Kimber, 1967); and Claude Fischler, Philippe Defrance and Lena Petrossian, *La Croyance astrologique moderne* (Lausanne: Editions l'Age d'Hommme, 1981).

56. T. W. Adorno, "The Stars Down to Earth: The *Los Angeles Times* Astrology Column" (1953), in his *Stars Down to Earth and Other Essays*, ed. S. Crook (London: Routledge, 1994).

57. Leo Lowenthal and Norbert Guterman, *Prophets of Deceit: A Study of the Techniques of the American Agitator*, foreword by Herbert Marcuse (Palo Alto, Calif.: Pacific Books, 1970).

58. Leo Lowenthal, "The Triumph of Mass Idols," in *Literature, Popular Culture and Society* (Englewood Cliffs, N.J.: Prentice-Hall, 1961), pp. 109–136.

59. See Heinz Steinert, *Die Entdeckung der Kulturindustrie, oder: Warum Professor Adorno Jazz-Musik nicht ausstehen konnte* (Vienna: Verlag für Gesellschaftskritik, 1992).

60. Robert C. Allen, "Introduction: Talking About Television," *Channels of Discourse*, ed. R. C. Allen (Chapel Hill: University of North Carolina Press, 1987), p. 15.

61. Ellen Seiter, "Semiotics and Television," in Allen, ed., *Channels of Discourse*, pp. 17–41.

62. E. Ann Kaplan, "Feminist Criticism and Television," in Allen, ed., *Channels of Discourse*, pp. 211–253.

63. John Fiske, "British Cultural Studies," in Allen, ed., *Channels of Discourse*, p. 272.

64. Meaghan Morris, "Things to Do with Shopping Centres," in During, ed., *Cultural Studies Reader*, pp. 295–319.

65. Arthur Asa Berger, *Manufacturing Desire: Media, Popular Culture and Everyday Life* (New Brunswick, N.J.: Transaction, 1996), pp. 190–192.

66. Henry Jenkins, *Textual Poachers: Television Fans and Participatory Culture* (New York: Routledge, 1992), pp. 73–74. Cultural studies professors regularly argue that viewing television is a complex and subversive activity. "Television is never passively received and its texts are as open to different interpretations as any rock and roll song"(Lawrence Grossberg, cited in and see the exemplary piece by Mike Budd, Robert M. Entman and Clay Steinman, "The Affirmative Character of U.S. Cultural Studies," *Critical Studies in Mass Communications* 7 [1990]: 169–184). See also Jodi R. Cohen, "Critical Viewing and Participatory Democracy," *Journal of Communication* 44, no. 4 (1994): 100–101; and Jim McGuigan, *Cultural Populism* (London: Routledge, 1992), pp. 153–154.

67. Morris, "Things to Do with Shopping Centres," pp. 296.

68. Lionel Trilling, *Matthew Arnold* (New York: Columbia University Press, 1939), p. 190.

69. John Henry Raleigh, *Matthew Arnold and American Culture* (Berkeley and Los Angeles: University of California Press, 1961), p. 1.

70. Levine, *Highbrow/Lowbrow*, p. 223.

71. This is the argument of Fred G. Walcott's fine study, *The Origins of Culture and Anarchy: Matthew Arnold and Popular Education in England* (Toronto: University of Toronto Press, 1970).

72. "Arnold's Speech on His Retirement" (1886), in Matthew Arnold, *Essays, Letters, and Reviews*, ed. F. Neiman (Cambridge, Mass.: Harvard University Press, 1960), p. 308.

73. "General Report for the Year 1852," in Matthew Arnold, *Reports on Elementary Schools 1852–1882* (London: Macmillan, 1889), pp. 4–7.

74. *Schools and Universities on the Continent*, ed. R. H. Super, *The Complete Prose Works of Matthew Arnold*, vol. 4 (Ann Arbor: University of

Michigan Press, 1964), p. 14. Arnold's great contemporary, John Stuart Mill, used a different line from Humboldt in his *On Liberty,* a line that addressed the goal of life as the development of the individual in his or her greatest diversity. Inasmuch as this was drawn from Humboldt's early book *The Limits of State Action,* it seems to suggest a laissez-faire, antistate bias in Mill. Arnold noted in *Culture and Anarchy* that soon after Humboldt wrote this, he became Minister of Education in Prussia, "and from this ministry all the great reforms which gave the control of Prussia education to the State . . . take their origin" (p. 124). See Editor's Introduction to Wilhelm von Humboldt's *The Limits of State Action,* ed. J. W. Burrow (Indianapolis: Liberty Fund, 1993); and Edward Alexander, *Matthew Arnold and John Stuart Mill* (New York: Columbia University Press, 1965), pp. 243–245.

75. *Popular Education in France,* in *Complete Prose Works of Matthew Arnold,* vol. 2, ed. R. H. Super (Ann Arbor: University of Michigan Press, 1962), pp. 3–29.

76. Matthew Arnold, "Ecce, Convertimur ad Gentes," in *Mixed Essays,* p. 362.

77. Matthew Arnold, "Equality," in *Culture and Anarchy and Other Writings,* pp. 219–220.

78. Arnold, "Equality," p. 233.

79. Arnold, "Ecce, Convertimur ad Gentes," p. 365.

80. Arnold, "Ecce, Convertimur ad Gentes," pp. 371–372.

81. Matthew Arnold, "My Countrymen," *Selected Prose,* ed. by P. J. Keating (London: Penguin Books, 1987), p. 192.

82. Matthew Arnold, "Heinrich Heine," in *Essays in Criticism: First Series,* ed. Sister T. M. Hoctor (Chicago: University of Chicago Press, 1968), p. 100.

83. Arnold, "Heine," p. 134.

84. To Sister Jane, November 15, 1883, *Selected Letters of Matthew Arnold,* ed. C. Machann and F. D. Burt (Ann Arbor: University of Michigan Press, 1993), p. 265.

85. "A Liverpool Address" (1882) in Matthew Arnold, *Five Uncollected Essays,* ed. K. Allott (Liverpool: University Press of Liverpool, 1953), pp. 87–88.

86. Indeed, he lampooned them in *Friendship's Garland,* his mock exchange with a German visitor to England.

87. Arnold, "A Liverpool Address," pp. 79–80.

88. Matthew Arnold, "The Future of Liberalism," in *Irish Essays and Others* (London: Smith, Elder, 1882), pp. 141–142.

89. Mill to Tocqueville, May 11, 1840, cited in and see the discussion in Alan S. Kahan, *Aristocratic Liberalism: The Social and Political Thought of Jacob Burckhardt, John Stuart Mill and Alexis de Tocqueville* (New York: Oxford University Press, 1992), p. 47.

90. John Stuart Mill, "M. de Tocqueville on Democracy in America," in *The Philosophy of John Stuart Mill*, ed. M. Cohen (New York: Modern Library, 1961), pp. 175–176.

91. Arnold, *Culture and Anarchy*, pp. 64, 119–120.

92. Arnold, *Culture and Anarchy*, p. 174.

Chapter Four

1. Jacques Le Goff, *Intellectuals in the Middle Ages* (Cambridge, Mass.: Blackwell, 1993), p. 82.

2. Paul Zanker, *The Mask of Socrates: The Image of the Intellectual in Antiquity* (Berkeley and Los Angeles: University of California Press, 1995), p. 2.

3. Mikhail O. Gershenzon, cited in Marshall S. Shatz and Judith E. Zimmerman, *Vekhi: Landmarks* (Armonk, N.Y.: Sharpe, 1994), p. xvii.

4. P. Struve, "Intelligentsia and Revolution," in *Landmarks: A Collection of Essays on the Russian Intelligentsia, 1909*, ed. B. Shragin and A. Todd (New York: Karz Howard, 1977), pp. 141–142.

5. Emile Zola, "Lettre à M. Félix Faure," in Zola, *J'Accuse . . . ! La Vérité en marche*, ed. H. Guillemin (Brussels: Editions Complexe, 1988), pp. 112–113. See Jean-Denis Bredin, *The Affair: The Case of Alfred Dreyfus* (New York: Braziller, 1986), pp. 248–249.

6. Eric Cahm, *The Dreyfus Affair in French Society and Politics* (London: Longman, 1996), p. 69.

7. Bernard-Henri Lévy, *Éloge des intellectuels* (Paris: Bernard Grasset, 1987), p. 48.

8. Paul Fussell, *Samuel Johnson and the Life of Writing* (New York: Norton, 1986), p. 38.

9. Joseph Addison, "The Aim of *The Spectator*," in *Selections from* The Spectator, ed. J. H. Lobban (Cambridge: Cambridge University Press, 1952), p. 10.

10. See Brian McCrea, *Addison and Steele Are Dead: The English Department, Its Canon, and the Professionalization of Literary Criticism* (Newark: University of Delaware Press, 1990).

11. Jonathan Beecher, *Charles Fourier: The Visionary and His World* (Berkeley and Los Angeles: University of California Press, 1986), p. 195.

12. Julien Benda, *The Betrayal of the Intellectuals*, (Boston: Beacon, 1955), pp. 60, 162.

13. Voltaire, "Lettres," *Philosophical Dictionary*, ed. T. Besterman (New York: Penguin, 1972), p. 274.

14. Antoine-Nicolas de Condorcet, *Sketches for a Historical Picture of the Progress of the Human Mind*, trans. J. Barraclough (London: Weidenfeld and Nicolson, 1955), pp. 136–137.

15. See the collection of materials, *Georg Lukács, Karl Mannheim und der Sonntagskreis*, ed. E. Karádi and E. Vezér (Frankfurt: Sendler, 1985); and Lee Congdon, *Exile and Social Thought: Hungarian Intellectuals in Germany and Austria, 1919–1933* (Princeton: Princeton University Press, 1991), esp. pp. 22–23.

16. See Colin Loader, *The Intellectual Development of Karl Mannheim* (Cambridge: Cambridge University Press, 1985), pp. 149–172.

17. See, generally, Anthony D'Agostino, *Marxism and the Russian Anarchists* (San Francisco: Germinal Press, 1977), p. 124.

18. "Machajski's May Day Appeal of 1902," printed as an appendix to Marshall S. Shatz's fine study, *Jan Wacław Machajski: A Radical Critic of the Russian Intelligentsia and Socialism* (Pittsburgh: University of Pittsburgh Press, 1989), p. 182.

19. Trotsky was quite familiar with Machajski's ideas, but Milovan Djilas may not have been. According to one account, "No evidence exists that Djilas ever heard of Machajski" (Michael M. Lustig, *Trotsky and Djilas: Critics of Communist Bureaucracy* [New York: Greenwood, 1989], p. 8).

20. Max Nomad, *Aspects of Revolt* (New York: Farrar, Straus and Cudahy, 1959), p. 4.

21. Max Nomad, *A Skeptic's Political Dictionary and Handbook for the Disenchanted* (New York: Bookman, 1953), p. 59.

22. See "Discussion with Noam Chomsky," ed. D. Richardson and J. Hess, *Black Rose* 1 [n.d. 1975?], pp. 63, 66; and, more generally, Robert F. Barsky, *Noam Chomsky: A Life of Dissent* (Cambridge, Mass.: MIT Press, 1997).

23. Noam Chomsky, "Interview," in *The Chomsky Reader*, ed. J. Peck (New York: Pantheon, 1987), p. 20.

24. Noam Chomsky, *American Power and the New Mandarins* (New York: Vintage, 1969). See my "The Responsibility of Intellectuals?" *Grand Street* (Summer 1989): 185–195, from which I borrowed a few sentences.

25. Noam Chomsky, "The Manufacture of Consent," in Peck, ed., *Chomsky Reader*, p. 126.

26. August Bebel, at 1903 Party Congress, cited in Wilfried van der Will and Rob Burns, "The Politics of Cultural Struggle: Intellectuals and the Labour Movement," in *Weimar Dilemma: Intellectuals in the Weimar Republic* (Manchester: Manchester University Press, 1985), p. 173.

27. Dietz Bering, *Die Intellektuellen: Geschichte eines Schimpfwortes* (Stuttgart: Ernst Klett, 1978); see pp. 148–262 for his discussion of "intellectuals" within Marxism.

28. Christopher Isherwood, *The Berlin Stories* (New York: New Directions, 1963), p. 64.

29. Richard Wright, in *The God That Failed*, ed. R. Crossman (New York: Bantam, 1959), pp. 115–116.

30. Milan Kundera, *The Book of Laughter and Forgetting*, trans. M. H. Heim (New York: Knopf, 1980), p. 5.

31. The entry for intellectuals in the massive *Dictionnaire Critique du Marxisme*, ed. G. Labica and G. Bensussan, 2d ed. (Paris: Presse Universitaire de France, 1982), does little more than summarize Gramsci (pp. 601–604).

32. Antonio Gramsci, *Selections from the Prison Notebooks*, ed. Q. Hoare and G. N. Smith (New York: International, 1971), pp. 9, 10, 15.

33. John P. Diggins, "Gramsci and the Intellectuals," *Raritan* 9, no. 2 (1989): 150.

34. Karl Mannheim (1921), cited in Dirk Hoeges, *Kontroverse am Abgrund: Ernst Robert Curtius und Karl Mannheim* (Frankfurt: Fischer, 1994), p. 229.

35. See Joseph Gabel, *Mannheim et le Marxisme hongrois* (Paris: Méridiens Klincksieck, 1987), esp. pp. 69–78.

36. Karl Mannheim, *Ideology and Utopia* (San Diego: Harcourt Brace Jovanovich, 1985), pp. 155–161.

37. Henk E. S. Woldring, *Karl Mannheim: The Development of His Thought* (Assen: Van Gorcum, 1986), p. 234. For a wide-ranging discussion of Mannheim's career and its reception, see David Kettler and Volker Meja, *Karl Mannheim and the Crisis of Liberalism* (New Brunswick, N.J.: Transaction, 1995). See also Leon Bailey, *Critical Theory and the Sociology of Knowledge: A Comparative Study in the Theory of Ideology* (New York: Lang, 1994).

38. Karl August Wittfogel, "Knowledge and Society" (1931), in *Knowledge and Politics: The Sociology of Knowledge Dispute*, ed. V. Meja and N. Stehr (New York: Routledge, 1990), p. 234.

39. Hans Speier, "Sociology or Ideology?" (1930), in Meja and Stehr, eds., *Knowledge and Politics*, p. 220.

40. Ernst Robert Curtius, "Sociology and Its Limits," in Meja and Stehr, eds., *Knowledge and Politics*, p. 114. For a discussion of German intellectuals and Curtis, see Joseph Jurt, "Curtius and the Position of the Intellectual in German Society," *Journal of European Studies* 25, no. 97 (1995): 1–16.

41. See Patrick Allitt, *Catholic Intellectuals and Conservative Politics in America, 1950–1980* (Ithaca: Cornell University Press, 1993).

42. Paul Johnson, *Intellectuals* (New York: Harper & Row, 1988), p. 342.

43. Scores of journalists and teachers have been murdered in Algeria over the last several years, mainly by Islamic fundamentalists; see Lara Marlowe, *Index on Censorship* 3 (1995).

44. Richard Hofstadter, *Anti-Intellectualism in American Life* (New York: Vintage, 1963), p. 9.

45. See David Riesman and Nathan Glazer, "Intellectuals and Discontented Classes" (1955), in *The Radical Right: Expanded and Updated*, ed. D. Bell (Garden City, N.Y.: Anchor, 1964), pp. 105–136.

46. "America and the Intellectual," *Time* (June 11, 1956): 65.

47. David Halberstam, *The Best and the Brightest* (New York: Random House, 1972), p. 43.

48. Hofstadter, *Anti-Intellectualism*, p. 393.

49. Ron Eyerman, *Between Culture and Politics: Intellectuals in Modern Society* (Cambridge: Polity Press, 1994), pp. 190–191.

50. Bruce Robbins, "The Grounding of Intellectuals," in *Intellectuals: Aesthetics, Politics, Academics* (Minneapolis: University of Minnesota Press, 1990), p. xi.

51. Ido Weijers, "Intellectuals, Knowledge and Democracy," in *Knowledge and Power: The Changing Role of European Intellectuals*, ed. P. K. Lawrence (Avebury, England: Hants, 1996), p. 33.

52. Pierre Bourdieu, *Homo Academicus* (Stanford: Stanford University Press, 1988).

53. For another sociological treatment with a wider focus of French intellectuals, see Rémy Rieffel, *La tribu des clercs: Les intellectuels sous la Vᵉ République* (Paris: Calmann-Lévy, 1993). For almost seven hundred pages, this volume analyzes schools, petitions, magazines, newspapers and the like.

54. Jean-François Lyotard, *Tombeau de l'intellectuel et autres papiers* (Paris: Éditions Galilée, 1984), pp. 11–22.

55. M'hammed Sabour, "Between Patronage and Autonomy: The Position of Intellectuals in Modern Society," in Lawrence, ed., *Knowledge and Power*, p. 19.

56. Jeremy Jennings, "Dilemmas of the Intellectual in Modern France," in *Intellectuals in Politics: From the Dreyfus Affair to Salman Rushdie*, ed. J. Jennings and A. Kemp-Welch (London: Routledge, 1997), p. 74.

57. Robbins, "The Grounding of Intellectuals," p. xiv.

58. Tony Judt, *Past Imperfect: French Intellectuals 1944–1956* (Berkeley and Los Angeles: University of California Press, 1992), pp. 296–297.

59. For a good critique of Judt, see Irwin M. Wall, "From Anti-Americanism to Francophobia: The Saga of French and American Intellectuals," *French Historical Studies* 18, no. 4 (1994): 1083–1100. See also the sharp exchange between Jean-Marie Domenach and Judt, "Les intellectuels française au temps de la guerre froide," *Commentaire* 16, no. 62 (1993): 403–412.

60. Jonathan Culler, *Framing the Sign: Criticism and Its Institutions* (Norman: University of Oklahoma Press, 1988), pp. 30, 54.

61. Michael Walzer, *The Company of Critics: Social Criticism and Political Commitment in the Twentieth Century* (New York: Basic Books, 1988), pp. 8–11.

62. Michael Walzer, *Interpretation and Social Criticism* (Cambridge, Mass: Harvard University Press, 1987), pp. 37, 39, 61, 64.

63. Andrew Ross, *No Respect: Intellectuals and Popular Culture* (New York: Routledge, 1989), pp. 210–211.

64. Edward W. Said, *Representations of the Intellectual* (New York: Pantheon, 1994), pp. xviii, 11, 32. I should note that I agree with much of Said's book. I should also note that he discusses my own book, *The Last Intellectuals*, identifying me as "a disaffected left-wing American intellectual called Russell Jacoby." Part of this description is accurate.

65. Stanley Fish, "The Unbearable Ugliness of Volvos," in *English Inside and Out*, ed. S. Gubar and J. Kamholtz (New York: Routledge, 1993), pp. 102–108.

66. Michel Foucault, *The Archeology of Knowledge*, trans. A. M. S. Smith (New York: Harper Colophon, 1976), pp. 203, 205.

67. Jacques Derrida, *Margins of Philosophy*, trans. Alan Bass (Chicago: University of Chicago Press, 1986), p. xxiii.

68. Jacques Derrida, *Points . . . Interviews, 1974–1994* (Stanford: Stanford University Press, 1995), pp. 60, 431–432.

69. Gayatri C. Spivak, *Outside in the Teaching Machine* (New York: Routledge, 1993), p. ix.

70. Spivak, *Outside in the Teaching Machine*, p. 57.

71. bell hooks, *Killing Rage: Ending Racism* (New York: Holt, 1995), pp. 8–10, 60–61.

72. Aijaz Ahmad, *In Theory: Classes, Nations, Literatures* (London: Verso, 1992), pp. 196–197.

73. Gerald Early, "American Education and the Postmodernist Impulse," *American Quarterly* 45, no. 2 (June 1993): 220–229.

74. Karl Mannheim, *Ideology and Utopia*, ed. L. Wirth and E. A. Shils (New York: Harcourt, Brace & World, 1959), pp. 262–263. These sentences are the final words of the original German edition, not the American version, which added various things, including another chapter. The German also has a more Marxist flavor than the English. The cited passage began, "Das Verschwinden der Utopie bringt eine statische Sachlichkeit zustande, in der der Mensch selbst zur Sache wird." See Karl Mannheim, *Ideologie und Utopie* (Bonn: Friedrich Cohen, 1929), pp. 249–250.

Chapter Five

1. I am using phrases from two translations of this sentence: "Towards the Critique of Hegel's Philosophy of Right," in Karl Marx and Friedrich

Engels, *Basic Writings on Politics and Philosophy*, ed. L. S. Feuer (Garden City, N.Y.: Anchor, 1959), p. 263; and "Critique of Hegel's Philosophy of Right: Introduction," in Karl Marx, *Early Writings*, intro. L. Colletti (New York: Vintage, 1975), p. 244.

2. Gunter W. Remmling, *The Road to Suspicion: A Study of Modern Mentality and the Sociology of Knowledge* (New York: Appleton-Century-Crofts, 1967).

3. Peter Sloterdijk, *Critique of Cynical Reason* (Minneapolis: University of Minnesota Press, 1987), pp. xxvii, 3.

4. Richard Rorty, *Contingency, Irony, and Solidarity* (Cambridge: Cambridge University Press, 1989), pp. 181–182.

5. Rorty, *Contingency, Irony, and Solidarity*, pp. 74, 80.

6. Eugene Halton, *Bereft of Reason: On the Decline of Social Thought and Prospects for Its Renewal* (Chicago: University of Chicago Press, 1995), p. 235. For a more measured discussion, see David A. Hollinger, "How Wide the Circle of the 'We'?" in *Scientific Authority and Twentieth-Century America*, ed. R. G. Walters (Baltimore: Johns Hopkins University Press, 1997), pp. 13–31.

7. Hauke Brunkhorst, *Der entzauberte Intellektuelle* (Hamburg: Junius, 1990), pp. 67–87.

8. Michael Walzer, *Thick and Thin: Moral Arguments at Home and Abroad* (Notre Dame, Ind.: University of Notre Dame Press, 1994), pp. 51–52.

9. Rorty, *Contingency, Irony, and Solidarity*, p. 94.

10. See Ronald G. Walters, "Signs of the Times: Clifford Geertz and Historians," *Social Research* 47 (1980): 537–538.

11. Dominick LaCapra, *Rethinking Intellectual History: Texts, Contexts, Language* (Ithaca: Cornell University Press, 1983), p. 16.

12. "Thinking and Reflecting" and "The Thinking of Thoughts," in Gilbert Ryle, *Collected Papers*, vol. 2, *Collected Essays* (London: Hutchinson, 1971), pp. 465–496.

13. Ernest Gellner, *Words and Things: An Examination of, and an Attack on, Linguistic Philosophy* (1959; London: Routledge & Kegan Paul, 1979), pp. 267–273.

14. Liam Hudson, *The Cult of the Fact* (New York: Harper & Row, 1973), p. 34.

15. G. J. Warnock, Preface, in Gilbert Ryle, *On Thinking* (Oxford: Blackwell, 1979), p. xiv.

16. Clifford Geertz, "Thick Description," in his *The Interpretation of Cultures* (New York: Basic Books, 1973), pp. 9, 16.

17. Carlo Ginzburg, "Just One Witness," in *Probing the Limits of Representation: Nazism and the "Final Solution,"* ed. S. Friedlander (Cambridge, Mass.: Harvard University Press, 1992), pp. 82–96.

18. Clifford Geertz, *After the Fact: Two Countries, Four Decades, One Anthropologist* (Cambridge, Mass.: Harvard University Press, 1955), pp. 2–3, 19.

19. Geertz, *Local Knowledge: Further Essays in Interpretive Anthropology* (New York: Basic Books, 1983), p. 161.

20. Clifford Geertz, "Deep Play: Notes on the Balinese Cockfight," in *The Interpretation of Cultures*, pp. 412–453.

21. Aletta Biersack, "Local Knowledge, Local History: Geertz and Beyond," in *The New Cultural History*, ed. L. Hunt (Berkeley and Los Angeles: University of California Press, 1989), p. 81.

22. Ronald G. Walters, "Signs of the Times," 556.

23. Vincent Crapanzano, *Hermes' Dilemma and Hamlet's Desire: On the Epistemology of Interpretation* (Cambridge, Mass.: Harvard University Press, 1992), pp. 66–67.

24. Clifford Geertz, "'Local Knowledge' and Its Limits," *Yale Journal of Criticism* 5, no. 2 (1992): 132.

25. Benedict Anderson, review of Geertz, *After the Fact*, in *London Review of Books* (August 24, 1995): 20. The passages appear in *After the Fact*, pp. 145–151.

26. Geertz, "Deep Play," p. 452. For a criticism of Geertz's approach to Balinese violence, see John Sidel, "Dark Play: Notes on a Balinese Massacre," *SEAP: Indonesia*, no. 63 (April 1977): 187–194; and the book it is discussing, Geoffrey Robinson, *The Dark Side of Paradise: Political Violence in Bali* (Ithaca: Cornell University Press, 1995).

27. For a tough-minded discussion of Geertz's writings on Indonesian agriculture, see Alec Gordon, "The Poverty of Involution: A Critique of Geertz' Pseudo-History," *Journal of Contemporary Asia* 22 (1992): 490–513.

28. H. Schulte Nordholt, *The Spell of Power: A History of Balinese Politics 1650–1940* (Leiden: KITLV Press, 1996), p. 7.

29. James Clifford, "Introduction," *Writing Culture: The Poetics and Politics of Ethnology*, ed. J. Clifford and G. E. Marcus (Berkeley and Los Angeles: University of California Press, 1986), p. 12.

30. Ernest Gellner, *Postmodernism, Reason and Religion* (London: Routledge, 1992), pp. 28–29.

31. William Wordsworth, Preface to *Lyrical Ballads* (1802), in *William Wordsworth*, ed. S. Gill (Oxford: Oxford University Press, 1986), pp. 604–605.

32. For an account, see Daniel Pipes, *The Rushdie Affair: The Novel, the Ayatolla, and the West* (New York: Birch Lane, 1990).

33. William Nygaard, *The Price of Free Speech*, foreword by S. Rushdie (Oslo: Scandinavian University Press, 1996), p. 72.

34. Muslim intellectuals show themselves to be tougher and more lucid. See *For Rushdie: Essays by Arab and Muslim Writers in Defense of Free Speech* (New York: Braziller, 1994). Bhikhu Parekh notes that in the Rushdie controversy British "political philosophers were largely silent" (B. Parekh, "The Rushdie Affair," *Political Studies* 38 [1990]: 709).

35. Robert Hughes, *The Culture of Complaint: The Fraying of America* (Oxford: Oxford University Press, 1993), p. 115.

36. Of course, the situation is not so simple. Some intellectuals rallied to Rushdie; others rallied to his censors. For instance, Feroza Jussawalla, a professor of English, finds Rushdie guilty as charged, although it is unclear whether she wants him murdered. "Through stylistic wordplay . . . Rushdie attempts to escape the responsibilities of the monstrosities he perpetrates. . . . The Muslims of Bradford and Brick Lane . . . now find themselves further victimized by someone, who, to compound matters, is one of their own" (Feroza Jussawalla, "Resurrecting the Prophet: The Case of Salman, the Otherwise," *Public Culture* 2, no. 1 [Fall 1989]: 106–117).

37. Charles Taylor, "The Rushdie Controversy," *Public Culture* 2, no. 1 (1989): 118–122.

38. Vijay Mishra and Bob Hodge, "What Is Post(-)colonialism?" in *Colonial Discourse and Post-Colonial Theory: A Reader*, ed. P. Williams and L. Chrisman (New York: Columbia University Press, 1994), p. 283.

39. Jim McGuigan, *Culture Populism* (London: Routledge, 1992), pp. 195–205. The last quotation is itself a citation of McGuigan's from Edward Said.

40. Gayatri C. Spivak, *Outside in the Teaching Machine* (New York: Routledge, 1993), pp. 217–241.

41. Wendy Brown, *States of Injury: Power and Freedom in Late Modernity* (Princeton: Princeton University Press, 1995), pp. 65–66.

42. Janet R. Jakobsen, "Agency and Alliance in Public Discourses About Sexualities," in *Feminist Ethics and Social Policy*, ed. P. DiQuinzio and I. M. Young (Bloomington: Indiana University Press, 1997), pp. 186–187.

43. Glenn Jordan and Chris Weedon, *Cultural Politics: Class, Gender, Race and the Postmodern World* (Oxford: Blackwell, 1995), p. 11.

44. Bill Ashcroft, Gareth Griffiths and Helen Tiffin, *The Empire Writes Back: Theory and Practice in Post-Colonial Literatures* (London: Routledge, 1989), p. 167.

45. Michel Foucault, *Power/Knowledge: Selected Interviews and Other Writings 1972–1977* (New York: Pantheon, 1980), pp. 189–190.

46. Michel Foucault, *Discipline and Punish: The Birth of the Prison* (New York: Vintage, 1979), p. 169.

47. Jean-Jacques Rousseau, *The Social Contract and Discourses*, intro. G. D. H. Cole (New York: Dutton, 1973), chap. 3, p. 168.

48. Iris M. Young, *Justice and the Politics of Difference* (Princeton: Princeton University Press, 1990), p. 116.

49. T. W. Adorno, "Zum Verhältnis von Soziologie und Psychologie," in Adorno, *Gesammelte Schriften*, vol. 8 (Frankfurt: Suhrkamp, 1972), p. 80.

50. Bill Ashcroft, Gareth Griffiths and Helen Tiffin, "Introduction," in *The Post-Colonial Studies Reader*, ed. B. Ashcroft et al. (London: Routledge, 1995), p. 55.

51. Chinua Achebe, "Colonialist Criticism," in Ashcroft et al., eds. *Post-Colonial Studies Reader*, p. 60.

52. Max Horkheimer, "On the Problem of Truth," in *The Essential Frankfurt School Reader*, ed. A. Arato and E. Gebhardt (New York: Urizen, 1978), p. 423, translation slightly altered. Max Horkheimer, "Zum Problem der Wahrheit," in *Kritische Theorie der Gesellschaft*, vol. 1 (Frankfurt: Marxismus-Kollektiv, 1968), p. 248.

53. Ann-Belinda S. Preis, "Human Rights as Cultural Practice: An An-thropological Critique," *Human Rights Quarterly* 18, no. 2 (1996): 308.

54. Alan J. Bishop, "Western Mathematics: The Secret Weapon of Cul-tural Imperialism," *Race and Class* 32 (October-December 1990): 51–65. A slightly abridged version appears in *The Post-Colonial Studies Reader*. Even a more judicious inquirer concludes we must move "beyond our Western mathematics"(Marcia Ascher, *Ethnomathematics: A Multicultural View of Mathematical Ideas* [Pacific Grove, Calif.: Brooks/Cole, 1991], p. 196).

55. Marcelo C. Borba, "Ethnomathematics and Education," in *Ethno-mathematics: Challenging Eurocentrism in Mathematics Education*, ed. A. B. Powell and M. Frankenstein (Albany: State University of New York Press, 1997), pp. 265–266. Anyone who believes that a university press im-primatur indicates scholarly excellence should check out this volume.

56. The citation is from Abdus Salam's Preface (p. iv) to Pervez Amirali Hoodbhoy's *Muslims and Science: Religious Orthodoxy and the Struggle for Rationality* (Lahore, Pakistan: Vanguard, 1991), which includes an eye-opening account of efforts to establish an "Islamic" science (pp. 169–187).

57. Meera Nanda, "Against Social De(con)struction of Science: Caution-ary Tales from the Third World," in *In Defense of History*, ed. E. M. Wood and J. F. Foster (New York: Monthly Review Press, 1997), pp. 74–96.

58. Alan D. Sokal, "Transgressing the Boundaries: Toward a Transfor-mative Hermeneutics of Quantum Gravity," *Social Text* 46–47 (1996): 217–245.

59. "Postmodern Gravity, Deconstructed, Slyly," *New York Times*, May 18, 1996, A1.

60. For their statement, Sokal's reply and other comments, see "Mystery Science Theater: Sokal vs. Social Text, Part Two," *Lingua franca* (July-August 1996): 54–64.

61. Nancy Fraser, *Justice Interruptus: Critical Reflections on the "Post-socialist" Condition* (New York: Routledge, 1997), p. 8.

62. Homi K. Bhabha, "Laughingstock," *Artforum* 35, no. 2 (October 1996): 15–18.

63. Stanley Fish, "Professor Sokal's Bad Joke," *New York Times*, May 21, 1996, A13.

64. Martin Gardner, "Physicist Alan Sokal's Hilarious Hoax," *Skeptical Inquirer* 20, no. 6 (November-December 1996): 14–17.

65. See David Nicholls, *Three Varieties of Pluralism* (New York: St. Martin's, 1974). For John Dewey's pluralism, see especially *Reconstruction in Philosophy* (Boston: Beacon, 1957); and Robert B. Westbrook, *John Dewey and American Democracy* (Ithaca: Cornell University Press, 1991).

66. William James, "A Pluralistic Universe," in *Essays in Radical Empiricism and a Pluralistic Universe* (New York: Longmans, Green, 1947), pp. 321–322.

67. Arthur O. Lovejoy, *The Great Chain of Being: A Study of the History of an Idea* (1936; New York: Harper and Brothers, 1960), pp. 293, 308.

68. Friedrich Schleiermacher, *On Religion: Speeches to Its Cultured Despisers*, trans. J. Oman (New York: Harper & Row, 1958), pp. 55, 110, translation slightly altered. See Friedrich D. E. Schleiermacher, *Kritische Gesamtausgabe*, Part 1, vol. 2, *Schriften aus der Berliner Zeit 1796–1799* (Berlin: Walter de Gruyter, 1984), p. 217.

69. Lovejoy, *The Great Chain of Being*, pp. 311–313.

70. Rajani K. Kanth, *Breaking with the Enlightenment* (Atlantic Highlands, N.J.: Humanities Press International, 1997), pp. 117–118.

71. Justus Möser's essay is cited in Karl Mannheim, "Conservative Thought," in his *Essays on Sociology and Social Psychology* (New York: Oxford University Press, 1953), p. 143. For a newer and revisionist view of Möser, see Jonathan B. Knudsen, *Justus Möser and the German Enlightenment* (Cambridge: Cambridge University Press, 1986).

72. See, generally, Georg G. Iggers, *The German Conception of History* (Middletown, Conn.: Wesleyan University Press, 1968).

73. Ernst Troeltsch, "The Ideas of Natural Law and Humanity in World Politics" (1922), included in Otto Gierke, *Natural Law and the Theory of Society 1500 to 1800*, ed. E. Barker (Boston: Beacon, 1957), p. 210. See Ernst Troeltsch, "Die deutsche Idee von der Freiheit," in his *Deutscher Geist und Westeuropa*, ed. H. Baron (Tübingen: Mohr, 1925).

74. Kenneth M. Stampp, *The Peculiar Institution: Slavery in the Ante-Bellum South* (New York: Random House, 1956).

75. *I'll Take My Stand: The South and the Agrarian Tradition*, by Twelve Southerners, intro. Louis D. Rubin, Jr. (Baton Rouge: Louisiana State University Press, 1977). See Michael D. Clark, *Coherent Variety: The Idea of Diversity in British and American Conservative Thought* (Westport, Conn.: Greenwood, 1983).

76. Michael Hill, "President's Message: Kith and Kin," *Southern Patriot* 3, no. 5 (September-October 1996): 1–2.

77. Maurice Barrès, *Scènes et doctrines du nationalisme,* vol. 1 (Paris: Librairie Plon, 1925), pp. 49, 59, 68.

78. Ernst von Salomon, "We and the Intellectuals" (1930), in *The Weimar Republic Source Book,* ed. A. Kaes, M. Jay and E. Dimendberg (Berkeley and Los Angeles: University of California Press, 1994), pp. 302–303.

79. Jane Flax, "The End of Innocence," in *Feminists Theorize the Political,* ed. J. Butler and J. W. Scott (New York: Routledge, 1992), pp. 450–452.

80. Luc Ferry and Alain Renaut, *French Philosophy of the Sixties,* trans. M. H. S. Cattani (Amherst: University of Massachusetts Press, 1990), p. 228.

81. Herbert Marcuse, *One Dimensional Man* (Boston: Beacon, 1964), pp. 255–256.

82. Herbert Marcuse, *Eros and Civilization* (New York: Vintage, 1962), p. 136. The phrase in quotes is from T. W. Adorno, "Versuch über Wagner," in T. W. Adorno, *Gesammelte Schriften,* vol. 13 (Frankfurt: Suhrkamp, 1971), p. 145.

83. Alfred North Whitehead, *Science and the Modern World* (1925; New York: New American Library, 1948), pp. 142–143, italics added.

84. "From the Other Shore," in Alexander Herzen, *Selected Philosophical Works* (Moscow: Foreign Languages Publishing House, 1956), p. 422.

85. See Eugene D. Genovese, *From Rebellion to Revolution: Afro-American Slave Revolts in the Making of the Modern World* (Baton Rouge: Louisiana State University Press, 1979), pp. 126–137.

86. William J. Watkins, "Our Rights as Men. An Address Delivered in Boston Before the Legislative Committee on the Militia, February 24, 1853," reprinted in *Negro Protest Pamphlets: A Compendium* (New York: Arno and New York Times, 1969), pp. 7–10.

87. See, generally, *The Fourth of July: Political Oratory and Literary Reactions 1776–1876,* ed. P. Goetsch and G. Hurm (Tübingen: Gunter Narr, 1992).

88. "The Meaning of July Fourth for the Negro" (July 4, 1852), in Philip S. Foner, *The Life and Writings of Frederick Douglass,* vol. 2 (New York: International, 1950), pp. 181–204.

Chapter Six

1. Aleksandr A. Blok, "The Intelligentsia and the Revolution" (1918), in *Russian Intellectual History: An Anthology*, ed. M. Raeff (New York: Harcourt, Brace and World, 1966), pp. 366–367.

2. Eugen Weber, "The Anti-Utopia of the Twentieth Century," *South Atlantic Quarterly* 58 (1959): 445.

3. Introduction, *The True Cost of Conflict*, ed. M. Cranna (London: Earthscan, 1994), p. xvii.

4. See Mike Moore, "So Where's the Peace Dividend?" *Bulletin of the Atomic Scientists* 51, no. 5 (September-October 1995): 30–34, and other articles in that issue. See also Ann Markusen, "How We Lost the Peace Dividend," *American Prospect* no. 33 (July-August 1997): 86–96; and Marek Thee, *Whatever Happened to the Peace Dividend?* (Nottingham, England: Spokesman/Bertrand Russell House, 1991).

5. Carnegie Commission on Preventing Deadly Conflict, *Preventing Deadly Conflict: Final Report* (Washington, D.C.: Carnegie Commission on Preventing Deadly Conflict, 1997), p. 3.

6. Stewart Lansley, *After the Gold Rush: The Trouble with Affluence* (London: Century Limited, 1994), pp. 1–2.

7. Zbigniew Brzezinski, *Out of Control: Global Turmoil on the Eve of the Twenty-First Century* (New York: Scribner, 1993), pp. xiii-xiv.

8. Samuel P. Huntington, *The Clash of Civilizations and the Remaking of World Order* (New York: Simon & Schuster, 1996), pp. 31, 303–304, 316.

9. Robert D. Kaplan, *The Ends of the Earth* (New York: Vintage, 1996), pp. 436–437.

10. Robert D. Kaplan, "Was Democracy Just a Moment?" *Atlantic Monthly* 280, no. 6 (December 1997): 55–80.

11. A number of scholarly organizations support conferences and journals in utopian studies. For an overview see Lynman Tower Sargent, "Contemporary Scholarship on Utopianism," *L'Esprit Créateur* 34, no. 4 (1994): 123–128. Syracuse University Press publishes the series "Utopianism and Communitarianism." The first volume was Ruth Levitas, *The Concept of Utopia* (Syracuse: Syracuse University Press, 1990).

12. Robert Theobald, *The Challenge of Abundance* (New York: Potter, 1961), pp. 108–109.

13. David Riesman, *Abundance for What?* (Garden City, N.Y.: Doubleday, 1964), pp. 182–183, 306–307.

14. George Kateb, *Utopia and Its Enemies* (New York: Free Press of Glencoe, 1963), pp. 1, 3, 134.

15. Alvin and Heidi Toffler, *Creating a New Civilization*, foreword by Newt Gingrich (Atlanta: Turner, 1995), pp. 15, 31, 43, 79, 81.

16. Michael L. Dertouzos, *What Will Be: How the New World of Information Will Change Our Lives*, foreword by Bill Gates (New York: HarperEdge, 1997), pp. xiii, 115, 137–138, 242.

17. Bill Clinton, with Al Gore, "The President's radio address," transcript, *Weekly Compilation of Presidential Documents* 33, no. 7 (February 17, 1997): 163.

18. See "Link Between Computer Use and Achievement Is Elusive," *Communicator* (Newsletter of the National Association of Elementary School Principals), November 1997.

19. "Book Shortages Plague L.A. Unified," *Los Angeles Times*, July 28, 1997, A1.

20. Kathyrn C. Montgomery, "Children in the Digital Age," *American Prospect* 27 (July-August 1996): 69–74.

21. Federal Trade Commission: Bureau of Consumer Protection; Center for Media Education, July 15, 1997. See also "Internet Sites for Children Raise Concerns on Privacy," *New York Times*, July 4, 1998, B3.

22. Dwight Macdonald, "The Triumph of the Fact," in *Against the American Grain* (New York: Vintage, 1965), pp. 399–401.

23. Orrin E. Klapp, *Overload and Boredom: Essays on the Quality of Life in the Information Society* (New York: Greenwood, 1986), pp. 112–113.

24. Sven Birkerts, *The Gutenberg Elegies: The Fate of Reading in an Electronic Age* (New York: Ballantine, 1995), pp. 75–76.

25. Richard Saage, *Das Ende der politischen Utopie?* (Frankfurt: Suhrkamp, 1990), p. 13.

26. Hannah Arendt, *Eichmann in Jerusalem: A Report on the Banality of Evil* (New York: Viking, 1964), pp. 287–288.

27. Christopher R. Browning, *Ordinary Men: Reserve Police Battalion 101 and the Final Solution in Poland* (New York: Harper Perennial, 1993), pp. 1, 161.

28. Critics who want to damn utopianism as the ultimate barbarism sometimes label Nazism utopian, but on what basis? For instance, the bi-

ographer and journalist Joachim Fest argues that both Nazism and communism were utopias—and both failed. Yet this requires stretching utopia till it is meaningless, by dubbing Nazism utopian since it is a "counter-utopia." See his *Der zerstörte Traum: Vom Ende des utopischen Zeitalters* (Berlin: Corso bei Siedler, 1991), pp. 41–57.

29. Élie Halévy, *The Era of Tyrannies* (Garden City, N.Y.: Doubleday, 1965), p. 266.

30. Kurt Glaser and Stefan T. Possony, *The Victims of Politics: The State of Human Rights* (New York: Columbia University Press, 1979), pp. 530–532.

31. Gabriel Jackson, *A Concise History of the Spanish Civil War* (New York: John Day, 1974), p. 174.

32. Gil Elliot, *Twentieth Century Book of the Dead* (New York: Scribner, 1972), pp. 1, 215.

33. For a discussion of Elliot's figures, see Glaser and Possony, *Victims of Politics*, pp. 42–45.

34. Carnegie Commission, *Preventing Deadly Conflict*, pp. 3, 11.

35. Julien Freund, *Utopie et Violence* (Paris: Éditions Marcel Rivière, 1978).

36. Edward Bellamy, *Equality* (New York: Appleton, 1897), p. 286.

37. See the discussion in Chapter 2.

38. Lewis Mumford, *The Story of Utopias* (1922; New York: Viking, 1962), p. 4.

39. Johan Valentin Andreae, *Christianopolis: An Ideal State of the Seventeenth Century*, trans. and ed. Felix E. Held (New York: Oxford University Press, 1916), p. 171.

40. Edward Bellamy, *Looking Backward 2000–1887*, ed. C. Tichi (New York: Penguin, 1987), p. 106.

41. Andreae, *Christianopolis*, p. 140.

42. Arthur Lipow, *Authoritarian Socialism in America: Edward Bellamy and the Nationalist Movement* (Berkeley and Los Angeles: University of California Press, 1991), pp. 33, 37.

43. Mumford, *The Story of Utopias*, p. 8.

44. Krishan Kumar, *Utopia and Anti-Utopia in Modern Times* (Oxford: Blackwell, 1991), p. vii.

45. Andreae, *Christianopolis*, pp. 237, 192.

46. Bellamy, *Looking Backward*, p. 110–111.

47. Melvin J. Lasky, *Utopia and Revolution* (Chicago: University of Chicago Press, 1976), p. 28.

48. J. H. Hexter, *More's Utopia: The Biography of an Idea* (Princeton: Princeton University Press, 1952), p. 95.

49. Thomas More, *Utopia and Other Essential Writings*, ed. J. G. Freene and J. P. Dolan (New York: New American Library, 1984), pp. 93–94.

50. Thomas Macaulay, "Lord Bacon," in *Critical and Historical Essays*, vol. 1 (London: Longmans, Green, 1866), pp. 399–401.

51. See Jerry Weinberger, *Science, Faith and Politics: Francis Bacon and the Utopian Roots of the Modern Age* (Ithaca: Cornell University Press, 1985); Perez Zagorin, *Francis Bacon* (Princeton: Princeton University Press, 1998), pp. 169–174.

52. Benjamin Farrington, *The Philosophy of Francis Bacon . . . with New Translations of Fundamental Texts* (Liverpool: Liverpool University Press, 1970), pp. 17, 72, 131. The quotations are from "The Masculine Birth of Time" and "The Refutation of Philosophies."

53. John Henry Cardinal Newman, *The Idea of a University*, ed. M. J. Svaglic (Notre Dame, Ind.: University of Notre Dame Press, 1982), pp. 89–90 (Discourse 5).

54. "English Traits," in *The Works of Ralph Waldo Emerson* (New York: Tudor, n.d.), vol. 2, pp. 174–175, 179.

55. To be sure, inasmuch as Macaulay was a critic of Bentham's Utilitarianism, some might not consider him a utilitarian. Yet it is fair to label Macaulay a utilitarian in the less technical use of the term. Indeed, he objected that Bentham's Utilitarianism led to no practical results. "The humble mechanic who discovers some slight improvement in the construction of safety lamps or steamvessels," wrote Macaulay, "does more for the happiness of mankind than the 'magnificent principle,' as Mr. Bentham calls it, will do in ten thousand years." Macaulay, "Bentham's Defence of Mill: Utilitarian System of Philosophy" (1829), p. 172; reprinted in *Utilitarian Logic and Politics: James Mill's "Essay on Government," Macaulay's Critique and the Ensuing Debate*, ed. J. Lively and J. Rees (Oxford: Oxford University Press, 1978).

56. William Paley, *Moral and Political Philosophy*, cited in Élie Halévy, *The Growth of Philosophic Radicalism* (Boston: Beacon, 1966), p. 500.

57. "Education," in James A. Froude, *Short Studies on Great Subjects*, vol. 2 (London: Longmans, Green, 1911), pp. 455–456, 464, 467.

58. Charles Kingsley, "How to Study Natural History," in his *Scientific Lectures and Essays* (London: Macmillan, 1885), p. 305. ["After life" here means later life, the time following the period of study.] On Victorian utilitarianism, see Walter E. Houghton, *The Victorian Frame of Mind 1830–1870* (New Haven: Yale University Press, 1957), pp. 110–136.

59. Leslie Stephen, *The English Utilitarians*, vol. 2 (London: Duckworth, 1900), p. 363.

60. *Autobiography of John Stuart Mill*, pref. J. J. Coss (New York: Columbia University Press, 1944), pp. 6, 34, 97, 101, 109, 163–164.

61. J. S. Mill, "Bentham," in *The Philosophy of John Stuart Mill*, ed. M. Cohen (New York: Modern Library, 1961), p. 25.

62. Sean O'Casey, *Sunset and Evening Star* (London: Macmillan, 1954), p. 250. Marcuse uses the passage as an epigraph to Part 2 of *Eros and Civilization*.

63. Leo Strauss, *Natural Right and History* (Chicago: University of Chicago Press, 1953), p. 4.

64. See Reinhart Koselleck, "Die Verzeitlichung der Utopie," in *Utopieforschung*, ed. W. Vosskamp, vol. 3 (Stuttgart: Metzlersche Verlagsbuchhandlung, 1982), pp. 1–8.

65. "Manifesto of Surrealism (1924)" in André Breton, *Manifestos of Surrealism* (Ann Arbor: University of Michigan Press, 1972), pp. 4–5.

66. See Michael Löwy and Robert Sayre, *Révolte et mélancolie: Le Romanticisme à contre-courant de la modernité* (Paris: Payot, 1992), pp. 223–225.

67. "The student movement's emphasis on imagination," writes an observer of the 1960s in Germany, reflected "its demand for the transformation of society through the liberation of the creative faculties" (Sabine Von Dirke, *"All Power to the Imagination": The West German Counterculture from the Student Movement to the Greens* [Lincoln: University of Nebraska Press, 1997], pp. 40–41).

68. Ernst Bloch, *The Utopian Function of Art and Literature: Selected Essays*, trans. J. Zipes and F. Mecklenburg (Cambridge, Mass.: MIT Press, 1988), p. 15. The sentence is from "Aufstieg und Fall der Stadt Mahagonny," Bertolt Brecht, *Stücke 2* (Frankfurt: Suhrkamp, 1988), p. 349. It

does not appear in the Auden/Kallman translation; see Brecht, *The Rise and Fall of the City of Mahagonny*, trans. W. H. Auden and C. Kallman (Boston: Godine, 1976).

69. Theodor Adorno, *Minima Moralia: Reflections from Damaged Life*, trans. E. F. N. Jephcott (London: NLB, 1974), p. 247.

INDEX